Alternative Lives of Jesus

ALSO BY ROLAND H. WORTH JR.
AND FROM MCFARLAND

*World War II Resources on the Internet* (2002)

*Biblical Studies on the Internet:
A Resource Guide* (2002)

*Secret Allies in the Pacific:
Covert Intelligence and Code Breaking Cooperation
Between the United States, Great Britain, and Other
Nations Prior to the Attack on Pearl Harbor* (2001)

*Church, Monarch and Bible in Sixteenth Century England:
The Political Context of Biblical Translation* (2000)

*No Choice but War:
The United States Embargo Against Japan and
the Eruption of War in the Pacific* (1995)

*Pearl Harbor:
Selected Testimonies, Fully Indexed, from Congressional
Hearings (1945–1946) and Prior Investigations
of the Events Leading Up to the Attack* (1993)

*Bible Translations:
A History Through Source Documents* (1992)

# Alternative Lives of Jesus

*Noncanonical Accounts through the Early Middle Ages*

Roland H. Worth, Jr.

McFarland & Company, Inc., Publishers
*Jefferson, North Carolina, and London*

LIBRARY OF CONGRESS CATALOGUING-IN-PUBLICATION DATA

Worth, Roland H., 1943–
    Alternative lives of Jesus: noncanonical accounts through the early middle ages / Roland H. Worth, Jr.
       p.    cm.
    Includes bibliographical references and index.

    ISBN 0-7864-1581-9 (softcover : 50# alkaline paper)

    1. Jesus Christ—Biography—Apocryphal and legendary literature.  I. Title.
BT520.W67   2003
232.9'01—dc21                                      2003010868

British Library cataloguing data are available

©2003 Roland H. Worth, Jr. All rights reserved

*No part of this book may be reproduced or transmitted in any form or by any means, electronic or mechanical, including photocopying or recording, or by any information storage and retrieval system, without permission in writing from the publisher.*

Cover images ©2003 PhotoSpin, Wood River Gallery,
   Artville and Art Today

Manufactured in the United States of America

*McFarland & Company, Inc., Publishers*
   *Box 611, Jefferson, North Carolina 28640*
      www.mcfarlandpub.com

# Contents

Preface .................................................... 1
Introduction ............................................... 3

## PART I: THE DOCUMENTS

1 **Detailed Surviving Gospels** ........................ 11
   The Infancy Gospel of James (also known as the
      *Protevangelium of James*)   11
   History of Joseph the Carpenter   19
   Infancy Gospel of Thomas   21
   Pseudo-Matthew   24
   Arabic Infancy Gospel   27
   Gospel of the Nativity of Mary   28
   Gospel of Peter   29
   Gospel of Nicodemus (consisting of *Acts of Pilate* and
      *Christ's Descent into Hell*)   32

2 **Fragmentary Surviving Gospels** .................... 36
   Gospel of the Hebrews (also known as *Gospel According
      to the Hebrews*)   36
   Gospel of the Ebionites   37
   Egerton Gospel (Papyrus Egerton 2)   38
   Unidentified Gospel (Oxyrhynchus Papyrus 840)   40
   Secret Gospel of Mark   40

3 **Surviving "Acts" and Other Documents** ............. 47
   Acts of John   47
   Pistis Sophia   48
   Epistle of the Apostles (*Epistula Apostolorum*)   49
   Toldoth Jeshu   49

## Part II: The Life of Jesus

**4  Mary and Joseph Before Jesus' Birth** .................. 53
   Birth and Childhood of Mary  53
   Betrothal of Mary to Joseph  57
   Annunciation of Jesus' Coming Birth to Mary  61
   Mary Visits Mother of John the Baptist  63
   Joseph Learns He Is to Be a Father  63
   Joseph Blamed for Mary's Pregnancy  65

**5  Birth of Jesus** ........................................ 68
   Jesus Born in Bethlehem  68
   Visit of the Magi  74
   Slaughter of the Bethlehem Children  76

**6  Egyptian Exile** ....................................... 79
   Flight into Egypt and Life While There  80
   Return to Palestine from Egypt  86
   Miracles of Healing and Protection While Still a Baby  87

**7  Youthful Years in Palestine** ......................... 92
   Childhood Miracles of Self-Protection  93
   Playful Childhood Miracles  94
   Childhood Miracles to Benefit His Parents  97
   Childhood Healings  98
   Childhood Resurrections  100
   Childhood Duplication of Food  101
   Childhood Protection of Others from
      Dangerous Animals  102
   Hurtful and Injurious Childhood Miracles  103
   Supernatural Childhood Executions  104
   Jesus' Supernatural Brilliance as a Childhood Student  107
   Jesus' Relationship to His Parents  111
   Death of John the Baptist's Mother  112
   Jesus' Jerusalem Pilgrimage at Age Twelve  114
   Jesus Is Commissioned to Preach at Age Twelve  116
   Death of Joseph  117
   Jesus Starts to Hide His Miraculous Abilities  119
   Jesus' Childhood Receipt of the Holy Spirit  120
   A Jewish Alternative Version of Jesus' Birth
      and Adolescence  121

Contents      vii

**8  Jesus' Adult Life and Teaching Ministry** .......... 124
    Roman Allusions to Jesus' Life and Death    127
    Jesus' Baptism by John    129
    Jesus' Forty Days of Temptation    131
    Jesus' Physical Appearance    133
    Jesus' Unique Physical Inability    134
    Appointment of Apostles    135
    Healing of a Man with a Bad Hand    135
    Every Meal a Miracle    136
    Jesus' Miracles: A Hostile Interpretation    136
    Jesus' Second Egyptian Stay    137
    The Second Transfiguration    138
    A Rich Man Seeking Divine Acceptance Stumbles
        Over His Own Riches    139
    Healing of Contagious Leprosy    140
    A Woman Accused of Sin    140
    A Challenge to Jesus' Ritual Purity in the Temple    141
    Jesus' Final Passover with the Disciples    143

**9  Betrayal, Arrest, and Trial** ....................... 144
    A Jewish Account of the Events    144
    Defenses of Jesus before Pilate by Friendly
        Witnesses    145
    Roman Subordinates and Standards Give Honor
        to Jesus    147
    Pilate's Challenge to the Jewish Leaders    148
    Mary's Grief over Jesus' Death    148
    Crucifixion of the Wrong Man    149
    Place of Crucifixion    150
    The "Departure" of Christ While Jesus Dies    150
    Earthquake at Jesus' Death    152
    Jesus' Disciples Pursued After His Death    152
    Pilate's Reaction to the Phenomena at Jesus' Death    153
    Joseph Asking for the Body of Jesus    154
    Punishment of Joseph for Burying Jesus    155

**10  Triumph Over Death** ............................ 157
    A Description of the Resurrection Event Itself    157
    The Decision to Hush Up the Guards' Report    161
    Appearance to Women at the Tomb    163

Departure of the Apostles to Galilee 164
Instruction to All the Apostles to Verify the
  Physical Reality of the Resurrection 165
Appearance to James to Convince Him to Break His Fast 166
Post-Resurrection Period of Teaching 167
Ascension into Heaven 167
The Imposture of Resurrection Exposed 169

*Notes* .................................................... 171
*Bibliography* ............................................. 185
*Index* .................................................... 193

# *Preface*

History did not end with the last book of the New Testament. The writing of "gospels"—both narratives and compilations of purported sayings of Jesus—did not end either.

Those such as myself who are primarily preoccupied by Biblical exegesis easily forget this. Yet if the biblical stories are commonly elaborated upon far beyond their scriptural roots in sermons, novels, and movies, should it be really all that surprising that the same instinct for "more" was present in the early centuries as well?

Hence it seemed a natural extension of my textual interests to venture into the area of how these stories were later elaborated on and expanded. Indeed some of these "extensions" became the root of major doctrinal innovation themselves. For example, the virginity of Jesus' mother becomes the perpetual virginity in this secondary literature, and the acceptance of the perpetual virginity, in turn, produced other major doctrinal and theological deductions that are difficult to imagine for someone working from the scriptures alone. Hence to understand what Christianity evolved into, one needs to be acquainted with not only its scriptural roots but also the nonscriptural foundations of doctrinal evolution.

Changes occurred not merely because learned theologians advocated them. They also occurred because they often had a natural resonance in the minds of much of the literate believing public. True, the popular literature simplified, amplified, and propagated in lay language the learned theses of the religious leadership. But they also broadened, popularized, and deepened the possible implications of existing beliefs that only later became embodied in official church doctrine. We have here a creative interaction between the elite and the masses whose consequences in doctrinal amplification no one could have predicted in advance.

Hence to set the evolution of Christianity in a broader perspective it seemed useful to undertake a concise summary of the popular literature that helped produce those changes.

Yet there is a secondary fallout from such a study. It is common for modern scholarship to look down upon the New Testament writings because of their narration of miracles and supernatural wonders of various types. Yet when one compares them with the later biblical imitations, one becomes profoundly aware of the restraint and caution with which the canonical literature approaches such matters.[1] As we examine the literature in detail we will discover a fascinating shift in attitude and perspective, away from the restrained embracing of the miraculous in the biblical literature to an enthusiastic (and sometimes grotesque) acceptance of idle wonders that seem designed to serve no purpose beyond the demonstration of raw power. Whether this was good or bad, spiritually edifying or destructive, is up to the individual reader to judge.

As with so many of my previous works, the vast resources of the William Smith Morton Library of the Union Theological Seminary in Richmond, Virginia, proved invaluable. Special thanks go to Tiffin M. Cooper, Circulation Librarian, who facilitated my continued use of the collection.

Roland H. Worth, Jr.
May 2003

# *Introduction*

As a "religion of the book," Christianity traditionally has put key emphasis upon the authority of the scriptures. Even in those bodies that explicitly uphold the authority of nonbiblical written tradition, the latter writings tend to be overlooked except by specialists and those vindicating a doctrinal point or attempting to discuss how doctrines and practices evolved over a period of centuries.

The earliest writings tend to have the greatest abiding interest. For example, First Clement (usually dated late first century) is clearly the product of a first class mind. Second Clement (c. A.D. 125–150) reminds this author of a well-intentioned pulpiteer, but not much more.

As one proceeds beyond this point, there is a tendency for the writings to lose their appeal. There are a number of reasons. A fundamental one lies in the fact that the doctrinal issues discussed are (to the modern mind) obscure and uninteresting. "Theology," both ancient and modern, has a regrettable inclination to obscurity and mind-numbing prose. Precision and exactitude drive out readability except for those deeply interested in the specific issue(s) being discussed.

As one goes beyond the strictly "church" writings into imitation gospel ones, the surviving examples tend to come even later. When they don't, they often exist in only scattered quotations. Some were written with clear-cut doctrinal axes to grind, and when their views lost out in the struggle for the intellect and organization of the post-apostolic churches, their gospels and apologetics rarely survived.

Hence the most exhaustive alternatives to the New Testament version of Jesus' life come from "orthodox" circles. These are often "imaginings" filling the holes in the canonical gospel accounts: What happened during Jesus' youthful years in Egypt? What happened during His youth, before He matured and His ministry began?

In other cases they are intended as supplemental to the relatively brief scriptural accounts of specific parts of Jesus' life. The human mind looks at a bare reference and wonders, as Paul Harvey the radio commentator puts it, about "the rest of the story."[1] The alternatives attempt to provide a description of what "might have been." By and large (with the obvious exception of those consciously out to do otherwise), the materials were written out of the best intent: not to contradict scripture, but to supplement it. Not to deny what had been written, but to provide more detail about areas of popular interest that were often sketchily discussed in the canonical records.[2]

Space precludes including all the accounts of Jesus' life that have survived from the Middle Ages and earlier. Perhaps this is for the best since it permits us to partly overcome the disproportion of story and narrative that occur in these sources. In regard to the birth of Jesus we are blessed with an abundance of material. In regard to the remainder of His life, the data, proportionately, can only be described as modest or, in regard to some aspects, outright skimpy.

For the infancy and childhood of Jesus, we use as a framework five major narratives that have survived: Infancy Gospel of James, Infancy Gospel of Thomas, History of Joseph the Carpenter, Pseudo-Matthew, and the Arabic Infancy Gospel. These are quite adequate to establish the general pattern of evolution of ancient thinking on Jesus' birth. Indeed, James, Thomas, and Pseudo-Matthew have been preserved in a number of copies, and their numbers argue that they had an ongoing appeal to a significant number of individuals. Hence not only did they survive, but we have good reason to grant them a significant degree of continuing popularity.

Joseph the Carpenter is especially important, however, because it deals with an individual who tends to become eclipsed by the development of the Marian ethos. Similarly the Arabic Infancy Gospel deserves attention both because of the cultural background being so significantly different from the other earlier accounts and because it, effectively, represents the full blossoming of the birth chronicles.

Variants of these various works also exist, but this book offers extracts of these variants only where they seriously supplement the material found in the other accounts.

For the years of Jesus' ministry, we are engaged in a much more patchwork endeavor. Whether heretical or "orthodox," there are relatively few surviving works that significantly deviate from or supplement the canonical material.

Turning to the arrest, trial, and resurrection of Jesus, we have only a few basic resources that cover much or all of the period. Extracts from ancient orthodox and heretical analyses, apocryphal "Acts" of the apostles, and other works flesh out and fill in additional details. On the borderline of this theme are the imaginary "reports" and "letters" of Pilate discussing the trial. Although it is a judgment call, since these are of such a very late date and do not contain dramatically interesting supplemental data, it seemed best to exclude them from our discussion.

Decades ago the great Catholic Bible translator John Knox gave a lecture in which he stressed the paradoxical nature of the King James Version of the Bible. On the one hand, its towering prose has never been beaten. On the other hand, when read in large segments it has a tendency to become mind-numbing. The apocryphal gospels (in their original or their English translations) rarely rise qualitatively to anything close to the KJV except its tales. It is perhaps because they represent a thought world so vividly different from both modern society and that of the canonical scripture writers that they lose much of their "punch" and impact when quoted in lengthy segments.

Although this book occasionally presents substantial quotes, by and large the documents are summarized. In cases where the surviving material is very brief, the entire document is sometimes quoted. In the case of the lengthy works that have been preserved, however, selective quotation maximizes their usefulness and the readability of this study.

The source for many of these quotations is *The Ante-Nicene Fathers*, which was published by the Christian Literature Publishing Company in the 1880s and 1890s. In his new Annotated Index, William DiPuccio rightly speaks of the continued value of this and its sister volumes of the *Nicene and Post-Nicene Fathers*, "Though the usefulness of a number of these volumes (especially in the ANF) has been surpassed by more recent translations, the NF and NPNF are still used and cited extensively. Moreover, despite the immense quantity of translations that have appeared in this century, this collection remains the only (English) source for many authors and works."[3]

Furthermore, the volumes are readily available in reprint form from various sources and, can be purchased for a reasonable price. Due to its copyright having lapsed, *The Ante-Nicene Fathers* is also available on the Internet, making it even more widely available to a new audience.

Unless otherwise noted, all translations derive from this source. Any non–ANF translations are noted either contextually or with an identification in a footnote afterwards.

Quotations are identified with chapter and section numbers rather than page numbers, since the latter will shift from one translation of a text to another. Chapter references are included in parentheses in the form of a "c" and the chapter number. Unless otherwise indicated, everything else in the immediate context comes from that chapter.

I have attempted to be respectful toward these ancient "romances" of the scriptural characters. In some cases, however, the glosses are so numerous and so blatant that a significant amount of space must be devoted to them. Blatant errors in reading the canonical texts provide us considerable insight into the impossibility that the authors were those claimed by the manuscripts. In addition, certain theological concepts are so far removed from the New Testament that one must assume many decades for their evolution. In other cases, attention is given to rival interpretations of the texts and how other ancient sources dealt with the same theme. Hence we are concerned not merely with what these documents say, but also with what they intended to teach their readers.

When accounts involving the same theme come from multiple sources, I have attempted to discuss them in the historical order in which they were written. An obvious problem with this arrangement is that we can't be sure of more than the very approximate date, with a potential error factor of decades or centuries. Even so, they were often written far enough apart that even very imprecise dating permits their presentation in their likely order of composition.

Even more difficult to determine is how faithfully the surviving texts, from centuries after their composition, faithfully reflect the earliest form. For our purposes we will assume that the similarity is close enough to look upon each document as reflecting, at least approximately, the theological view of its original even if it has been somewhat expanded since the original composition. In at least some cases, one is inclined to suspect later theological rewriting as the new trends matured and blossomed. Alternatively, a significantly different form of the same work may have existed in different places.

I have also made an effort to get inside the mind of the authors. Wherever one stands on the theological spectrum, from atheist to fundamentalist, it is extremely easy to mock the naivety, exaggeration, and lack of consistency of these documents. To do justice to them, however, we must recognize not only their profound weaknesses— even in terms of consistent storytelling— but also the psychology that made such improbabilities reasonable in the mind of the authors.

Hence repeatedly I probe for the type of reasoning that would have allowed authors to seriously put forward these narratives for the reading public. Our modern psychology rebels against the credibility of the material, even as fiction. We may not always judge fully or correctly on such matters, but the effort must be made if we are to treat the materials with the seriousness they deserve.

There was an interaction between the believing community and its leadership in regard to the creation, use, evolution, and acceptance of these materials. R. Joseph Hoffmann effectively argues that "preachers from the second to the fourth century knew the value of folklore, legend, and tall tale in spicing a sermon and made free use of what they heard or read" in such lessons.[4] By their allusions, they gave de facto approval of the works that contained them. In some cases, he suggests, they may even have been the author of such formal accounts[5] or, at least, of some of the stories that were later incorporated in them. (Contemporary preachers who use fictitious anecdotes to illustrate a point likely understand this interaction between the needs of a sermon and available storytelling narratives.)

Sectarian movements, of course, had their own agenda and brought forth their own works to justify their convictions. The "sayings" work called the *Gospel of Thomas* is a good example.[6] Such groups might also utilize the "orthodox" narratives available to them and might or might not interpolate their own selected materials to make them a better fit for their ideas.

Although this book concentrates chiefly on what once were connected narratives, some other Jesus stories deserve inclusion as well, typically because the contents were developed independently in such works. Many of these are quoted here from the useful translation and compilation of Bernhard Pick,[7] though I have modified the source attributions into a more contemporary English form. For example, Hieronymus becomes the more familiar Jerome and *Contra Pelagium* becomes *Against the Pelagians*.

To conserve space I have omitted nearly all of the "sayings" of Christ that have survived in everything from patristic quotation, to fragmentary papyri, to more or less complete apocryphal doctrinal (versus biographical) gospels. Although these are well deserving of their own evaluation as to credibility and reliability, in this book we are concerned with are the life events—real and imagined—of Jesus. Hence the "sayings," in and of themselves, have only marginal relevance to the current study.

In some of these "sayings" text, however, there is an occasional attempt to establish historical roots for an abstract teaching by describing some alleged event in Jesus' life. In such cases the material fits into the broad theme of noncanonical accounts of Jesus' life and is therefore included in this book. Yet even here the emphasis is on life events rather than teaching.

Because I will make so many references to the five major narratives, I have adopted the following verbal shorthand:

### Abbreviations of Often Cited Infancy Accounts

James = Infancy Gospel of James
Joseph = History of Joseph the Carpenter
Infancy Thomas = (Infancy) Gospel of Thomas
  (Latin and First Greek forms)
Pseudo-Matthew = Pseudo-Matthew
Arabic Gospel = Arabic Infancy Gospel

# Part I

# The Documents

CHAPTER 1

# *Detailed Surviving Gospels*

In the next three chapters we deal with the major sources of data utilized in this study. This in-depth treatment is intended to benefit the reader by analyzing each source's date, origin, and usage and to assist in deciding the relative credibility of each source as an alternative to the canonical accounts. For some, an in-depth treatment is not, in our judgment, really required. On the other hand for certain works—such as the *Gospel of Peter*—which have come to attract a disproportionate amount of attention compared to what they once did (and may in the future), an in-depth treatment is virtually inescapable. Likewise the *Secret Gospel of Mark* came out of nowhere in the 1970s and has garnered an immense amount of attention that may also be looked upon as both premature and exaggerated in its evaluation of the work's importance and ongoing significance.

## *The Infancy Gospel of James*[1] (also known as the *Protevangelium of James*)

### Contents and Purpose

This is even more the story of Jesus' mother than it is of Jesus' own birth. Mary's own childhood and youth until her betrothal to Joseph takes up the first ten chapters. Chapters 11 and 12 speak of her learning of her pregnancy from an angelic messenger. The following four chapters concern Joseph's moral integrity being challenged in light of Mary's pregnancy.

Chapters 17 to 20 take the story into Bethlehem itself, and the stress is on how Mary remained a virgin even as and after the child was delivered. Then comes a chapter dedicated to the visit of the Magi. The final three chapters discuss in detail the effort to kill the infant John the Baptist in order to assure that the Messiah has been eliminated. Jesus becomes virtually a supporting actor in a narrative starring others.

Mary's perpetual virginity — even after marriage — is heavily emphasized in the narrative. In the Biblical accounts Mary's virginity is the means to explain that Jesus was supernatural and legitimate from conception; here it is turned into a tool to emphasize Mary's uniqueness (her perpetual virginity). This element indicates that we are dealing with a mindset that had evolved beyond the interpretation of Jesus' status into one attempting to enhance the status of His mother.

In the history of doctrinal and organizational religious evolution, one of the repeated implicit issues is what causes issues and doctrinal change. Are they "invented" (for reasons good or bad, idealistic or self-seeking) by the religious leadership and then crusaded for among the masses, or are they born in the fellowship at large and then latched onto by the elite in response to their popularity (and sometimes in an attempt to enhance their own leadership credentials)? In such cases who is the leader and who is the follower?

Given the early date of the Protevangelium it seems clear that "popular piety ... first gave rise to the formation of the dogma of the perpetual virginity of Mary."[2] Only then was it latched upon by the theoreticians of faith and built upon to deduce further alleged insights into her spiritual status.

The preoccupation with Mary fully justifies the title given it in the oldest surviving manuscript — Papyrus Bodmer V (see below) — "The birth of Mary. Revelation of James."[3] The first half specifies the major theme; the second half, the purported authorship.

The elevation of Mary's status can be interpreted as either a goal in itself or a rebuttal against such accusations as that she was a mere poor woman and that her pregnancy had been a case of adultery. Either way, the rhetoric and assumptions utilized, once they became deeply rooted, would have encouraged the evolution of the veneration of Mary even if the stories did not originate out of that motive.[4]

W. S. Vorster attempts to minimize the Marian glorification element that seems inherent in the narrative. He concedes that the maximization of Mary's significance was a major use of the book, but he wonders whether that ultimate usage actually reflects authorial intent. "Granted the fact that the virginal conception, virgin birth and enduring virginity (cf. 20:1) is narrated by PJ, one should nevertheless be careful to conclude that its purpose is to glorify Mary. The purpose of the story should rather be looked for in PJ as a retelling of the birth story of Jesus from the perspective of his mother."[5]

However, when half of the book (in chapters) is devoted to Mary's birth, heritage, and character and the rest conspicuously builds up her importance, it is hard to see how one can properly embrace such an alternative. The book's original author may well have been out to explain why Mary in particular was chosen to be the mother of Jesus, but clearly he felt that in order to justify that selection Mary's own morals, ethics, and parents had to have been extraordinary as well. The possibility that being a moral, upstanding Jewess might have been regarded as adequate background in and of itself was clearly impossible for him to accept. Hence Mary's "qualifications" to be the mother of Jesus had to be magnified in order for her to be the proper choice to bear this child.

Adam F. Findlay also attempts to reorient our thinking away from the work's being a Marian defense: he argues that it is designed to defend Jesus against allegations of illegitimacy.[6] We run into the same problem once again: It is hard to see how the defense of Jesus is the goal of the work when He is almost—and this is only a mild exaggeration—a secondary figure in the narrative. Indeed, the case can be made that the only reason Jesus is of importance to the text is to have an excuse to discuss and build up the stature and image of His mother. This was hardly likely to have been the author's conscious intent, but from the perspective of what he has actually written the argument would be a credible one.

Furthermore, this work was intended for internal church circulation. How then would the apologetic aim of defending Jesus against outside cynics have been fulfilled? One could argue that it was written to reassure Christians and to build up their confidence against such attacks. It wasn't written to defend the faith to outsiders but to its own adherents. Hence, from that standpoint, it might be regarded as an "apologetic" work. Yet even if that is part of the agenda, the amount of space devoted to Mary precludes that being either the purpose or even the primary purpose— unless we wish to argue that the building up of the prestige of both mother and child were co-equal on the author's agenda.

Even so, B. Harris Cowper, in his nineteenth century work on these materials, is right in stressing that we are dealing in a matter of degree. Although exuberant in its praise of Mary and her virtues (thereby indicating that at the time of composition such a mindset already existed and appealed to a significant number of people), compared to much later works it is much more modest and restrained in its presentation and claims.[7]

Another who wishes to graft onto the work a major apologetic theme, one that uses Mary as a tool to a greater end, is Bart D. Ehrman. He argues that Mary's miraculous conception, super-spirituality (in a positive rather than negative use of the term) and perpetual virginity were intended to be interlocked with Jesus' birth rather than viewed independently of it. As he sees it "these points allowed this forged account to serve an important instructional purpose for orthodox believers, especially as they confronted groups of Ebionite Christians who denied the notion of Jesus' miraculous birth altogether."[8] Hence, although its long-term impact on Mariology was more important, in the short-term its apologetic defense of Jesus was the pivotal point.[9]

Unless we are to believe that the Protevangelium was regarded as scripture — something few if any would dare venture — are we to believe that a nonscriptural account would be more compelling and evidential to "heretical" movements than one perceived as Biblical? If the latter did not fully convince them, would this one? Furthermore, if what was widely regarded as "scripture" (Matthew and Luke, in particular) did not convince the Ebionites, would they not even more clearly reject this tale, which even its users would not elevate to that status? Looked at from the standpoint of *intra*-orthodox propaganda, the same reasoning would remain true: if the books they regarded as authoritative did not conclusively establish the truth they believed in, what more could this work do? In light of such considerations, one would be better advised not to seek an apologetic motive at all.

(Whether the concept of a clearly defined "canon" existed this early or not is irrelevant to our line of reasoning. The ideas of clear apostolicity — either direct or through their disciples — clearly did exist, and the same mental contrast of definitively reliable versus material of a more dubious nature would still have come into play. We use the terms "canonical" and "Biblical" in this context as verbal shorthand for this broader concept, though the concept of canonicity probably did exist far earlier than often assumed, but that is almost irrelevant to our line of reasoning.)

It seems far more likely that the pious believers among whom this work circulated had no particular axes to grind — not even orthodox ones. At this early stage, they simply wanted to know more of what Jesus' life had been like. And if they couldn't know the surety, then they could envision what it might have been like. Like the reader of *Ben Hur* in the nineteenth and twentieth centuries, the audience was seeking edification and encouragement, rather than an authoritative work from someone who was personally acquainted with the events.

Willem S. Vorster suggests three reasons for the preparation of relatively early works such as the Protevangelium.[10] The most compelling one is the first on the list (and the one we just alluded to): the desire to know more than the New Testament provides.[11] Yet the unwillingness of the much earlier canonical material to engage in such speculation still gives one considerable pause even if one feels considerable appeal in this scenario: was there that much less interest in the first half-century or so of

Christianity? Or did the speculation only really begin after the church had laid down for itself significant roots over a large part of the empire and had been grounded in the traditional version for many decades?

If the latter, one must speculate how much valid (or even responsible speculative) material had been handed down. The detachment of the Protevangelium from first century conditions may well serve as a quiet warning that, by the time large parts of the church became intrigued by the issue, it was far cut off from any but modest fragments of genuine historical tradition concerning the matter.

The second motive for the apocryphal writings, Vorster suggests, was to develop more fully the Christology of the faith. It sought to integrate the birth of Jesus to this system of thought.[12] Yet the canonicals had already trodden this ground well. What works such as James do is interject a distinctive new element — they strive to make a far larger room for Mary within the bounds (or in competition with?) the traditional Christology that already existed.

The final motive lay in the desire to explain how the Messiah — openly predicted in the canonical version to be born in Bethlehem — came to be linked so firmly with Nazareth.[13] Yet what do the Protevangelium and other such infancy accounts do but pad out in far greater and more imaginative detail what the canonical versions had already explained? Within an overwhelming Jewish context one might understand such greater elaboration, but the text of these infancy gospels indicates a very modest grounding in first century Judaism. In short, they did not originate from the desire to deal with a potential dilemma that early Jewish critics might raise but are written to meet the perceived needs of a much later Gentile-dominated church in which the Jewish segment was of such a modest proportion that even blatant errors could easily creep into the account.

Hence, the still existing "natural curiosity" to know the unknown — in this case, more details of Jesus' birth and early years — seems likely to have been the direct motivation in composing these works. The authors desired to "edify" (spiritually build up) the Christian mainstream through these pious tales. The fact that they chose the pivotal importance of Mary in the proceedings is itself telling in revealing how they best thought this honorable goal could be accomplished.

And even here, a composition written far too many decades after the events argues that they were consciously intended to be read as historical romances, appealing tales of what might have been and what could have been and with no intent of misleading anyone into literally believing these *had been*.[14] As time went by their narratives tended to become acceptable and "literalistic" glosses on the meaning of the scriptural text and became the precedent for translating spiritual hyperbole concerning Mary into dogmatic and binding "truth" for the church at large.

## Manuscripts and Translations

James is the earliest noncanonical alternative life of Jesus that has survived either intact or nearly so. As such, it is not surprising that its contents and theology had a marked impact upon the development of similar later works that treated much the same area.[15]

The original language of the work was Greek.[16] In that language alone more than thirty complete or partial Jameses have survived.[17] Of the manuscripts, however, only one is earlier than the eleventh century.[18] Papyrus Bodmer V, contains the text from either the third or fourth century,[19] but certain parts of the later dominant text are missing from it.[20]

A very literal translation into Syriac was made, while the one into Ethiopic felt free to stray from the original text.[21] The popularity of James is also indicated by its preservation in Arabic and Coptic[22] as well as Armenian and Georgian.[23]

Since Syriac will be mentioned many times in what follows it should be noted in passing that it became the official "church" language of Christian worship in the East. This reality probably encouraged the preservation of various works in that tongue that would otherwise have disappeared when found in other languages. Syriac itself comes in two dialects and both are forms of Aramaic, preserving both its words and grammar but utilizing a different type of alphabet.[24]

Although an Old Latin translation could have existed, and probably did, it has not survived.[25] Nor has any in the form of Latin that took its place. The decisive factor that caused the work to lose its audience was probably the listing of it among the papal condemned works in the Gelasian Decree of the sixth century. This assured that few in the West would dare knowingly copy it.[26]

The papacy was reflecting a deeply entrenched hostility to the work in the region that would have discouraged its widespread use even without its intervention. This opposition has been explained on several grounds. James assumes a previous marriage by Joseph and presents him explicitly as a widower. In the West there was great hostility to this concept.[27] Jerome had come down emphatically against the work and this certainly did not help either.[28]

In addition Pseudo-Matthew developed a substantial birth narrative that originated among Latin writers themselves.[29] Works such as Joseph the Carpenter (though based in part on James) were available and these covered much the same territory.[30] For some reason, their contents did not suffer the objections made to James, even though it included the controversial assertion that Joseph had outlived a previous spouse.

## Authorship

The closing sentences of the final chapter identify the book's author as an otherwise unidentified "James." He wrote it "in Jerusalem," either just before or just after Herod had died when the city went through a period of "commotion" and unrest. (The language is vague and the chronological reference can be read either way.) This is presumably the same Herod as the one who attempted to kill Jesus and dates the writing as during Jesus' infancy.[31]

The "James" intended is normally assumed to be the brother of Jesus who bore that name.[32] If one believes that the brothers of Jesus were also sons of Mary (rather than being merely half-brothers), the identification would be impossible for James if he had been a younger brother and not alive at the time of Herod's death. Even if the half-brother scenario was adopted, why in the world would such a document be written at such an early date? There seems neither reason nor rationale for the action. It wasn't as if Jesus were a member of the royal family and an obvious claimant to the throne. He was rather an unknown Jew of obscure family.

## Date and Place of Origin

The mistakes in understanding the religious mores of first century Palestine preclude its origin in this period.[33] The errors in understanding the Old Testament argue that its author was not a Jew[34] nor a Gentile who was a close student of that material. The mistakes in misreading the New Testament texts argue that he was not all that close a student of that testament either. (A number of these points will be mentioned in our discussion of the specifics of the book.) This does not mean that he was ignorant of either testament; just that he was not a close student of them and that it shows in his mistakes.[35]

Furthermore it deals with a question that one would not have thought of unless Matthew and Luke were available: how did the close relative John (the Baptist) survive the massacre?[36] Actually this was a self-manufactured problem: there was no reason to assume that John was born in Bethlehem at all since his mother's pregnancy was several months in advance of Mary's. Furthermore, there was no scriptural reason to assume that she was living in Bethlehem (the sole site the canonical text refers to the massacre having been carried out).

Yet they could have been there. It would add drama to the situation. So it is quite reasonable that some readers of the scriptural text had created for themselves this interpretive difficulty. Yet for that to have happened, the two gospels would already have to be available and in sufficiently general circulation for the "answer" to be of wide interest.[37] Hence the first century date claimed by the book itself is utterly improbable. It must come from a later period.

At the other extreme is the cut-off date for the work. Clement of Alexandria may have referred to the book's contents and Origen definitely did.[38] Since the first died in A.D. 215 and the second in 254, the maximum date for at least the first version of the book would need to be no later than the late second century.[39] Depending upon which sources one believes are utilized by the work and what individuals utilized James without citing it by name, the date could be as early as A.D. 150.[40] Others prefer not to be pinned down to such a specific date and speak of it being composed sometime during the broad spectrum of the second century[41] or the middle of that century.[42] Those willing to push the date back even further argue that the work "date[s] probably from the first or second century...."[43] A first century origin, however, is extremely improbable for the reasons already examined.

Revisionary work on the gospel is certain. Bodmer Papyrus V is believed to have been written during the third century or fourth century (see above) yet it lacks Joseph's "first-hand" account of how the animals and birds were standing still while he searched out a mid-wife.[44] Just as Origen testifies to the existence of the work, his differing version of Zacharias' death than the one found in it argues that the current version was added or blended in at some later point.[45]

The place of writing is extremely speculative. The types of errors found in the work — especially geographic ones— argue against its author being a resident of geographic Palestine.[46] On the other hand, there is only the most tenuous evidence of internal allusions that would point to specific alternatives.[47] Ron Cameron opts for Syria because "gospel harmonies" were popular in that area (but this is not a gospel harmony!), though he concedes that a variety of other locations are "not at all impossible."[48] More useful is the fact that the bulk of such narratives appear to have originated in Syria,[49] making one expect that this one may have done so as well. Some have found the work's language promoting/idealizing perpetual virginity to reflect the pro-chastity rhetoric of Syria.[50]

# History of Joseph the Carpenter

## Contents

At the beginning of Joseph, Jesus addresses the apostles and gives them the great commission to preach the gospel to the entire world, a commission the canonical gospel places after the resurrection rather than during Jesus' earthly ministry (cf. Matthew 28:18–20). In the final three chapters (c30–32), Jesus again shifts to words of encouragement to the apostles, though in this case with the explicit warning of the coming Antichrist (c31–32).

The actual life and marriage of Joseph to Mary are treated in only a few chapters (c2–9). The bulk of the book (c10–29) is devoted to a prolonged description of Joseph's death at the advanced age of 111 (c1).

## Translations and Place of Origin

Joseph appears to have been translated into Sahidic Coptic, from which it was rendered into the Bohairic dialect of the same language. It was later translated into Arabic, though some think that a Syriac edition lies behind it.[51]

The preoccupation of the book with Joseph's death has been used to argue for an Egyptian origin to the work. Certainly, there was such a preoccupation in Egyptian Coptic works concerning the death of Mary.[52] To anticipate a parallel interest in Joseph's demise would only be natural. At the very least it would certainly explain the significant degree of interest in the work, as manifested by the number of full and (mainly) partial Coptic manuscripts that preserved it.[53]

## Authorship

The narrative claims to be the written down form of Jesus' personal memories of His earthly father, Joseph. As such an apostolic origin would virtually be required and is so claimed. According to the account, "The holy apostles have preserved this conversation, and have left it written down in the library at Jerusalem" (c1). The text is presented not as a rewriting of an apostolic account but (except for part of the introduction in the first chapter), as if quoting the apostles themselves: "And we apostles, when we heard these things from our Savior, rose up joyfully, and prostrated ourselves in honor of Him" (c30).

The fact that Jerusalem was razed in the war with Rome (A.D. 70) prevented any library from being preserved there and the probability that a genuine apostolic memoir somehow made its way back to Jerusalem at a later date would be minimal at best. On the other hand, the allusion could well indicate that an earlier document claiming such an origin had been utilized and that the circulation of it in the Joseph narrative both preserved it and made it available to a wider audience.

## Date

The theological stance of the book is clearly long post-apostolic. The introductory words of chapter 1, "in the name of God, of one essence and three persons," can profitably be contrasted with the concept of the supernaturalness of Jesus as presented in the first chapter of the gospel of John. Although "trinitarian" (for lack of a better word), the canonical presentations nowhere rise to this kind of level of specificity.

This could be considered merely part of the copyist's prologue rather than that of the supposed apostolic authors themselves. Such can not be the case in the words put in Jesus' mouth in chapter 5, "and I chose [Mary to be My mother] of my own will, with the concurrence of my Father, and the counsel of the Holy Spirit. And I was made flesh of her, by a mystery which transcends the grasp of created reason." Although Father, Son, and Spirit are all three introduced in some texts in the canonical scriptures (the baptism of Jesus is, perhaps, the most obvious example), the relationship of the three is never spelled out in such explicit language.

Another element that does not match the hypothetical authorship in the first century is found toward the end of the document. Here the apostles are explicitly quoted as saying of Jesus, "Thou hast ordered us to go into all the world and preach the holy Gospel; and Thou hast said: Relate to them the death of my father Joseph, and celebrate to him with annual solemnity a festival and sacred day" (c30). Distinctively "Christian" feast days—as contrasted with those of the Torah—came into popularity only long after the apostolic period.

An intriguing concept of Elijah (Elias) is presented that finds no root in the canonical accounts. Enoch is only mentioned in one of the shorter epistles (Jude) and there as a prophetic speaker rather than as a survivor of death. Here, though, the apostles speak of how "they had not to undergo death. For truly they dwell in the habitation of the righteous even to the present day, nor have their bodies seen corruption" (c.30). Jesus endorses this theory, referring to how these two people "remain alive to this day, keeping the same bodies with which they were born" (c31). They would, however, ultimately return and be killed by the Antichrist (c31–32).

Since a first century date is untenable, where do we date it? A date in the fourth or fifth centuries has been argued for on the ground that it is preserved in both of the major dialects of Coptic, indicating that it had gained widespread interest and usage by that time. Others argue for a later date because of the emphasis of the book on observing the feast day set for Joseph.[54]

## Infancy Gospel of Thomas

### Contents

In older works, this is often simply called the "Gospel of Thomas." In light of both its contents and the increased awareness of a teachings text which is also given the same name, we will call this "Infancy Thomas." It has survived in two Greek forms as well as a Latin one. For the purpose of this work we will be citing the First Greek Form of the work (a/k/a Form "A" or the "Long Form") since it is far longer than the second and will examine only the first three chapters of the Latin since those contain materials not preserved in the Greek. They share in common an emphasis on the supernatural actions of Jesus while an infant or a child.

The Greek account: The childhood miracles presented run the gauntlet from idle wonders that were playful (c2) or helped his parents (c11, 13), to healing (c10, 16–17), miraculous duplication of food (c12), and to raising the dead (c9, 18). On a destructive note, there were miracles intended to inflict harm (c3) and even death (c4–5). Much space is devoted to Jesus' brilliance as a student (c6–8, 14–15). Finally there is a description of Jesus' visit to a Jerusalem feast at age twelve (c19).

These alleged miracles are in marked contrast to the canonical ones. In only two cases do the traditional gospels come close to describing destructive wonders. In one case we have the "cursing" of the fig tree and its withering (Matthew 21:18–19). In another we find exorcised demons who are permitted to substitute possession of pigs for their human victim and the pigs promptly panic and kill themselves in the sea (Matthew 8:31–34). Neither, however, concern human beings as their "victims." One would also find difficulty in claiming a scriptural precedent for either the playful wonders or the miracles to assist His parents.

In Infancy Thomas we have clearly moved into a conceptual world in which such actions are regarded as credible even though the narratives themselves are presumably regarded as fictitious by their original authors. Certainly this would have been the case at a much earlier date. Indeed, John explicitly labels the turning of water into wine at Cana of Galilee as Jesus' first miracle (John 2:11). If such tales as those found in Infancy Thomas existed at that time, he clearly intended to exercise his authority to squash them.

The Latin account: Before leading into a Greek type text (as to contents), a new beginning has been added. This briefly discusses Jesus plucking grain while a young child and His one year stay in Egypt. This includes two incidents that antagonized the local population. Originally presented to the modern public in translation from the Latin, later discoveries unearthed this material in a single Greek manuscript of the work as well.[55] Because the bulk of texts that contain the manuscript preserve it in the Latin, we will continue to simply label this material the Latin account.

## Manuscripts and Translations

The work is not given the heading of a "gospel" in the manuscripts.[56] The term "paidika" ("childhood events") is preferred.[57] This may have been a conscious effort to distinguish the material from the canonical records.[58] This would have several advantages. The material is different and to utilize a different term befitted that fact. It would also steer clear of the danger of being read as a competitor with the canonical stories, with all the potential danger of being labeled unorthodox as well.

The great popularity of the work can be seen in the fact that it was circulated in Greek, Latin, Slavonic, and Syriac,[59] as well as Arabic and Georgian.[60] From Latin it was translated into both German and Celtic.[61] These manuscripts exist in a variety of lengths.[62] Whether Greek or Syriac was the original language has been a matter of intense discussion and most would hesitate in firmly endorsing either specific option.[63]

Of the surviving manuscripts, the earliest is in Syriac and was written during the fifth[64] or sixth century.[65] In contrast, the earliest Greek manuscript comes from the fourteenth century.[66] In light of the date of the Syriac texts, one can reasonably establish the latest date for the work's composition as sometime in the 400s or 500s.[67]

The work was utilized by the Gnostics, but there is nothing explicitly gnostic in the work itself although it can certainly be interpreted within such an intellectual framework.[68] Since it could equally well be interpreted within an "orthodox" construction, it lacked the doctrinal distinctiveness (heresy to its opponents) that would have discouraged its preservation among them. For example, Jesus' childhood exoteric explanation of the true meaning of the letters of the alphabet could be laying the foundation for a gnostic revelation of other and more exotic hidden truths. On the other hand, it could simply be doing no more than what it appears on the surface, presenting Jesus as a childhood prodigy. The discussion of Jesus in the temple at age twelve would have provided another opportunity to creatively enlarge the material to promote their type of reasoning about hidden truths and realities.

The key to determining the degree of the appeal of the work to gnostics would be evident if we had an early copy of the work as circulated among them. If it magnified and went even further about Jesus' esoteric insights, we could easily see why the work would be of special interest to them. This would still leave unresolved whether the surviving manuscripts are doctrinally "purified" abridgments of a gnostic original or whether the gnostics took the opportunity to "expand" the material at such points to promote their own agenda.[69]

## Authorship

The author is described in the First Greek form as an "Israelite philosopher" in the heading to the entire work and in chapter one as simply an "Israelite" writing to believers in Jesus in the Gentile world. But what Thomas? The heading to the Second Greek form clarifies this by referring to him as an "apostle" (though the text of chapter 1 still merely refers to him as an Israelite). Since the additional material in the Latin form is a conscious addendum, there is no heading to the part where the transition is made to the Greek traditions. When that point is reached (c4) Thomas is simply described as "the Israelite and apostle of the Lord."

But why would an "apostle" know of Jesus' childhood years in such detail? Some ancients thought that the full name would have been "Judas Thomas" and that this was one of Jesus' brothers.[70] At this point the theory becomes irrevocably locked into the dispute of whether Jesus' brothers were full brothers (hence younger than Himself) or half-brothers, the result of Joseph's alleged earlier marriage. If the former, one wonders how and why he could have come into contact with such detailed information. If the latter, he could easily have been old enough to personally know the details. The apocryphal willingness to depict Joseph as a widower argues that the latter authorship was most compatible with their authors' world view. Although there is no reason to consider the attribution as valid, it does indicate the author's intended "point of view" in telling the story.

## Date

Since Irenaeus (c. A.D. 185) refers to the schoolboy arguments about Jesus learning the alphabet, it has been argued that some form of this book clearly existed in the late second century[71] and had become sufficiently circulated to be referred to by him. The *Epistula Apostolorum*, typically dated mid-second century, also refers to the incident.[72] There is a very marked difference in how the two documents approach the incident, however. The pseudo-apostolic epistle describes it as if accepting it as valid and genuine history. In contrast Irenaeus calls the story a "falsehood" circulated by the Marcosian sect.

Based upon these citings, the work would likely be dated as coming from the second quarter of the second century.[73]

There is, of course, the possibility that the story was circulated as either a written or oral tale for an unknown period before being picked up and inserted in Infancy Thomas. The degree of detail in the Irenaeus account argues, however, that even if this be the case it has been faithfully incorporated in its original form.[74]

The fact that the Gospel survives today in three different major forms (two Greek and one Latin) itself argues that it is unsafe to assume that the earliest form was as long as any of the versions we have.[75] Others prefer to argue that it began in a longer form and was edited downward in length to protect against criticism and the charge of unorthodoxy.[76] What further complicates the picture is that in some passages Greek Form B is actually longer than A,[77] which could suggest that all surviving forms are actually variants of a significantly different (and longer?) original.

## Pseudo-Matthew

### Contents

Although no one seriously believes that the theoretical authors of the preceding narratives really wrote them, only this account has traditionally born the candid "pseudo" as part of its description. Since it is both accurate and traditional, we have retained it here.

Chapters 1–17 are an elaboration of the Infancy Gospel of James. In spite of its significant length — perhaps even because of it, since no narrative can be permitted to be but so long — James' account of Mary's visit with the mother of John the Baptist is not included.

Chapters 26–34 are clearly built upon the Infancy Gospel of Thomas, although the author has felt free to both modify and expand the earlier version. Chapters 37–39 and 41 similarly are based upon the earlier work.

Hence the real core of originality are chapters 18–25, 35–36, 40, and 42. The degree to which the author has borrowed from two major identifiable sources (though he has felt free to rework them) makes one wonder whether part or all of the remainder is based upon a now vanished source as well. Some have pointed to an affinity between these chapters and the Arabic Infancy Gospel,[78] indicating that one may be utilizing the other or that both are tapping into a similar document or body of popular tales.

## Significance and Manuscripts

More explicitly and emphatically than its predecessors, Pseudo-Matthew elevates the importance of the virgin Mary as an object of piety and holiness, although the minds of the earlier writers had clearly been moving in the same direction. Due to centuries of rising elevation of her status in popular religious mythology, this more advanced stage of theorizing is hardly surprising. Indeed, if anything, it may be surprising that the tendency is not even more profound.

A major textual problem concerns chapters 25–42. These are absent from Pseudo-Matthew in most surviving manuscripts,[79] yet their joining together in other cases argues that there was a tradition of providing the material in both a short and a more "complete" form. Indeed, since the material has modest (but significant) additions to that found in the Infancy Thomas, it seems one would have to postulate either the existence of another childhood gospel whose beginning has been lost (but whose conclusion has been added to this work) or at some stage a conscious expansion of Pseudo-Matthew was made by a later writer.

## Authorship

The text is preceded by a letter purporting to come from the two bishops Cromatius and Heliodorus. They acknowledged the existence of "apocryphal books" discussing both the birth of Jesus as well as that of His mother, but confessed their unwillingness to use them because "in them [are] many things contrary to our faith." They had received the report that Jerome had come across a Hebrew language volume written by Matthew himself which recorded these events. They urged him to translate the material into Latin not so much for their own value but as a means to exclude "the craft of heretics, who, in order to teach bad doctrine, have mingled their own lies" with the accurate story of the nativity of the two.

Then follows a return letter purporting to be from Jerome. Jerome agreed to translate the work even though "the holy Apostle and Evangelist Matthew himself did not write for the purpose of publishing." Indeed he had composed it "somewhat secretly." We immediately wonder: If this were so, why should anyone arrogate to him/herself the publishing of a genuine apostolic work the author never intended to be generally circulated? If one prefers the other horn of the dilemma, why would an apostle write a work never intended for publication in the first place?

Passing by these obvious questions—and one can't help but suspect that the historical Jerome was quite astute enough to have grasped them if such a purported apostolic document had crossed his path—this

"Jerome" insisted that not only was it in Hebrew "by his [Matthew's] own hand" but was also "in the possession of very religious men, to whom in successive periods of time it has been handed down by those that were before them." That a first century manuscript had survived all these centuries is itself improbable; that it would have been preserved in Hebrew (a language a shrinking number of Christians knew or had any concern with) even less so. "This book they never at any time gave to any one to translate," which also raises severe questions as to its genuineness if they had perceived it as an apostolic work.

When the work was finally translated and distributed it was done with heretical additions and intent. Jerome pledges that his version has purged it of such evil accoutrements and that it makes available what Matthew really wrote.

To the extent that this letter contains any genuine material may lie in the claim that an orthodox-minded churchman had consciously taken a quasi- or anti-orthodox work and either translated it into Latin or purged an existing Latin version of its questionable material.

The second purported letter also asserts the Hebrew origin of the work, its apostolic composition, and its heretical mistranslation. In a remark that sounds more likely to have come from the genuine Jerome, if he had been hesitatingly and unwillingly talked into translating a dubious work, there is the candid admission that its historic reliability could not be assured: "…[W]hether these stories be true or inventions, the sacred nativity of St. Mary was preceded by great miracles, and succeeded by the greatest; and so by those who believe that God can do these things, they can be believed and read without damaging their faith or imperiling their souls." In short, if the work turns out not to be genuine, it consists, at worst, of edifying pious tales of no harm to the faithful even if they believe them.

The material, as we saw above, borrows from James and Infancy Thomas.[80] The letters attached to the beginning of Pseudo-Matthew clearly indicate that the taint of heresy was common among the available childhood gospels and it is the author/compiler's clear goal to explain why this narrative is free from such contamination. Even at this date such works are under the odor of automatic suspicion, at least among those who are its intended audience.

That leaves unanswered whether the author considered James and Infancy Thomas heretical either in their current form or the version he utilized. The former is unlikely since the comparison of his rendering with the earlier ones shows a clear-cut expansion of the narratives. More likely he had a version of the two works even more fanciful than the one he permits to survive his editorship. Unless, of course, we assume that all of the talk of avoiding heresy was simply a self-defense mechanism to permit the work to circulate among the orthodox when he knew full well that all he was doing was expanding (rather than editing out) material from earlier works.

That the claimed authorship of the work by Matthew is thoroughly improbable is seen by the great detail surrounding such a narrow segment of Jesus' life: "How is it likely that the Apostle Matthew who was so restrained in his account of the infancy of Christ, would have added much later a long supplement of twenty chapters?"[81] What the actual author/editor apparently assumes is that because he is so fascinated by Jesus' youthful years and by the preceding life of Mary, that the apostles would have been as well. Assuming that the canonical Matthew is, indeed, from that apostolic source (and the author of Pseudo-Matthew certainly did), the canonical work's modest space devoted to this part of Jesus' life argues that his interests were far different from his later imitator.

## Date

The earliest surviving manuscript comes from the eleventh century.[82] A date of composition in either the eighth or the ninth century, however, has been suggested as likely,[83] with some favoring an even earlier date somewhere between A.D. 550 and 700.[84] The 550–700 dating (the earlier one goes in that range) only refers to the initial section concerning Mary and the birth of Jesus; the Egyptian and childhood of Jesus materials came to be grafted on at a later date.[85]

The original language, contrary to the claims of the introductory letters attached to the narrative, appears to have been Latin.[86] In that language, more than 130 manuscripts have survived though there is significant difference in details of the text among them.[87]

# *Arabic Infancy Gospel*

## Summary

The story begins with the birth of the child Jesus (c1–9) and then deals at length with the stay in Egypt (c10–25).

Some believe that chapters 1–10 find their roots in James.[88] Although there is, broadly speaking, a parallel it is so inexact that if there is a borrowing it is likely one from memory rather than from a copy of the text actually in front of the author.

There is a clearer reliance upon Infancy Thomas. This is especially true in chapters 36, 38, 43–50, and 53. Some of the material is reasonably close in wording and content, yet the author has felt free here to embroider upon the narrative — sometimes at length — and to broaden out the contents of certain of the specific incidents as well.

## Manuscripts and Translations

The work was introduced to the modern western world via a 1697 translation into Latin. The manuscript this was based upon disappeared but a few alternative Arabic manuscripts were later discovered in Italy.[89] The Arabic is itself likely a translation of a Syriac original.[90] It was the nature of such inventive works, however, that its contents were not frozen in a permanently authoritative form. Hence the text may have been considerably expanded and modified by those who undertook the translation to make it better fit the imagination and preconceptions of those who would be reading it.[91]

## Authorship

The book makes no explicit or implicit claim in regard to the matter. All the author does is express the confidence that God would help him in the effort: "With the help and favor of the most High we begin to write a book of the miracles of our Lord and Master and Savior Jesus Christ, which is called the Gospel of the Infancy: in the peace of the Lord. Amen" (foreword).

## Date

If the assumption is valid that the work is based upon an earlier form originally written in Syriac (and it likely is), the initial version could have been composed as early as the fifth or sixth century.[92] It can not be overstressed that there the degree of similarity and difference in substance and detail between them is purely conjectural.

# Gospel of the Nativity of Mary

In a trend noted in several earlier works, the emphasis is even more on Mary than on her Son. Indeed, the text ends with Joseph's angelic guided decision to marry her in spite of her obvious pregnancy and barely mentions Jesus' own birth. Although one may question Montague R. James' assertion that this is an inferior work to narratives such as Pseudo-Matthew, he clearly hits the mark in describing it as being "an amplification of the earlier chapters of that work in more elegant Latin, and with all the detail blurred and smoothed down."[93] Being based upon Pseudo-Matthew, its composition must, of course, be placed at a later date than that work.

Erroneously attributed to Jerome,[94] this purported authorship doubtless gave it some of its initial stature. Also encouraging its utilization was the development of its Marian theology into an even more explicit and clear-cut fashion. Hence it was very popular during the Middle Ages, and the embodiment of its contents in the thirteenth century *Legenda Aurea* magnified the impact of its contents even further.[95]

## Gospel of Peter

### Contents

This is a detailed description of the trial, death, and resurrection of Jesus. One of the unanswerable questions about the work concerns how much text existed before the current narrative begins. There is simply no way of being sure whether this was strictly a "Passion Narrative"—centering on the final days of Jesus—or whether, like the canonicals, it originally encompassed the entire life.[96]

### Manuscripts

The only manuscript with a significant segment of the work (known as the Akhmim Greek text) is the one discovered in 1886 in Egypt. The fact that the copyist has inserted decorative ornaments both at the beginning and end argues that this copyist only had available the section of the text that he duplicates.[97] This was written in Greek during either the eighth or ninth century.[98] The manuscript consisted of thirty-three pages (parchment) and also included text from such diverse works as First Enoch, the Apocalypse of Peter, and the Acts of the Martyrdom of Julian.[99]

Three factors have been involved in its dating: "the handwriting [style], the format of the codex, and the location of the monk's grave" in which it was found.[100] The earliest graves date to the fifth century and the last to the fifteenth. The particular corpse that had the manuscript was found far closer to the oldest graves than to the newest.[101] The first editors of the published text thought it derived from the eighth century at the earliest. Later analysts have been receptive to a date as early as the sixth or even the fifth century.[102]

Two short fragments published in 1972 are often connected with this Gospel. These appear to come from the early part of the third century or, possibly, even the latter years of the second;[103] in other words, in the area of the year 200.[104]

The first of these two fragments is P. Oxy. 2949. Although reflecting the same narrative as the Gospel of Peter, this appears to be a significantly different version of it.[105]

The second is P. Oxy. 4009 and the connection here is far more conjectural. Also in Greek, this contains none of the material from the Akhmimic version but is sometimes thought to come from the same work.[106]

One early scholar divided the text into fourteen chapters (each containing a distinct incident or narrative section) and another into sixty verses. Since both forms are still utilized we have given the chapter number first and then the verses contained in that section afterwards.

## Place of Origin and Date

Several lines of evidence have been introduced to argue that the work originated in Syria, probably Antioch, its major city and intellectual center. Those ancients who refer to the work came from Syria. Similarities between the picture of the resurrection here and in the *Ascension of Isaiah* have also been pointed to.[107]

Since Bishop Serapion of Antioch utilized the work around A.D. 175 (in composing a refutation), the Gospel has to date earlier than that.[108] The discovery of the text found in our "Gospel of Peter" appears to verify that this Gospel of Peter was the same as the one cited by the second century Bishop.[109] Serapion explicitly refers to it having been authored by those of the same movement from whom he obtained a copy. In other words, it was believed by him and them that the work had originated in Syria.[110] This view is still generally accepted.[111]

As already noted, although short sections came to light in the early 1970s, what is available of the bulk of the text comes from a manuscript discovered in 1886. How closely the 1886 text represents the earliest form of Peter is unknown. There are significant differences between it and P. Oxy. 2949, the more recently discovered fragment.[112] Hence P. Oxy. 2949 later evolved into the 1886 text or two varieties of the text were perpetuated independently.[113]

If either of these is the same basic work as the rejected gospel of Bishop Serapion, then it would not be surprising if canonical elements were later added to disguise the unorthodox materials or if unorthodox materials were purged to make the material acceptable to an orthodox readership.[114]

One would be unlikely to find anyone who would assert the earlier works in this chapter are genuinely first century or even very close to it. The Gospel of Peter, in the second half of the twentieth century, spawned much speculation that the case might be dramatically different in regard to this work.

One school of thought argues that "the traditions underlying the Gospel of Peter ... go back to the first century and ... are independent of and as old as those of the New Testament Gospels."[115] How one would conclusively prove independence versus evolution of canonical thought into a modified form presents an immediate and difficult obstacle for this thesis. Furthermore, even assuming either approach, how much distinctly new material has the GP author added? How do we distinguish it from the pre-existing traditions— independent or dependent upon the canonicals?[116] For that matter, even in regard to the pre-existing materials, to what extent did they preserve credible alternative tellings of Jesus' death?

The defenders of this pre–Markian hypothesis make plain that pivotal to their view are the assumptions (1) that the canonical gospels are neither historical nor contain a major historical core within their interpretation of the events of Jesus' life and death and (2) that Jesus' resurrection never occurred and that all accounts of it are subjective "imaginative response[s] to the trauma of Jesus' fate."[117] Accepting these as a priori "givens," then it is quite reasonable to assume that such a significantly different account as that found in the Gospel of Peter could be at least as ancient as the canonical approach.

This neither proves not disproves either their claims or their dating, but vividly illustrates that it is virtually impossible to have an assumptionless scholarship. Indeed, such attitudes seem to be the driving force behind the Jesus Seminar and similarly minded individuals in their efforts to push radically backwards to an ultra-early date various noncanonical writings.[118]

Indeed, it is but a step from arguing the first century origin of the root materials to advocating the possibility that the canonical accounts were based, at least in part, upon the Gospel of Peter.[119] If so, its non-recognition in the following century or two is perplexing since they were in many ways in a far better position than we to directly judge how ancient a document (and its sources) actually were. Indeed, in light of the pivotal importance put upon the death and resurrection of Jesus in the New Testament epistles, the inclusion of a work dealing exclusively with that subject would have been a natural action if there had been a document available that was believed to genuinely represent accurate and authoritative apostolic traditions.

James H. Charlesworth and Craig A. Evans stress the improbability of this work being earlier than Mark. There are historical problems such as the apparent belief that Herod had authority in Jerusalem (1:2).[120] "Furthermore, the distance from the Jewish world and religion, as reflected for example, in the words 'their feast' (2:5), and 'it is written for them' (5:15), do not fit into the early Palestinian Jesus Movement that antedated Mark."[121]

Even some who argue for a relatively early date (a "final" version as early as A.D. 110, in this case) concede the difficulties in taking the work as reflecting genuine history. As Claudia Setzer observes, "It contains many implausibilities (e.g. the Jewish crowd crucifies Jesus) and mistakes (e.g. the Feast of Unleavened Bread lasts only three days). The author seems to know little about Palestine in the 30s (e.g., Pilate needs to ask permission from Herod)."[122]

It also deals with matters that would not have been regarded as potential problems until after the gospels were written, such as why the body of Jesus would have been given to Joseph at all.[123] Furthermore, the picture of the Jewish role in the death is painted far darker and more intensely than in the synoptics, as if it were a purpose of the author to emphasize it far more emphatically.[124]

# *Gospel of Nicodemus* (consisting of *Acts of Pilate* and *Christ's Descent into Hell*)

## Contents

Claiming to be the work of Nicodemus, a covert disciple of Jesus who was a member of the Sanhedrin, the story is, essentially, that of the trial and execution of Jesus even though the resurrection and post-resurrection events play a secondary role in the narrative. Called "The Gospel of Nicodemus" (after its purported author) its subject matter makes "The Acts of Pilate" (its earlier title) an accurate description of the work from the standpoint of its contents. In the thirteenth century the transition of name from "Acts of Pilate" to "Gospel of Nicodemus" began to take its place.[125]

Grafted on to this in many manuscripts is "Jesus' Descent into Hell," an apologetic work supposedly telling Jesus' contemporaries about what He had seen and done in the interim between death and resurrection. The two stories had an immense impact upon both literature and the popular imagination during the Middle Ages.[126]

## Authorship

Although claiming to be the record of Nicodemus, a secret disciple of Jesus, the account is heavily reliant on large segments of the canonical

Biblical text. It would have us believe that a major line of accusation against Jesus presented to the Roman Pilate was His defiance of the religious traditions (such as regulations of Sabbath work) that were the norm of the day. The historical Pilate, of course, would have had virtually no interest in this since his role was that of defending Rome's interests and not that of the local monotheistic religious establishment.

## Date

Several relatively early assertions by ancient church writers have been taken as an allusion to the Acts of Pilate section of the Gospel of Nicodemus. As early as Justin in his first *Apology*, there are references to a report by Pilate concerning Jesus' trial that were preserved in the government archives.[127] The credibility of this has been undermined, in the mind of some, because Justin also refers to the records of Quirinius' census and since — many believe — no such census occurred it easily follows that the existence of Pilate's records of the trial were also non-existent.[128] This objection, of course, is based upon the assumption that Quirinius' census never took place. It could equally well be argued that it would have been an extraordinarily foolhardly apologetic move to challenge people to look for records that one full well knew were not there.

In other words, it is not Justin who was wrong but modern critics. Hence if one is to reject Justin's assertions on these matters, it would be far more prudent to claim that he thought and believed such documents existed but was simply ill-informed. (But would it not have been a recklessly foolhardly apologetic to go that far out on the limb if he had not been confident of his assertions?)

The filing of some type of report would not have been an unnatural act. But there is a very large conceptual leap indeed from a report of some kind to some form of *this* work. If Pilate filed such a report one would not expect it to be as long as this treatise, nor would one have anticipated anything overly complimentary to Jesus and His claims since he represented a polytheistic state, whose leader was recognized as a "god."

What we could expect would be one of two approaches: Pilate could pass the blame to the Jewish authorities on the assertion that the risk to public order was so grave that to deny their wish for Jesus' death would have been extraordinarily unwise, however unfortunate its sad repercussions were for the accused. Alternatively, he could have heaped the blame on Jesus for not permitting him any excuse for freeing Him. In short, whatever existed would have been far different than the document we are considering.

Justin, however, refers to miracles at this time by Jesus. That we can confidently expect Pilate would not have mentioned, even assuming there had been any. Since the canonical versions do not introduce the matter, this argues that there was some other source in Justin's day that did and that it was believed to come from Pilate[129]: A document such as the surviving Acts of Pilate—"Such as," not necessarily "same as."

By the time we reach Tertullian we find that ancient church scholar referring to a report of Pilate that was so emphatic that Tertullian counted Pilate as a Christian in conviction even if never in formal allegiance.[130] Certainly the Acts of Pilate could be read in such a manner. Yet when Eusebius cites Tertullian on the subject it only concerns a purported "Letter" and no reference is made to a lengthy "Acts" type of document, which has led some to suspect that what we today call the Acts of Pilate or Gospel of Nicodemus still did not exist.[131]

When Epiphanius writes circa 375 that the Acts of Pilate could be used to calculate the exact date of Jesus' death, we clearly have arrived at either the current work or a closely related version since it can be utilized in exactly that manner.[132] But at what point prior to this did these Acts actually come into existence? The evidence of Tertullian points in the direction of this kind of document as does that of Justin, though not necessarily this particular work.

Our oldest surviving manuscript is only from the fifteenth century.[133] Due to significant differences in the manuscripts it is quite possible that it circulated in multiple forms for a lengthy period of time.[134] Hence great caution must be exercised in assuming how far back our text actually existed in something approaching the current form.

A date between approximately A.D. 150 and 200 has been suggested by Ron Cameron, though the evidence is sufficiently unclear that he concedes the possibility of an origin a century later.[135] Whatever other genuine or pseudo-Pilate materials may have existed in the early second century, there is simply nothing to clearly connect the current work with such materials, unless we are to assume a far shorter and less pro-Jesus version that was much later "padded out" at length. Hence a third or even early fourth century date seems far more reasonable, for sufficient time still must be left for it to have gained sufficient attention and popularity in order to come to Epiphanius' notice about 375.

## Place of Origin and Manuscript Forms

Ron Cameron suggests Syria as the more likely site, but concedes that the evidence is so conjectural that locations from Rome to Asia Minor to Egypt might be equally possible.[136]

Greek Form "A" (or "First Greek Form" in older works) is the one that will be utilized in our study since it is the oldest form. (Any citations from "B" are entered with a B and a slash in front of the chapter number.) Some date its composition, based upon the prologue, to A.D.[137] (Note how this dating makes it significantly later than whatever work was known to Epiphanius.) Others prefer a date around 600.[138] It is found in Armenian, Coptic, Georgian, Latin, and Syriac.[139]

Greek Form "B" is basically a condensation of the material of "A" except in two chapters (10 and 11), in which the crucifixion is described in far more detail. The omissions permit the recrafting of the conclusion to permit a logical inclusion of the Descent narrative, which otherwise is an obvious addition to a work that stands on its own two feet.[140]

The Latin forms come in a version that both closely echoes the Greek and one that does not. Even in the one closest to the Greek the length of the speeches have been greatly increased.[141]

CHAPTER 2

# Fragmentary Surviving Gospels

## Gospel of the Hebrews (also known as Gospel According to the Hebrews)

### Multi-Sources Cited as One Document

In the early ninth century, the Patriarch of Constantinople, Nicephorus, speaks of the Gospel of the Hebrews being 2,200 lines longer. For comparison, canonical Matthew is only 300 longer,[1] thereby indicating that whatever form of the work was available to the Patriarch, it was a quite lengthy composition.

The surviving fragments indicate that this was a "narrative" gospel in contrast to the "sayings" type manifested in works such as the well known (Coptic) Gospel of Thomas. Yet even this generalization would be quite challengeable. One problem in determining what quotations come from this work is that the title (or its equivalent) is used by ancient writers of what appears to be different works— at least two[2] and possibly three.[3] In either analysis, one now flies under the name "The Gospel of the Nazoreans" and the other with the traditional label "Gospel of the Hebrews" (in the three-fold division, two distinct works are given this title).[4]

In our citations we have maintained the ancient usage of using the same name to apply to all of this material. This is done for the sake of convenience and because the constituent parts no longer exist as distinct sources, and it is impossible to fully verify the deductions made concerning their separate existence and nature.

### "Gospel of the Hebrews"

These quotations and allusions provide internal indications that its author(s) were deeply imbued with the traditional "Wisdom" literature approach to religious and ethical thinking found among a certain type of ancient Jewish writers.[5] Estimates of the date of its composition have varied from the early years of the second century[6] to some time in the first half of the century[7] to a little later than mid-century.[8]

P. Vielhauer argues for an Egyptian origin on the basis of the fact that the main references to the work come from both Origen and Clement, both of whom conducted their ministry in Egypt.[9] This view of the place of its origin is widely shared.[10]

## "The Gospel of the Nazoreans"

This appears to have been a narrative type gospel such as the canonicals are.[11] Its original language is a subject of considerable difference. Some of the quotations attributed to this source, it has been argued, make much better sense as being based upon a Greek language document.[12] John S. Kloppenborg, however, argues that it was an Aramaic "translation" from Greek, and consisted of a mildly modified canonical Matthew.[13] Others prefer the scenario of the work having originated in Aramaic.[14]

The time of origin was likely during the first two quarters of the second century.[15] Because Jerome speaks of an important Nazorean group in the city of Beroea, Syria, Kloppenborg speculates that this could have been the site of its composition.[16]

# Gospel of the Ebionites

## Contents and Underlying Theology

This has been the title of convenience given to the account because the Ebionites utilized it.[17] Although the movement is referred to by a few other ancient theologians, only Epiphanius preserves any of the text of this gospel. Ambrose, Jerome, and Origen refer to the "Gospel of the Twelve" and the "Gospel according to the Twelve." These have been taken by some to be references to the same account since the narrators in all these cases are the apostles, as in the case of the Ebionite Gospel.[18]

The belief was expressed both in Epiphanius and other ancient references, that the Gospel of the movement was based upon canonical Matthew but with free censorship and modification to make it more amenable to the group's theology. A major example would be the removal of all accounts of the birth of Jesus. A minor alteration, but perhaps pointing to the group's vegetarianism, is found in the omission of locusts from the diet of John the Baptist.[19]

When one feels free to remove text to make it more religiously acceptable, there is little reason not to find in its additions a theological motive as well. Jesus' dislike of partaking of the final Passover (quoted later) may well represent further support of the group's vegetarian preferences.

In addition to the claim that it was based upon Matthew, the available fragments themselves verify that there is an on-going narrative in the work. A "sayings" style gospel might well be a unifying factor for an elitist "Gnostic" type group proud of its "exclusive truths" and unconcerned with its slender numbers. On the other hand, even any Gnostic movement hoping for a broad base needed a narrative style account of Jesus' life for the benefit of the rank and file. The Ebionite Gospel served this purpose.

## Date and Place of Origin

Since Irenaeus in the second half of the second century knew of the work (by name not by personal access), it is reasonable to assume it came into circulation at least a few decades earlier. So we are speaking in terms of an origin at mid-century or earlier.[20] The problem here is that Irenaeus' knowledge of the work later referred to under that name is highly arguable since he does not quote it nor refer to it in a manner to make the identification clear cut.[21] Hence the work might well be from a significantly later date.

Two major arguments support the writing of the work in the Transjordan region. The strongest is that this was the center of the Ebionite movement.[22] The fact that Epiphanius is the only writer to quote from it, and that he is known to have conducted part of his ministry in that area, both explains his interest in the work and ability to quote directly from it.[23] The caveat has to be added to this that the popularity of a work in a certain region does not necessarily prove that it was composed there.[24] (A modern example might be useful: If a massive disaster were to wipe away American civilization, the most likely place for a Book of Mormon to be uncovered by some future archaeologist would be Utah. Yet Joseph Smith [or whoever he may have "borrowed" the text from] certainly did not compose it in that state.)

# Egerton Gospel
# (Papyrus Egerton 2)

## Contents and Connection with Other Works

This "gospel" is named neither after the subject matter, its purported author, nor even its discoverer. Instead the "Egerton" refers to the Englishman who funded the purchase of the material.[25] The very limited segments that survive of the work implies that it was, in the main, a narrative rather than sayings gospel. In the body of this study we have quoted from fragment 2, which contains a healing narrative. Fragment 4 records a nature miracle, but the text is so incomplete that its contents and purpose is largely conjectural.[26]

The work likely represents an otherwise unpreserved gospel. Although it could be the same as one of the obscurer gospels about which little is known but a name, that hardly advances our knowledge since only a few short passages of the current work have survived. Nor do we have any guidance as to which of these other works it might be connected with. The possibility that it might represent part of the unpreserved earlier section of the Gospel of Peter can safely be rejected because the tone and content of the surviving Peter text is so drastically different.[27]

## Date and Place of Composition

H. Idris Bell and T. C. Skeat place the latest date for the writing of this narrative as early second century.[28] In a later work they place the earliest dates as approximately A.D. 80–90 and the latest as 120.[29] H. T. Andrews argues, "The Gospel shows no heretical tendencies and is comparatively free from exaggeration, suggesting that it may date from the early second century, or even the late first century."[30]

One stream of thought dates it much earlier. Ron Cameron opts for some point in the second half of the first century, but concedes it could be a little later.[31] Similarly, David R. Cartlidge and David L. Dungan view it as perhaps "as early as the middle of the first century; it can be no later than the early second century."[32]

J. K. Elliott estimates the codex fragments themselves as from approximately A.D. 150 and the composition of the work as, possibly, at the beginning of that century.[33] Joachim Jeremias opts for a date prior to 150 as well.[34] Jon B. Daniels, however, speaks of both the composition and copying of the current fragments as being in the second half of that century.[35] Yet other scholars feel more comfortable by speaking in terms of a second century date and not attempting to pin it down any further.[36]

The sole external evidence of date comes from the paleographical evidence. The style of writing fits the earlier part of the century, but unknown (and probably unanswerable) is how late into the century the same style was maintained.[37]

If the narrative was written in the same country where the fragments have been found, then Alexandria, Egypt is the only likely place for composition. This is argued from the early date of the work and the fact that such a large metropolis was the most likely place in the country to have a significant size Christian community.[38] Others prefer to separate the two aspects and opt for a place of composition in or around Palestine and Syria.[39]

## *Unidentified Gospel (Oxyrhynchus Papyrus 840)*

### Contents

Beginning with the end of a sermonic point about the danger of suffering eternal punishment, the bulk of what has survived deals with a verbal conflict in the Jerusalem sanctuary between Jesus and His foes on the subject of ritual purification. The text is among those uncovered at Oxyrhynchus in Egypt and is the only currently known copy.

The manuscript fragment has been thought, by some, to be from either the Gospel of the Hebrews or the Gospel of Peter. Since only a few extracts of the former exists and since what survives of the latter only begins after Jesus' arrest, there is little on which to base the derivation claims.

### Use of Text and Date

It is not uncommon to encounter the interpretation that the text was carried as a kind of magical amulet by the Christians among whom it circulated.[40] The script style utilized is dated by Phillip Sellew as likely third century.[41] Others think fourth century is probable or, less likely, the fifth.[42] The actual date of origin of the account is even more difficult to estimate, with some passing the subject by in silence[43] while others suggest a date prior to A.D. 200.[44] or "in the second half of the first century C.E., most likely [originating] in Syria."[45]

## *Secret Gospel of Mark*

### Contents and Discovery

This was a conscious expansion of the gospel of Mark in which the author inserted the additional materials he thought desirable. Since it received considerable favorable attention in the last decades of the twentieth century, we will give it greater consideration than might seem justified by the amount of text involved and the fact of the extraordinary late date of the sole attestation of the text.

This intriguing document has not survived from the ancient world. The document citing its contents, though supposedly written by Clement of Alexandria (which would place it in the late second century) is preserved only through a copy written at the end of a 1646 book.[46] The style of the script is such that it appears to have been added a century or more later.[47] Although preserved in Greek, where the copyist obtained the original and the whereabouts of its current location are unknown, if it has escaped the ravages of time at all.

From the standpoint of scholarly study, the document poses a particularly vexing problem. A facsimile was not printed nor have other scholars been able to gain access to the original. Justly or unjustly, this type of situation automatically sets off mental alarm bells in how one evaluates the genuineness and credibility of the material.[48]

## Credibility of "Clement's" Purported Letter

According to the reputed letter of Clement that quotes the work, Mark first wrote an account of Jesus' life in Rome for the benefit of those being taught about Christianity. This has been interpreted as canonical Mark[49] and as written for the preparation of individuals for their baptism.[50] The former may well be correct but the latter unlikely. As one reads the book of Acts, the universal custom described is baptism being offered upon the same day as the instruction (Acts 2), and individuals being baptized as soon as they request it (Acts 8). The idea of an obligatory period of instruction prior to baptism (though arising early) does not fit the canonical data or period.

According to Clement, Mark expanded the material into a wider ranging account after Peter's death and while living in Alexandria. This Secret Mark was intended for private circulation among the spiritually elite. This was later obtained by the heretical Carpocratians who not only bent its teaching but circulated their own corrupted version of the work.

That Clement had access to a document purporting to be from Mark is not impossible nor his belief that it actually originated in that source (which is not the same thing as his opinion being accurate). Various commentators have pointed out that Clement apparently believed that the *Preaching of Peter* originated with that apostle (*Strom.* 2.15.68; 6.5.39–41) as well as the *Apocalypse of Peter* (Eusebius, *Hist. Eccl.*, 6.14.1).[51] Hence, unless the document blatantly contradicted the canonical documents, he was apparently willing to give them the benefit of any doubt.

More alarmingly, the Clement of the Secret Mark letter accepts the propriety of not writing down for the general believing population the most important spiritual truths, but preserving them only for the inner circle of the movement. His complaint is that the Carpocrates had taken it and added or substituted their own materials permitting lascivious and unrestrained behavior. So his grievance is two fold: that a rival group (a) has gained access to the same spiritual material he has and (b) have allegedly twisted and distorted it.

The second is a quite credible reading of how Clement would have reacted to the misuse of the works he regarded as credible and/or authoritative, but what remains to be established is whether the historical Clement would have approved the idea of maintaining a secret set of "truths" that believers in general could not and must not have access to. He was certainly one who believed most were incapable of understanding deeper truths (see below), but there is a profound difference between recognizing their intellectual and spiritual limitations and denying them the data to even make the effort to understand.

One also encounters the ethical difficulty of defending and explaining why Clement ordered and how he rationalized a half-lie: Deny, he urges, that the Secret Gospel is Mark's when the followers of Carpocrates cite it. Yet the real objection is that they had added to it. Since any canonical work could be expanded, would not that have been the more likely line of rebuttal if the work were regarded as equally genuine and authentic?

The discoverer of the Secret Gospel concedes that Clement's known writings deny the Caprocatian claim of having a secret gospel that originated with Mark.[52] He concedes that, based upon this alleged new fragment from the church father, Clement's Secret Gospel and the Caprocatian "were basically the same."[53] In another work, the discoverer concedes that there are differences between statements and implications found in the previously known works of Clement and this one. He suggests that they "can be explained by the supposition that the letter represents Clement's secret teaching, as opposed to that in his published works."[54] If this be true, was not Clement himself functioning on the kind of debased level of moral non-integrity that he attributed to his opponents?

Laying aside this ethical dilemma, do the acknowledged writings of Clement give evidence that he believed in the concept of a secret teaching of Jesus? Here the answer hinges upon what the term "secret" is assumed to mean — teaching denied others so it might be reserved for an inner elite or teaching that most were incapable of comprehending?

Salvatore R. C. Lilla argues that Clement believed that the scriptures "were purposely written in symbols so that the truth might be kept hidden from the multitude and revealed only to a few initiated."[55] But if the hiding of the intent of the message (and he has in mind parables in particular) could be adequately done within the confines of written gospels available to all, why would one expect a book of the "secret" explanations to be committed to writing? Why has the distinction between written and unwritten disappeared? If such a written explanation were needed by an individual, did it not automatically prove the reader's "unworthiness" (at least, "unpreparedness") to receive and understand it?

Furthermore, the pivotal basis of the very argument postulates that crucial distinction between text available to all and explanations that are not. The extracts of the Secret Gospel in the purported letter of Clement are additional accounts of alleged events, not explanations of them. (We will return to this dilemma later.) How then do they fit into the sought for pattern? How could they be that which was to be kept secret?

Along the same line of the previous argument, Lilla argues that Clement of Alexandria believed that Jesus "spoke in parables in order to prevent His teaching from being divulged and communicated secret doctrines to those few among His disciples who were worthy of apprehending them."[56] (See the discussion a little later in this section.) This interpretation of Clement's teaching is "confirmed," he insists, by the discovery of Clement's letter about the Secret Gospel of Mark.[57]

As evidence for Clement's belief in a secret tradition, he cites two acknowledged texts from the church father's writings.[58] A look at the broader context of each passage argues that he has confused "secret" in the sense of difficult to be understood with the Gnostic use of the term as teaching denied to all but the elite.

For example, in one of the standard English translations,[59] *Stromata* 2.10 begins with the remark, "These three things, therefore, our philosopher attaches himself to: first, speculation; second, the performance of the precepts; third, the forming of good men; which, concurring, form the Gnostic." Yet the remainder of the section stresses that it is through the study and analysis of scripture — not other sources such as direct revelation or secret gospels — that this true Gnostic receives his enlightenment. It is conspicuously *not* from a source denied believers in general.

More germane is *Stromata* 1.12.[60] The chapter begins with the provocative heading, "the mysteries of the faith not to be revealed to all." This chapter begins with the assertion, "since this tradition is not published alone for him who perceives the magnificence of the word; it is requisite, therefore, to hide in a mystery the wisdom spoken, which the Son of God taught." On the other hand, since this word had been "published" it was already available; it was not hidden in the sense of being consciously denied all but the spiritually superior.

The problem lay not in people being denied access to the "truth" but in their ability to comprehend it, in the fact that not everyone could "perceive the magnificence" of the word. Clement then notes that this inability of many to adequately comprehend the truth represented a hindrance that he faced in his own effort to communicate truth through the written media. In both cases of original text and exposition, the teaching is not physically hidden from others, but the limitations of others affect how it is proclaimed and whether it can be understood.

Then Clement makes a remark more useful to the idea of a secret tradition, "But the wise do not utter with their mouth what they reason in council." The idea here is of things that "they reason in council," i.e., in private — there are things better left for the more knowledgeable to argue about when among themselves rather than drag others into a matter that is over their heads. This is not a secret tradition but an exposition of known tradition and how it is to be applied, presumably on difficult and troublesome topics.

Further evidence that this is meant comes in the words that immediately follow, which stresses the openness of the message rather than it being hidden:

> "But what ye hear in the ear," says the Lord, "proclaim upon the houses"; bidding them receive the secret traditions of the true knowledge, and expound them aloft and conspicuously; and as we have heard in the ear, so to deliver them to whom it is requisite; but not enjoining us to communicate to all without distinction, what is said to them in parables. But there is only a delineation in the memoranda, which have the truth sowed sparse and broadcast, that it may escape the notice of those who pick up seeds like jackdaws; but when they find a good husbandman, each one of them will germinate and produce corn.

To some the teaching is nothing but "parables," something beyond their comprehension. To them, Clement insists, there is no obligation to share the insights to be derived from their private "council" together discussing such texts. Again, the idea is not that they are to be denied what is useful and desirable, but denied what — to them — will seem useless and meaningless controversies and discussions. Hence, if there really had been another Mark available in Alexandria, we have no reason to believe that Clement would have denied any one access to it. What he would have denied, based upon his own genuine remarks, is any involvement in the intricacies of interpretation on matters above the heads of his listeners.

To use a modern parallel: He was not going to attempt to communicate to those on a middle school level the abstruse controversies that delight the minds of college professors and academics. It was not intended to be demeaning or "secret," just an acknowledgment of the limitations of the audience. (And, quite probably, more than a touch of philosophical snobbery on the part of Clement himself.)

Clement's brief appeal to the parables of Jesus as precedent for "secret" teaching fits in well with this: The teaching was publicly proclaimed to all and its meaning privately explained to the apostles. The message itself was openly available, not its intent. Hence there was only precedent for a "secret" explanation of a public teaching. (Even in regard to the interpretation, it should be noted that Jesus rebuked His apostles for their inability to comprehend the point of the parables [Mark 4:13]. In other words, they weren't as esoteric and mysterious and needful of deep insight to understand as they and, later, Clement, thought they had to be. They were seeking for a "deepness" in content in material intended to be the exact opposite—simple rather than complex explanations and exhortations.)

Clement did believe that there were precious truths that were not recorded in the gospels but that these had been handed down orally. "This gnosis [in context, given by divine revelation] has come down to our day, having been handed down in succession to a few from the Apostles in unwritten form" (*Stromata* 6.7).[61] He does not see this gnosis codified in any written document, the so-called Secret Gospel included. Indeed, from his own remarks and that of other ancients, it seems likely that a major purpose of writing at all was to preserve and spread these unwritten traditions.[62] If this be the case, is it likely that he would support the existence of a book of secret traditions that would not be similarly available for any believer seeking greater enlightenment?

## Credibility of the Secret Gospel Depicted in the Letter

What little of the text that is quoted itself raises problems. The bulk of it concerns the resurrection of a young man. Afterwards Jesus remains with him (and, presumably, the entire family) for about a week. Jesus spends one entire night instructing him in His teachings.

What in this is there to further the "free living" doctrines and practices of the Carpocratians? Admittedly, a little imagination could read into the night of instructions a veiled allusion to a homosexual encounter, but unless one goes that route what is there to have motivated the textual addition?[63] The same might be read into the disconnected and unexplained later reference of the work concerning two naked men. Clement argues that the Capocratians were out to further their agenda, but the specific additions do not seem to do so in the concrete and clear-cut fashion one would expect.

John D. Crossan combines the two events mentioned in the previous paragraph and concedes that they could be intended to have a homosexual implication. He argues, however, that the references make better interpretive sense as a reference to nude night time baptism.[64] In light of societal prohibitions against nudity, naked baptism would obviously have to be at night. There is some evidence indicating that at least Gnostic groups practiced such.[65] There are also canonical texts from Paul that can be creatively read in such a manner: the putting off of the old person and putting on of the new in particular.[66] Putting on a new nature/person is the point, not clothing, however, so this would not seem to have any genuine relevance.

Furthermore, nude baptism would not have been the norm in the apostolic era. The command to baptize (Matthew 28:18–20) had nothing in it to imply or require such a practice. Furthermore, the mass baptism in Jerusalem in Acts 2 was obviously done in daylight and involved both genders. Crossan's baptismal reading of the text could well be right, however, as fitting the reality of a sectarian movement and changing practice.

The baptismal reading of the text takes it as an illustration of mainstream as well as divergent Christianity. If so, we are pushed back, once again, to what made the work so offensive based upon the little that has been preserved. Faced with this difficulty, F. F. Bruce suggests that, "as with the *Gospel of Thomas,* it was the interpretation and not the written text that was regarded as esoteric."[67] If so, then the "Secret"/ Gospel actually did not reveal the "Secret(s)" after all, making it a misnomer at best.

Some have gone so far as to suspect that our canonical Mark is an abridgement of this Secret Gospel (at least in Clement's version of it).[68] It is far sounder, based upon our analysis of Clement's remarks on the origin of the work and the particular material he cites from it, to deny that either the letter or the Secret Gospel went back to his age. That it represents an unknown individual protesting against an expanded Mark at some later date (by invoking a respected earlier leader) would be a more attractive option — if we prefer to accept the pre-medieval antiquity of the purported letter and alleged gospel at all.

CHAPTER 3

# Surviving "Acts" and Other Documents

Although the gospels (both lengthy and fragmentary) are the most obvious source of information on Jesus' life,[1] other materials provide additional narrative that deserve attention as well.

## Acts of John

### Contents and Manuscripts

With John's missionary work and miracles its main preoccupation, the account also provides occasional "flashbacks" to incidents that occurred during Jesus' ministry. In context, these are clearly incidental to its major themes rather than primary to its purpose.

If, as the *Stichometry* of Nicephorus claims, these Acts were originally the same length as the Gospel of Matthew, then between two-thirds[1] and about 70 percent of it has survived into the modern age.[2] The "traditional" chapters 1–17 are now looked upon as not properly part of the work.[3] This misattribution was caused, in part, by the fact that there is no one single manuscript that contains the entire work. Instead, it has had to be pieced together from various sources, each of which seemed to be part of the book or one of similar intent or purported authorship.[4]

### Authorship and Date

Theoretical places of origin have divided scholars between Egypt, Syria, and Asia Minor.[5] The work came to be connected in the West with sectarian interests and movements.[6] In the East, though it was not looked upon as canonical, its stories were often viewed with considerable favor and preserved in excerpts in the writings of those considered unquestionably orthodox.[7]

The authorship of the Acts of John may have been the fourth century writer Leucius (Charinus). In the ancient world he was regarded as the author of a number of pious fictions, including ones purporting to be from the apostles. The linking of him to any specific work — this one in particular — remains speculative though intriguing.[8]

Although certain incidents are based upon earlier traditions,[9] how early that places these Acts (since surviving manuscripts are not themselves that ancient) hinges, in large part, upon one's theological convictions and one's theory of the development of the canon and nature of early Christianity. To the extent one views most of the canonical New Testament as a de facto generally recognized early standard and that anything that dramatically differs from it is likely to be of a later date, the more likely one is to date this and similar works in the second or third or later century, depending upon the external and internal evidences for each specific work. To the extent that one believes that there was no generally accepted consensus in late first century/early second century Christianity as to its core beliefs, doctrines, and basic authoritative works, the more likely one is to accept an ultra-early, even first century origin for such materials.

As to the Acts of John in particular, some believe it possible (though not probable) that it was composed in the first century or soon thereafter. Ron Cameron, on the basis of alleged "internal evidence," argues for a early second century date, though conceding that it might actually come from the following century.[10] Other specialists in the field argue that the work appears to date from the fourth century.[11] Most believe that its existence before the time of church historian Eusebius is unlikely.[12]

## Pistis Sophia

This gnostic work is a mystical explanation of faith, given in dialogue between Jesus, Mary (His mother), and certain other disciples.

The Askew Codex, which preserves the work, was obtained by a London doctor of that name in 1772. Where, when, and by what means his bookseller had obtained this Coptic language manuscript is unknown.[13] The codex is dated as having been written between 350 and 400.[14]

It is divided into four sections or "books." There are duplications of discussions and the speakers do not always retain the same name throughout even individual books. Although who is under discussion is reasonably clear in spite of this obstruction, such phenomena strongly argue that the current manuscript has been compiled from earlier works.[15] The first and fourth "books" have been dated as likely composed between 250 and 300.[16] Egypt is regarded as the likely place for the four sections to have been written and eventually combined into a single work.[17]

## Epistle of the Apostles (Epistula Apostolorum)

Basically, this is a series of conversations between Jesus and His disciples after the resurrection, purportedly sent out in letter form by the apostles. There are, however, a few references included about Jesus' life while on earth. Chapter 5, in particular, blends together a summary of several of His miracles that are recorded in the canonical accounts.

Oddly enough the work is nowhere mentioned in ancient Christian literature,[18] a factor which seemingly carries the unavoidable implication that its usage was extremely restricted. Once a Coptic version was discovered in 1895, fragments were then recognized as coming from the same composition in both Ethiopic and Latin.[19] The earliest surviving segments are found in Ethiopic and appear to date from the last part of the fourth century or the early fifth.[20] Preservation in multiple languages (even in fragments) certainly argues for its significant circulation geographically, yet the lack of favorable or critical references in ancient literature argues that it was not viewed either as a major impediment nor as a major work defending or defining the faith either.

Although the work is not considered Gnostic, it has been judged compromising by some for its use of gnostic type language and imagery in a form that was compatible with non-gnostic faith.[21] Ron Cameron goes so far as to argue that it intentionally mimics the gnostic style literature in order to combat it.[22] Mimicry or not, such language easily opened it to suspicion on accusations of doctrinal compromise in the eyes of the orthodox, while its restraint in openly embracing gnosticism compromised its appeal to that movement as well. Finally, even if orthodox, it simply did not express itself in the manner one expected the prevailing attitude to be presented. This also undercut its literary appeal to later generations in the strain of Christianity that ultimately triumphed.[23]

Some have suggested that it was not only composed in the first century but, quite possibly, in the first half.[24] A date in the middle or late second century[25] is far more likely due to the divergence in writing style, purpose, and content from the canonical literature and because it presupposes the existence and acceptance of such material.

## Toldoth Jeshu

The existing form may not date before the ninth century but its broad storyline was denounced a century earlier by the Bishop of Lyons, Agobard, in a book entitled *De judaicis superstitionibus* ("Concerning Jewish Superstitions"). Some of the storyline is the same as even earlier fragments that have survived in Aramaic describing Jesus in highly negative terms. Even before then, both Tertullian and Origen refer to a volume circulating in Jewish circles in their day containing stories providing an unflattering description of Jesus' life and activities. Hence the *Toldoth Jeshu*, in spite of any narrative innovations it probably contains, likely preserves the basic attitudes and interpretations that had been available for many centuries.[26]

Stephen Gero[27] and Morris Goldstein[28] both suggest the sixth century as a reasonable estimate for its original composition. Goldstein, in particular, suggests that it was most likely at mid-century under the anti–Jewish persecution of Justinian.[29] Craig A. Evans tentatively suggests the eighth century as the time of its writing.[30] Hugh J. Schonfield speaks a minimum date of the ninth century[31] but believes the earliest form dates to the fourth.[32]

The distribution of the work within the Jewish communities seems to have been modest.[33] On the other hand, the survival of a number of copies, prepared over centuries, argues that the subject matter retained enough interest to justify its preservation among copyists. Occasionally, outsiders came into contact with the work and quoted or otherwise referred to it.[34] Martin Luther, for example, both read it and translated it into German.[35]

# Part II

# The Life of Jesus

CHAPTER 4

# Mary and Joseph Before Jesus' Birth

## Birth and Childhood of Mary

### Infancy Gospel of James

As the Infancy Gospel of James tells it in chapter 1, Mary's father was Joachim, a man so wealthy and spiritually attuned that he brought double the offerings that were required for his sacrifices to God. On a certain occasion a critic rebuked him, arguing that there was no need to bring such gifts because he had no descendants. Scripturally speaking the claim was without merit. On the emotional level, however, one can easily imagine it prying open long suppressed feelings of guilt.

Hence the rebuke provoked a major bout of both grief and self-examination. He searched the tribal registers of the genealogies and discovered "that all the righteous had raised up seed in Israel." Did that mean that he was unrighteous? Not necessarily, for ancient Abraham had not fathered a child until his old age. So Joachim resolved to go apart from his wife and set up a tent. There he would fast for forty days and nights and not leave for either "food or for drink." The forty days of fasting immediately reminds one of Jesus' own forty days of fasting conjoined with temptation.

This fast, however, was undertaken under far different circumstances, in a last ditch prayerful effort to have God right the situation. If not, death would be the alternative. Indeed, in this case death was anticipated because when Anna learned of it (c2), she spoke of her "widowhood."

At the same time she cried out her sorrow over her own childlessness. Recalling the happy days of her youth she "put on her wedding garments" and went out to pray to God who had blessed the barren Sarah with a child from Abraham. In her prayer (c3) she protested that she was less than even the birds of the air and the animals of the field for at least they could produce offspring.

This bout of self-pity was broken up by an angelic appearance (c4). Her child would be one "spoken of in all the world," indicating the importance that Mary would play in the Divine scheme of things. Joachim had been informed of the coming birth shortly before and was returning to arrange for the offering of a large number of animals to celebrate the good news. (The manuscript evidence is divided on whether Mary's mother conceived by direct supernatural act independent of intercourse [as with Jesus] or whether the miracle lay in making possible the conception that occurred due to the normal marital sexual relationship.[1])

In return for having a child, the mother pledged that it would be delivered to the temple to "minister to Him in holy things all the days of its life" (c.4). The child was brought to term, born in the normal ninth month, and nursed by her mother (c5). At six months of age she could walk and at a year of age, the father held a major feast at which she received the blessing from the important priests who were his guests (c6). At age three she was delivered to the temple as a gift for the Lord (c 7).

One thinks in terms of Hannah and her son Samuel being passed into the hands of the priest Eli to become a life-time servant of Yahweh.[2] This was a peculiar one-time situation and had nothing to do with the temple, which, at that time, did not yet exist. When it did come into being (and was rebuilt after its various destructions), the custom of children being, in effect, adopted into the Temple never existed.[3] Even less imaginable was female children being so treated.

Stephen Benko points to this as part of a body of evidence indicating that the author was not only unfamiliar with first century Jewish practice, but also was likely influenced by pagan religious practices in his depiction of temple Judaism,[4]

> It is quite impossible, to mention only a few examples, that Mary, as a child, was at the "third step of the altar" in the temple (7:3; 8:1), and even more impossible that she had access to the Holy of Holies (13:2) where only the high priest could enter, and even he only once a year (Hebrews 9:3, 7). Furthermore ... bringing a woman into such close relation to priestly functions is not Jewish but pagan. In Greco-Roman religions, priestesses and other female religious officials, such as the Vestal Virgins in Rome, were known, but in Judaism they were not.

## History of Joseph the Carpenter

When we turn to History of Joseph the Carpenter, the same background is taken for granted though summed up in one concise chapter.

She was brought to the temple when she was three. She lived there for nine years, until she was twelve. At that point the priests sought out a man to be her spouse. She is described as "blessed, holy, and pure" and her parents go unmentioned (c2).

## Pseudo-Matthew

When we read Pseudo-Matthew, we find more than the first third of the book is based upon a retelling and expansion of the material recorded in James. Joachim is presented not only as an exemplar of faithfulness to God and charity to his fellow mortals but the nature of that benevolence is spelled out in far greater detail. "Therefore his lambs, and his sheep, and his wool, and all things whatsoever he possessed, he used to divide into three portions: one he gave to the orphans, the widows, the strangers, and the poor; the second to those that worshipped God; and the third he kept for himself and all his house" (c1). This generosity was rewarded by God with an even greater abundance.

For the first time we discover when he married: "And at the age of twenty he took to wife Anna, the daughter of Achar, of his own tribe, that is, of the tribe of Judah, of the family of David. And though they had lived together for twenty years, he had by her neither sons nor daughters "(c1).

When he came to the temple to sacrifice, "the priest, Ruben" rebuked him, arguing that "it is not lawful for thee to stand among those who are doing sacrifice to God, because God has not blessed thee so as to give thee seed in Israel" (c2). Although there was a total fabrication of the teaching of the Torah, Joachim retreated for five months to his flocks and did not return home at all during that period. So long was the separation that Anna poured out her fears in prayer-that not only was she childless, but she feared her husband must be dead as well. An angel then appeared to her and reassured her that she would, indeed, have a child.

At the same time this was happening (c3), "a young man" (angel, later in the chapter) appeared to Joachim and inquired why he had not gone home. Since God had not blessed him with children by her, he felt so much "shame and reproach," he replied, that he would rather stay in the fields with the animals. The angel assured him that she

> has conceived a daughter from thy seed, and thou in thy ignorance of this hast left her. She [the child] will be in the temple of God, and the Holy Spirit shall abide in her; and her blessedness shall be greater than that of all the holy women, so that no one can say that any before her has been like her, or that any after her in this world will be so. Therefore go down from the mountains, and return to thy wife, whom thou wilt find with child.

Since five months had passed, we know, today, that it could hardly have been Joachim's child. Either the author was unaware of such fundamentals of reproduction or he believed that it was not only a miraculous birth, but a birth not involving sexual intercourse at all. This would make it just a shade less miraculous than the birth of Jesus which is pictured in terms not only of being miraculous but being to a virgin, i.e., one who totally lacked sexual experience. The agenda of enhancing Mary's status would certainly be well served by this assumption.

Even though he offered an animal in sacrifice, Joachim was still uncertain what to do. He had seen a "vision"; but could he trust it? When he fell asleep, the same angel reappeared and reassured him of the uniqueness of the child to be born: "such fruit as no prophet or saint has ever had from the beginning or ever will have." So the instruction was repeated to promptly get back to his wife. The fact that it took him thirty days to complete the return, vividly illustrates the previous chapter's reference to the flock being in "a far country."

An angel appeared to Anna and commanded her to meet her husband at the "Golden" gate into the city, a command which she fulfilled. When Mary was three, her parents took her to the temple and placed her "in the community of virgins, in which the virgins remained day and night praising God (c4). And when she was put down before the doors of the temple, she went up the fifteen steps so swiftly, that she did not look back at all; nor did she, as children are wont to do, seek for her parents." By miraculous infusion of the Holy Spirit, Anna then poured out her joy in a psalm of praise to God for having blessed her with a child (c5).

During the temple years, Mary was an infant spiritual prodigy, more like thirty years of age in behavior and attitude than a mere three (c6). Three hours daily she prayed, then worked at weaving for six hours, only to return to a second three hours of prayer, which only came to an end when an angelic visitor provided her food to eat. (The food she obtained from the priests went to the poor.) In spite of this heavy load of spiritual and temporal obligations, she still found plenty of time to become "learned in the wisdom of the law of God," to engage in "praises and vigils of God," and to sing His praises.

With these virtues came what we today would call a touch of spiritual paranoia. "She was afraid lest in her laughter, or the sound of her beautiful voice, she should commit any fault, or lest, being elated, she should display any wrong-doing or haughtiness to one of her equals."

Inadvertently she created a new societal custom. So determined was she to pray throughout the day that she found herself greeting others with the words, 'Thanks be to God.' And from her the custom first began of men saying, 'Thanks be to God,' when they saluted each other."

There are fundamental historical errors in this material. As noted earlier, although we read in the Old Testament of Samuel being dedicated to the service of God and living at the site of worship, Samuel's is the only known case. Such service was the rarest of rarities for a male child and is totally unheard of for a girl.[5] In addition Mary would have been about ten when Herod's temple was brought into service, significantly too late in her life for the stay described in the text.[6] To the extent that a youthful home is ascribed to her it is Nazareth rather than Jerusalem (Luke 1:26).[7]

## Gospel of the Nativity of Mary

Although going over the same ground as Pseudo-Matthew, the Gospel of the Nativity of Mary serves as a useful capstone of the earlier narratives because it adds the most clear-cut advocacy of her perpetual virginity. Indeed, her own mother is told that after she entered the temple "she shall abstain from every unclean thing; she shall never know man, but alone, without example, immaculate, uncorrupted, without intercourse with man, she, a virgin, shall bring forth a Son…" (c4).

# *Betrothal of Mary to Joseph*

## Infancy Gospel of James

In James' story, Mary's special status in the sight of Yahweh was miraculously demonstrated to the priests in the temple. Throughout her years there "she received food from the hand of an angel." When she reached the age of twelve the priests began to worry whether she could maintain her sexual purity (but see below) and decided to pray for her as to how best to handle the potential problem. The high priest was instructed by an angel to "assemble the widowers of the people" from throughout Judaea in order to find her a husband (c8).

Typically, interpreters have taken their objection to her presence to mean that she would soon begin menstruation and thereby ritually pollute the temple in that sense (Levitcus 15:19–30).[8] If this were the case, why was she accepted for apparently permanent residence in the temple in the first place since the onset of menstruation was inevitable? Sexual abstinence might or might not be feasible on a lifetime basis, but the beginning of menstruation was inevitable.

According to the Leviticus 15 text, the ceremonial pollution was limited to sexual relationships and touching that which she sat or slept on or anything on the bed or chair. Nothing is said about the place she resides (in the narrative of Mary, it being the Temple in particular) becoming polluted.

To find anything excluding her from the temple, one would have to rely upon the Leviticus requirement that she bring to the priest at the entrance the necessary offerings at the end of her period of uncleanness. The presence of that factor would hinge upon the location of the living accommodations within the broader temple complex.

Narratively, it is quite possible that the author did embrace the misconception that menstruation was inherently defiling to even the attached buildings joined to a holy site. If so, this would be simply another example of his lack of detailed acquaintance with the scriptural texts. Narratively he needed some excuse to get Mary out of the temple and into the home of Joseph, and the current priestly doubts serve as an excuse to provide this result.

As the story continues, each widower brought with him a rod or staff, and all of these were collected by the high priest. He then entered the temple and prayed. Returning to their owners, a miracle promptly occurred: "a dove came out of [Joseph's] rod and flew upon Joseph's head." The high priest argued that this meant, he had "been chosen by lot to take into thy keeping the virgin of the Lord" (c9).

Joseph was understandably reluctant to undertake the task. "I have children, and I am an old man, and she is a young girl. I am afraid lest I become a laughing-stock to the sons of Israel." [9]

The text could assume that she was to be there as a kind of ward, with Joseph functioning in a guardian role until whatever time — if ever — she married. As the centuries went by this likely was the interpretation placed upon the text. Within even a second century context — the most likely time for the origin of this work — one would have anticipated amusement or shock that an unmarried male (even a widower) would be assigned such a task, especially when he no longer has a spouse to assure his honorable behavior. Hence the presumption of marriage to Joseph would be the most likely original intention of the passage.

The high priest reminded Joseph of Old Testament incidents in which those who defied God's will had been "swallowed up" by the earth. Out of fear this would happen, he "took her into his keeping" to live in his home while he went out to "build my buildings" as his carpenter trade required (c9). The fact that he could be away for varying lengths of time due to his work rings true; the fact that he would take a woman into his home before the betrothal period ended defies the realities of first century society.

## History of Joseph the Carpenter

Although Mary's menstruation could be the cause of her removal from the temple in James' account, here it becomes quite explicit. Joseph moved toward a clearer menstrual interpretation: "Let us search out a man, righteous and pious, to whom Mary may be entrusted until the time of her marriage; lest, if she remain in the temple, it happen to her as it wont to happen to women, and lest on that account we sin, and God be angry with us" (c3).

Joseph is pictured as a priest who supported himself and his family by carpentry. By his first wife he had four sons and two daughters. As customary in that society, he taught his sons the same trade and they accompanied him on his building excursions to other places (c2). Oddly, he is depicted as having to travel "to the shop where he wrought at his trade of a carpenter" (c4), even though we would anticipate this to be in or attached to the home.

Those in charge of arranging a guardian selected "twelve old men of the tribe of Judah," including Joseph (c4). (That those of this tribe could not serve as priests [Hebrews 7:13–14] apparently missed the observation of the writer.) A "lot" was cast — no mention of anything miraculous as in the earlier account — and Mary was given over to "be with him till the time of your marriage" (c4).

## Pseudo-Matthew

In Pseudo-Matthew, the reason for Mary leaving the temple loses the element of both potential personal fault (potential sexual misbehavior) or the gaining of sexual maturity (and the accompanying menstruation). Here it becomes a matter of rigid temple policy.

First of all, it is implied that she was an attractive young lady whose spirituality and abilities made her an appealing potential spouse. The priest Abiathar wished to have her marry his son and offered many "gifts" to the religious leaders to obtain the privilege (c7). Mary vetoed this by insisting that it was her destiny to forever remain a virgin. The priests responded that one method of worshipping God was to bear children, as had always been the custom in the nation.

Mary countered that perpetual chastity was better. In a gloss on the scriptural texts she appeals to the example of Abel, one of whose great virtues (one absent in the scriptural text) is that he died a virgin. Then there was Elias, who went through life without marriage as well. The temple itself had taught her to cherish virginity. Acting upon this childhood teaching and these alleged scriptural precedents — actually creative interpretations of the text with little or nothing to back them but the imagination of the interpreter — she had vowed to never have sexual relationships with any man.

The immediate cause of her having to leave the temple came from the fact that the Pharisees had successfully insisted that it was "now a custom" that no girl who reached fourteen should remain in the temple any longer (c8). Hence all the tribes (leaders of them? all available males? probably the latter) are summoned to Jerusalem.

The high priest addresses them with the historically erroneous claim that "since this temple was built by Solomon, there have been in it virgins, the daughters of kings and the daughters of prophets, and of high priests and priests; and they were great and worthy of admiration. But when they came to the proper age they were given in marriage... But a new order of life has been found out by Mary alone, who promises that she will remain a virgin to God." Hence there was the need to determine whose household she should enter.

(If it were all that important for her to remain a virgin life long, what better place to do so than the temple itself? Would not perpetual virginity there be far more likely to assure that result than living in a man's household where she could have been the victim of abuse? If we equate virginity with purity, what more appropriate place could there be? The need to interlock perpetual virginity with the Biblical framework of a marriage to Joseph ruled out the development of such a scenario.)

The priests first cast a lot as to which of the twelve tribes would take her. Judah was selected. The next day all available males of Judah were to appear with a rod. Their rods were collected and, by direct order of God, placed in the holy of holies. When they came back the following day to collect their rods, a dove would appear from the one to whom Mary was to be handed.

But it did not happen. So the high priest entered the holy of holies (in real life, prohibited except once a year [Hebrews 9:7]) in order to offer a sacrifice (which, again in real life would have been offered outside the holy of holies [Hebrews 9:6]) and to pray to God to solve the difficulty. An angel appeared and explained that they had somehow missed "the shortest rod" of the lot and had not taken it out.

The rod was Joseph's. He "was an old man" and was embarrassed to ask for it back and had let the error go by in silence. As soon as he received it from the high priest a beautiful dove flew out of it toward the skies. Joseph was not happy with the idea of taking the woman. "I am an old man, and have children; why do you hand over to me this infant, who is younger than my grandsons?" Joseph was cautioned that if he defied God's will he could perish as had people in the days of old.

In this version Joseph is clearly far more astute and worldly-wise than in the earlier versions, for he seeks time to think and pray about it and takes measures to protect his own reputation:

I shall be her guardian until I can ascertain concerning the will of God, as to which of my sons can have her as his wife. Let some virgins of her companions, with whom she may meanwhile spend her time, be given for a consolation to her. Abiathar the high priest answered and said: Five virgins indeed shall be given her for consolation, until the appointed day come in which thou mayst receive her; for no other can be joined in marriage (c8).

Her claim of perpetual virginity is one that is conveniently pushed to the background. She is now Joseph's problem and so far as he is concerned, she will marry. None of the sexual connotations normally attached to the relationship are disavowed. The only issue in doubt is which of his sons would be the husband if Joseph continued to refuse the role. "No other" than one of these could be joined in marriage to her.

## Annunciation of Jesus' Coming Birth to Mary

### Infancy Gospel of James

According to James' Infancy Gospel,[10] a council of priests decided that a new veil was needed for the temple. To prepare it, they asked Mary to lead a group from the tribe of David that would consist of herself and seven additional "undefiled virgins"—implying that the marriage has not been consummated. It was her task to cast the lots to decide which individuals would sew the various colors into the veil (c10).

Historically speaking there was no such thing as a tribe of David,[11] though one could imagine the tribe he was a member of sometimes applying such an epithet to themselves as a way of enhancing group honor. Ancient traditions also present a problem with the narrative because they indicate that not eight but eighty individuals were involved in the preparation of the veil.[12] The smaller number makes Mary's headship of the project more practical (given her youth) and serves that useful narrative purpose.

While she went out to get water, an angel appeared to her and told her that she would bear a child. She, at first, took this to refer to the normal process of procreation and childbearing, but the angel promptly corrected her by stressing that this pregnancy would occur by "the power of the Lord" (c11).

### History of Joseph the Carpenter

All mention of the annunciation to Mary is completely omitted in Joseph the Carpenter. It happens "offstage" so far as the development of the story.

## Pseudo-Matthew

As Pseudo-Matthew tells it, six women (Mary and her escorts) were given the responsibility of working on a new veil for the temple (c8). Since Mary was "younger than all" the rest she got to sew the purple thread. (But since Mary was described as being cast out of the temple because she had reached the mandatory leaving age of fourteen, how did these others get passed over though older? Why hadn't Mary been permitted to stay as well? Here is a story consistency glitch that the writer misses.)

Mockingly, her escorts gave her the nickname "queen of virgins." An angel quickly appeared and told them all that this nickname would actually come "most true."

The following day Mary went out to fill a pitcher with water (c9). An angel appeared to her to tell her that she would bear a child who would be a "King" and "reign from generation to generation." Her own importance was stressed as well: "For, lo, the light from heaven shall come and dwell in thee, and by means of thee will shine over the whole world." Something approaching a co-redemptress interpretation of Mary's role is implied though, oddly enough, her virginity at the time of conception is not emphasized.

## Arabic Infancy Gospel

The Arabic Gospel made only the most passing, indirect allusion to the annunciation. At some point on the day of birth (not identified by the text), Jesus had spoken to Mary from the cradle about this earlier announcement: "I am Jesus, the Son of God, the Logos, whom thou hast brought forth, as the Angel Gabriel announced to thee; and my Father has sent me for the salvation of the world" (c1).

## Epistle of the Apostles

In the Epistle of the Apostles Gabriel becomes an incarnation of the unborn Jesus (c14). "I alone was a minister unto myself in that which concerned Mary," for it was His custom to act in such a manner. After the announcement of the coming birth, "Her heart accepted me, and she believed [she believed and laughed, Ethiopic], and I formed myself and entered into her body."[13]

## Mary Visits Mother of John the Baptist

### Infancy Gospel of James

In a blatant inflation of his status as described in Luke 1, in James' account Zacharias is changed from being a mere priest who happened to be serving in the temple as part of his periodic service to the rank of being high priest (c8). After arranging for the preparation of a new veil, Zacharias is visited by the angel that strips him of his speaking abilities (c10).

At this point Mary went to visit her kinswoman Elizabeth. Elizabeth felt honored that "the mother of my Lord should come to me." For no obvious reason in plot development, Mary is described as having "forgotten the mysteries of which the archangel Gabrial had spoken." So she "gazed up into heaven and said: Who am I, O Lord, that all the generations of the earth should bless me?" At this point Mary was sixteen years old (c12). (A majority of James manuscripts give this as the age, but a minority have everything from twelve to seventeen.[14])

Since a husband had been sought for Mary when she reached twelve (c8), three or four years had now gone by. Yet she had just prior to the meeting with Elizabeth been described as one of "the undefiled virgins of the family of David." Moving into Joseph's home (which happens immediately after Joseph is miraculously selected to be her spouse) traditionally carried the connotation of moving from betrothal into the formal married state.

Hence we are supposed to believe that for three or four years the marriage had remained unconsummated. This would be a matter of shame for a first century Jewish husband and flies in the face of societal anticipations and demands. Furthermore, there is nothing in the text of James prior to this point to make us anticipate a permanent state of virginity. Her permanent service to God had been pledged by her mother (c4), not her permanent virginity.

### History of Joseph the Carpenter

The visit of Mary to Elizabeth is unmentioned in the account of Joseph. Indeed, Elizabeth's pregnancy goes totally unmentioned. In a similar manner, these elements go unmentioned in Pseudo-Matthew as well.

## Joseph Learns He Is to Be a Father

### Infancy Gospel of James

Mary returned home as her pregnancy became obvious (c12) James tells us that Joseph had been away engaging in his craft of building (c13).

At this point she was six months pregnant and he was horrified because he recognized that he would be blamed for what had happened. Since there has been no reason given in the narrative to anticipate her permanent virginity, this would, obviously, be untrue. Indeed, since the text had earlier stressed his great age in comparison to her, her pregnancy would have been taken as a sign of honor and pride for him — as a mark of his success as a husband.

Joseph was tempted to divorce her but was afraid that something supernatural might be involved in the conception (c14). With the New Testament in front of one, this would not be an unnatural thought in the post-apostolic centuries. However, a first century individual would only have had the Old Testament writings and those only deal with miraculous conceptions of women who have been unable to conceive after extended periods of the normal marital sexual relationship. The time period involved in this case was far too short for the suspicion or anticipation of supernatural intervention to play a role.

## History of Joseph the Carpenter

In Joseph, we read that he returned home after being away for an unspecified period of time. Mary was fourteen years old at this point (c4) and three months pregnant (c5). Barring his being married to her and enjoying the sexual intimacy that goes with it — in which case he would be well aware of every contour of her body — one can't help but wonder whether the pregnancy would be all that noticeable in the loose fitting clothes of the era. Even with that degree of familiarity, three months is still an early point for the pregnancy to become obvious.

The narrative difficulty notwithstanding, the discovery of her pregnancy "greatly perplexed" him and he "thought of sending her away secretly. But from fear, and sorrow, and the anguish of his heart, he could endure neither to eat nor drink that day" (c5). In the middle of the day, Joseph had a dream in which Gabriel appeared to him to bring assurance that Mary was without moral guilt. He was "to take Mary as thy wife: for she has conceived of the Holy Spirit." Her Son would rule the nations (c6).

## Pseudo-Matthew

After spending nine months away on a house-building project, Joseph returned home to find Mary pregnant (c10). Mary's escorts vouched for her integrity: she had had no opportunity to have slept with a man. Their best speculation was that an angel had caused her to become pregnant. Joseph dismissed that as nonsense and wondered how he was going to explain the situation when he next went to the temple.

That night an angel appears to Joseph to explain that her conception was supernatural and that he was to marry her (c11). He shared this "vision" with Mary and her escorts and confessed, "I have sinned, in that I suspected thee at all."

## Joseph Blamed for Mary's Pregnancy

### Infancy Gospel of James

According to James, when Joseph took Mary with him to the temple, her pregnancy was quite visible and horrified the scribe who first saw it (c15). Reporting this to a priest, he informed him that Joseph "has defiled the virgin whom he received out of the temple of the Lord, and has married her by stealth, and has not revealed it to the sons of Israel." This is totally incredible in light of the story that has been told so far. Since they had been intentionally seeking out widowers, what would they have expected except marriage? If not to himself, then to one of his other sons? No mention of perpetual virginity had been enjoined and if that had been the intention, prudence alone would have required that they put her in the household of a stable married couple of good spiritual and social standing. (Perhaps we are dealing here with a later addition to the work when just such a perpetual vow was assumed to have been in existence.)

A tribunal was convened to hear the matter. Mary was challenged with the query of how she could have permitted a pregnancy to occur since she had been "reared in the holy of holies and didst receive food from the hand of an angel"? In real life no woman was permitted into the holy of holies, only the high priest and that only once a year.

The priest challenged Joseph and he protested his innocence as well. Both parties were required to "drink of the water of the ordeal of the Lord" to verify their innocence or guilt (c16). According to the Old Testament, guilt produced death upon drinking of this water. In the canonical scriptures, however, only the accused woman drank of it, not the accused male.[15] Since neither perished, the priest in charge dismissed the case, "If the Lord God has not made manifest your sins, neither do I judge you."

### History of Joseph the Carpenter

In the Joseph account, there is no call to reckoning before a priestly court of either Mary or Joseph.

### Pseudo-Matthew

Pseudo-Matthew notes that when word spread that Mary was pregnant, "officers of the temple" arrested both of them and took them there (c12). They accused him of seducing her — an odd accusation since we saw (above) that when she was given into his custody the priests were clearly thinking she would marry. They had no reason to assume that their intention had not been fulfilled. Since pregnancy normally accompanies marriage, pregnancy would not be an abnormality; the lack of pregnancy would be. Perhaps in terms of Pseudo-Matthew's plotting, the idea is that at that earlier point Joseph had spoken of giving Mary to one of his sons. Since that had not happened (as demonstrated by his being her escort to the temple and not one of the sons) and since she remained in his home, he himself must be to blame for her condition.

(His being away nine months and just arriving back would make it biologically impossible for him to be the father. On the other hand, Pseudo-Matthew believed that Mary's father had gotten her mother pregnant with his seed though away five months. Hence one must suppose that in the sexual theory assumed by the author that this could have been the result of a sexual encounter with Mary at some point before leaving on the building project.)

Both individuals are made to drink of the water of testing to see if they were guilty of sexual misbehavior. As described here, Joseph does so first and the rationale is that "when any one that had lied drank this water, and walked seven times round the altar, God used to show some sign in his face. When, therefore, Joseph had drunk in safety, and had walked round the altar seven times, no sign of sin appeared in him." (In the Old Testament form of the ritual, death occurred and nothing involving walking around an altar was in the ritual.)

Mary was then subjected to the same test and came through equally cleared of guilt. Reconciling the obvious pregnancy with their "verified" guiltless status divided the judges. She was pregnant, many thought, therefore she must be guilty. Joseph may not be, but the child is somebody's. Mary responded that she had vowed to remain a virgin, she had remained a virgin and she would forever remain such. (Only now does the perpetual virginity motif reappear and they are implicitly rebuked by being reminded that she had adhered to original intention even though their intentions had been different.)

This turns the tide of opinion in the crowd. "Then they all began to kiss her feet and to embrace her knees, asking her to pardon them for their wicked suspicions. And she was sent down to her house with exultation and joy by the people, and the priests, and all the virgins."

Such claims of innocence would not have cleared the Vestal Virgins of ancient Rome — among whom occasional pregnancies, embarrassingly, did occur. Nor would it be met with anything but mirth today. Indeed, if any woman except Mary made such a claim in Pseudo-Matthew's day would it have been accepted? Hence we clearly have a case where the desire to glorify Mary defies the psychology of the people of the author's own age as well as that of the first century and our own. Working from the assumption that such acceptance and praise is how people "should" react, he assumes that the ancients "would" have reacted that way. This speaks much, perhaps, of his piety but not of his realism.

CHAPTER 5

# Birth of Jesus

## Jesus Born in Bethlehem

### Infancy Gospel of James

At this time, the Emperor Augustus' decree that the population be enrolled for taxation purposes came into play. As James tells it, Joseph decided to take his sons with him, but hesitated before deciding to take Mary as well. Near Bethlehem she had a vision of two groups of people, "one weeping and lamenting, and the other rejoicing and exulting" (c17).

Recognizing that her time for delivery was near, Joseph "found a cave there and led her into it; and leaving his two sons beside her, he went out to seek a midwife in the district of Bethlehem" (c18). From here through chapter 20, the text shifts into the first person and claims to be the words of Joseph himself, perhaps indicating the conscious interpolation of a separate work. The cause of its inclusion and its origin is not explained by James, however.

As Joseph sought for the midwife (c18) he noticed that the birds and the animals had ceased moving about. They were no longer eating or flying but were all looking heavenward. Even the sky itself (clouds, presumably) had stopped its movement. This cessation of motion has been interpreted as a vision.[1] Psychologically speaking it is more likely a recognition that in times of crisis, time itself seems to slow down and it is as if we are moving in time but the world around us is frozen in place.[2]

Depending upon how naïve one assumes the author and his audience to have been, it is possible to assume that the narrative was intended to be taken literally.[3] Some have attempted to find a canonical precedent for such literalness by citing the earthquake and eclipse narrated in connection with Jesus' crucifixion and death.[4] With these "natural" phenomena, however, one can easily imagine tangible real life events since both have occurred time and again. The "freezing" of movement in nature found in James is something far different for, on a "literal" basis, it is without precedent.

Some have introduced the words of Ignatius, writing to the Ephesians, as evidence that in his day such a belief existed concerning the time of Jesus' birth. In regard to Mary's virginity, her childbearing, and Jesus' death, Ignatius describes these as "three mysteries of shouting which were wrought in the silence of God."[5]

Although James' reference to the suspension of movement would seem to carry the necessity of silence as well (since there would be nothing to cause noise), Ignatius is speaking of the "silence of God" rather than that of nature as in James.[6] The fact that the best explicit reference to such freezing of movement at the birth of an important figure is found in the narrative of the birth of Buddha[7] argues either that the conception was one that was widespread[8] or that, on some psychological level, it was one that could appear in many different cultures as most befitting the birth of a great man.

After observing the strange phenomena around him, at this point (c19) Joseph encountered a woman and told her that he was seeking a midwife. Instead of emphasizing the urgency of the needed assistance — the natural reaction of a frantic husband — he emphasized that the woman about to give birth is only "betrothed" and not formally his wife. Furthermore the child had been "conceived of the Holy Spirit." In real life, this would have encouraged the woman to think him either a madman or the child the result of an illicit affair. In either case, she would have been more inclined to wash her hands of the entire affair rather than become involved in such a dubious situation. Joseph's time for explanations might have occurred after the birth but not before it.

Perhaps the narrative purpose for such an unnatural protestation lies in the desire to prepare the woman (and the reading audience) for the equally miraculous preservation of Mary's virginity in spite of giving birth. That becomes more important than the credibility of his volunteering to a total stranger the startling claim of the nature of Mary's conception.

The woman, who turned out to be a midwife such as he sought, was able to tell that something incredible was happening because "a luminous cloud overshadowed the cave" (c19). For some reason she took for granted that this meant that "salvation has been brought forth to Israel." (Based upon Old Testament precedent, a divine manifestation of some type would have been more likely rather than this "Christian" expression of the ancient hope.) The cloud "immediately" disappeared and a bright light took its place from within the cave. As its brightness declined, the infant appeared without any assistance from her. (Most manuscripts refer to the cloud as a shining one; a minority describe it as dark.[9])

A friend of the midwife insisted upon physically verifying that Mary was still a virgin, (c. 19, 20)[10] though there had been no reason given her for assuming that Mary would still be such. Scripturally speaking, there is no Biblical, supernaturally-produced conception that hints at such a situation occurring prior to this time, so there would have been no reason for a Jew to anticipate it in this case.

Be that as it may, when she made the examination her hand burned so intensely that it felt like it would burn off. She desperately prayed for relief and an angel then told her that if she would but hold the infant she would be cured. This she did, making the assumptive proclamation (again without anything making it a natural thought in the context) that "a great King has been born to Israel" (c20).[11]

The concept of Mary as a virgin in childbirth had a long fight before it became the dominant judgment. Even Clement of Alexandria, who accepted the belief, conceded that it was a minority stand even at his time. "Most people, as it appears, even now believe that Mary ceased to be a virgin through the birth of her child, though that was not the case; for some say that after her delivery she was found when examined to be a virgin."[12] Clement was clearly aware of a tradition embodying what James records, though it is fascinating that, though it matches his own convictions, he distances himself from it by merely describing it as "some say" that such an examination occurred. He seems to have been in the difficult position of wishing to embrace the position taken by a written narrative whose overall reliability he does not wish to embrace.

Central to early Christianity's claims was a belief in a literal bodily resurrection of Jesus. Why then should the concept of an ever virgin mother begin to have such an appeal? Stephen Benko argues that it was a matter of cultural adaptation to the religious preconceptions of a far different region than the Palestine in which it had originated[13]:

> For minds accustomed to thinking in the categories of the prevalent pagan culture, the mother of the Son of God could have no lesser dignity than the Great Mother of the gods, the favorite subject of popular piety in the East. So the author lifted Mary out of the ordinary and elevated her to a goddess-like figure. Her feet did not touch the ground until she was taken to the temple, her bedchamber was made into a sanctuary, and the "undefiled daughters of the Hebrews" attended her. Even after her marriage to Joseph she labored in the company of "pure virgins" at making a veil for the temple, much the same way that the girls of Athens worked at making the new peplos for the statue of the Virgin Athene.

## History of Joseph the Carpenter

In Joseph, Mary's presence at the registration of taxpayers was caused by sympathy and deep human concern, because "the time of her bringing forth was at hand" (c7). The birth itself is described succinctly and without the elaborations of James. "Indeed Mary, my mother, brought me forth in Bethlehem, in a cave near the tomb of Rachel the wife of the patriarch Jacob, the mother of Joseph and Benjamin." The odd geographic correlation of the birthplace of Jesus and the burial place of Rachel argues that by this time a more concrete location had come to be regarded as the birth spot, in contrast to the vaguely described "cave" of James.

## Pseudo-Matthew

Pseudo-Matthew also sets the stage for the birth narrative by noting that the tax enrollment was due to the decree of Caesar Augustus (c13). In his version, Mary accompanying Joseph is not a matter of personal choice but necessity since they both traced their ancestry through "the tribe of Judah" and both needed to be enrolled.

Nearing Bethlehem Mary saw a vision of two groups of people, one happy and one overcome with sadness. Unlike James, Pseudo-Matthew explains its significance. "She saw the people of the Jews weeping, because they have departed from their God; and the people of the Gentiles rejoicing, because they have now been added and made near to the Lord, according to that which He promised to our fathers Abraham, Isaac, and Jacob: for the time is at hand when in the seed of Abraham all nations shall be blessed."

This interpretation of the vision was given by an angel who appeared after a weary Joseph had dismissed her words as unimportant. Then the angel ordered the beast Mary was riding to stop and instructed Mary to get down and go into a deep cave, one so long that light never reached its end. As soon as she did so the entire cave was lit up with mid-day brightness. (Since it does so: is the supernatural light caused by the unborn Jesus' presence or that of Mary? Most likely the later since Jesus was not yet born.)

As soon as the child was born, He stood upon His feet and "the angels adored Him." While this happened Joseph had been out seeking midwives and had brought back two. Although the child had been born, Joseph was concerned about complications and urged Mary to give permission for them to approach her, which she promptly granted. After examining the patient, the midwife Zelomi cried out, "Lord, Lord Almighty, mercy on us! It has never been heard or thought of, that one should have her breasts full of milk, and that the birth of a son should show his mother to be a virgin. But there has been no spilling of blood in his birth, no pain in bringing him forth. A virgin has conceived, a virgin has brought forth, and a virgin she remains."

The midwife Salome doubted these claims and wished to examine Mary's physical condition herself. Because of her "unbelief, since without a cause" she had doubted Mary's continued virginity, her hand withered up in terrible pain. An angel told her that if she would "adore" and "touch" the newborn, she would be healed. As soon as she touched his clothes this, indeed, happened.

Some shepherds arrived and reported having heard angels "singing a hymn at midnight" and proclaiming the child's birth. "Moreover, a great star, larger than any that had been seen since the beginning of the world, shone over the cave from the evening till the morning. And the prophets who were in Jerusalem said that this star pointed out the birth of Christ, who should restore the promise not to Israel, but to all nations."

The canonical version in Luke has the child born in a place where animals ate (for that is what a "manger" was), i.e., it was a stable.[14] Pseudo-Matthew attempted to reconcile the Lukian narrative with the version it had adopted from James by having Mary, on the third day after the birth, leaving the cave "and entering a stable" (c14). There she "placed the child in the stall, and the ox and the ass adored Him."

Another means of reconciling the two (though not utilized by Pseudo-Matthew) is to argue that a cave was itself used as a stable — either a natural one or one dug out for that purpose. Since this phenomena was found in the region in later centuries it would not be improbable for something similar to have been familiar in the first century as well.[15] Certainly the tradition of birth in a cave goes back at least to the days of Justin.[16]

Pseudo-Matthew claims that this was the embodiment of two prophecies. "Then was fulfilled that which was said by Isaiah the prophet, saying, "The ox knoweth his owner, and the ass his master's crib. The very animals, therefore, the ox and the ass, having seen Him adore Him." A second prediction from a person unmentioned in the scriptures is then cited. "Then was fulfilled that which was said by Abacuc the prophet, saying: Between two animals thou art made manifest."

On the required eighth day Jesus was circumcised (c15). After the period of ceremonial purification required of Mary was completed, they took the child to the temple and offer the required sacrifices. At this point the text interlocks with canonical Luke, by recording the reaction of the elderly Simeon and Anna to the child.

## Arabic Infancy Gospel

The Arabic Gospel avoids the heavy Mariology of the earlier accounts by avoiding their conjectures and praise of her early years. Instead, it

## 5. Birth of Jesus

immediately jumps to the time of the census and Jesus' birth (c1). Responding to Augustus' decree, Mary brought the trip to an abrupt end outside the city by telling Joseph that it was time for her to deliver (c2). Omitting all reference to the canonical text's description that there was no room in Bethlehem, she insists that she can go no further and urges that they use a nearby cave. Though it was sunset, Joseph hastened out to find someone to assist with the birth. Finding an elderly woman, he urged her to accompany him.

By the time they arrived, the child had already been born (c3). The cave was filled with light more beautiful than any candles or lamps could provide and more magnificent than the sun itself. Then in a token but quite explicit piece of Mariology, the woman describes her as "not at all like the daughters of Eve" (how in the world could physical appearance be *that* much different?). To this comes the response, "As my son has no equal among children, so his mother has no equal among women."

As "payment" for coming, the woman asks for her "palsy" to be removed. (Nothing has been explicitly stated to indicate that healing could either be expected or was even possible.) Mary instructed her to "place thy hands upon the child" and as soon as she did she "was immediately cured. Then she went forth, saying, "Henceforth I will be the attendant and servant of this child all the days of my life."

The supernatural light had now disappeared for we find a fire being lit after the shepherds arrive (c4). A heavenly chorus erupted in song and the elderly lady is convinced that "mine eyes have seen the birth of the Saviour of the world."

On the eighth day the child was circumcised "in the cave" (c5). The elderly Jewish woman saved the foreskin and provides it to her son with the strictest of instructions not to sell it for any amount of money. Jesus was then taken to Jerusalem and on the required day the necessary offerings were made at the temple.

While there, "angels, praising Him, stood round Him in a circle" (c6). This caused two elderly spiritual individuals to notice him and to show their affection for the newborn. (Their words of praise — but no mention of seeing angels praising the newborn — are mentioned in Luke 2.)

## Some General Observations

Although the doctrines concerning Mary that were pioneered by James were ultimately developed in a church approved fashion, it is useful to remember that they were equally amenable to evolution in a very different fashion — one that was officially deemed heretical. As Jaroslav Pelikan writes,[17]

Some of the legends about the Virgin contained in the *Protevangel of James* were the inviolate virginity of Mary not only in conception but in birth, as well as the related idea that she gave birth to Jesus without suffering birth pangs, and therefore the explanation that the "brothers of Jesus" spoken of in the Gospels must have been the children of Joseph the widower from his first marriage. Although it is not clear, there are grounds to suppose that some of these legends about the Virgin Mary may implicitly have represented as well a hesitancy to ascribe total humanity to her divine Son, as that hesitancy was already being expressed in other sources nearly contemporary to the *Protevangel of James*.

Irenaeus, to whom we owe the first large-scale exposition of the parallel between Eve and Mary, is likewise one of the sources from whom we learn that such a hesitancy among the followers of the Gnostic teacher Valentinus had led them to assert that Jesus had not been "born" of the Virgin Mary in the usual sense at all, but had "passed through Mary as water runs through a tube," not only without birth pangs but without the involvement of the mother except in a purely passive sense. Christian art would eventually counter this tendency by its portrayals of the pregnant Mary.

## *Visit of the Magi*

### Infancy Gospel of James

Before they could leave the city "there was a great commotion in Bethlehem of Judaea, for Magi came, saying: Where is he that is born king of the Jews?" (c21). Herod called them to Jerusalem to discuss the matter. In the canonical gospels, of course, they go to Jerusalem first, the most logical course to undertake, since it was the religious and de facto political capital of the land. Nor is there any explanation of why they would even accidentally stop in Bethlehem (a small town) while on the way to the political center of the country. Stopping in Bethlehem first represents the type of thinking that would come naturally to Christian generations later but not to individuals living at the time of the events.

In James' telling it is clear that the "star" is not an astrological conjunction of planets or some similar phenomena. "We have seen a star of great size shining among these stars, and obscuring their light, so that the stars did not appear; and we thus knew that a king has been born to Israel, and we have come to worship him."

Then comes the traditional story of the star leading them — but this time to the "cave" of James' narrative rather than to the more ambiguous location in the canonical account. The number of Magi is not given but they have three gifts, "gold, and frankincense, and myrrh." Similarly mirroring the Biblical account they are warned not to return to Herod. Unfortunately the geographical ignorance overshadows these similarities for they are instructed "not to go into Judaea" to return to Herod.[18] In real life, of course, Bethlehem itself was in Judea. Some have suggested that this was a slip of the author's pen and that he meant either "not to go into Jerusalem" or that he meant "not to remain in Judea."[19] Perhaps, but an odd slip nonetheless.

## History of Joseph the Carpenter

The visit of the Magi goes unrecorded in Joseph the Carpenter. Pseudo-Matthew, however, does not pass it by. This visit does not occur until two years have passed since birth (c16). The Magi came from an unidentified point in "the east" with "great gifts" (c16). They inquired first "of the Jews" where the new king had been born and word of the query reached Herod. Herod then demanded of the religious leaders where one would look for such a predicted king. Bethlehem, they answered.

Using the Magi as his unknowing intelligence agents to prepare the way for murder, he instructed them to find the child and bring back word so that he himself might worship the new king. After leaving, the star reappeared and they followed it to where Jesus and His parents were residing in an otherwise unidentified "house."

The author attempts to blend contradictory traditions as to how many wise men there were. He makes token allusion to the belief that there were a significant number of them, having "each of them" (leaving the matter ambiguous) provide a piece of gold as gift to the child and His parents. He also incorporated the *three* Magi tradition, in particular, by having each one give gifts, one of gold, one of frankincense, and one of myrrh.

## Arabic Gospel

The interaction of the Magi and King Herod is not told in systematic order in the Arabic recounting. Herod's query of the priests as to where the child would be born and his instruction to them to return after finding the child (c9) is only recorded at the end of the narrative describing their visit. The number of Magi is not mentioned, only that they brought the three gifts of "gold, and frankincense, and myrrh" (c7). Wishing to provide something in return, Mary provides them one of the swaddling-bands as a memento of their visit. Instead of being warned not to return to Herod, their motive in leaving is described differently, "And in the same hour there appeared to them an angel in the form of that star which had before guided them on their journey; and they went away, following the guidance of its light, until they arrived in their own country."

The deviation from the Biblical record is odd. A star was useful in guiding them to a previously unknown place. Heading back to their own land would surely have required little or nothing beyond the instruction to "go."

When they arrived back in their homeland the rulers and leaders inquired what they had seen and they provided a description of their trip and the newborn (c8). "Wherefore they celebrated a feast, and, according to their custom, lighted a fire and worshipped it, and threw that swathing-cloth into it; and the fire laid hold of it, and enveloped it." When it went out, it had been miraculously preserved. Recognizing this as a supernatural sign, they carefully preserved it among the Magi treasures.[20]

## Slaughter of the Bethlehem Children

### Infancy Gospel of James

As James tells it, Herod knew about the Magi's disappearance so quickly that Jesus' parents were still in Bethlehem when the murders began. "Mary, having heard that the children were being killed, was afraid, and took the infant and swaddled Him, and put Him into an ox-stall" (c22). So far as James' account goes the family seemingly never leaves Bethlehem[21]; it goes totally unmentioned. How then did the child escape death? Ronald F. Hock believes, probably correctly, that the text intends to imply that the child was hidden in the feeding trough of the stall.[22]

Instead of stressing how Jesus Himself managed to survive, the remainder of the book shifts to how John the Baptist survived the bloodletting. His being in the line of fire is provided no explanation at all. Scripturally, of course, there is no reason for believing that he was in Bethlehem at any time and certainly not at the same time as Joseph and Mary. There is nothing in the New Testament text to suggest that he had the same ancestral home as Joseph, the reason for Joseph himself being there.

Hence the claim of some that it answers the implicit Lukian question of how a child born so close in time to Jesus was not targeted for death as well[23] does not seem to be relevant. If there was no reason for him to be in the same city, especially at the same time, there was no "problem" to resolve.

As James tells it, a miracle protected the mother and infant, "And Elizabeth, having heard that they were searching for John, took him and went up into the hill-country, and kept looking where to conceal him. And there was no place of concealment. And Elizabeth, groaning with a loud voice, said: "O mountain of God, receive mother and child. And immediately the mountain was cleft, and received her. And a light shone about them, for an angel of the Lord was with them, watching over them" (c22).

Which, logically, makes John superior to Jesus since Jesus and His parents—in the canonical gospel—had to flee into another country while John was protected by angelic intervention without such a flight. James' desire to tell a good story clearly has caused him to overlook the theological problem he has inadvertently created.

Herod demanded of Zacharias the high priest the location of his son for he "is destined to be king over Israel" (c23). A not illogical deduction: who better to be father of the king than the high priest? Zacharias refused to divulge the information and he was murdered during the night hours at the entrance to the temple itself. The bloody body was only discovered the next day "beside the altar" (c.24). A heavenly voice threatened that an "avenger" would come to do justice for the slain leader.

Then the body of Zacharias disappeared before it could be retrieved — presumably removed and covertly buried by Herod's agents[24]— and the remaining blood had "turned into stone." Three days of mourning followed before he was replaced as high priest. Simeon was the replacement as high priest because he had been promised that he would live to see the coming of the Messiah (an allusion to Luke 2:25–26). Not surprisingly, there is no evidence of either Zacharias or Simeon as high priests in the ancient sources.

## History of Joseph the Carpenter

The author of Joseph is apparently ignorant of the Biblical story of the wise men. This is argued not merely due to the omission of it, but to the fact that Herod's knowledge of Jesus' birth is brought to him not by the Magi but by "Satan" (c8). A major historical blunder is that he makes the Herod who tried to kill Jesus the same as the Herod who beheaded John the Baptist. In terms of the Joseph text, standing alone, this makes no sense, for the anti-infant crusade in Bethlehem was separated by decades from the execution of the adult John. Perhaps the author, unaware that a different Herod was involved in the execution, means to imply that Herod persistently opposed God's servants throughout the coming decades of his life. Alternatively this could be a garbled summary of the story in James of Herod the Great trying to kill John as part of the extermination of all possible messianic claimants.

## Infancy Gospel of Thomas

In the Greek of the Infancy Gospel of Thomas, the narrative begins with incidents after the return from the stay in Egypt. In the Latin form, however, it begins with the need to go into Egypt to escape the death threat. This is concisely summed up in the context of a brief allusion to the Biblical narrative, "When a commotion took place in consequence of the search made by Herod for our Lord Jesus Christ to kill Him, then an angel said to Joseph: Take Mary and her boy, and flee into Egypt from the face of those who seek to kill Him. And Jesus was two years old when He went into Egypt" (c1).

The Biblical text speaks of the instruction to flee as coming before the actual effort to kill the children. The author is more astute than many readers of the canonical record, however, in perceiving that Jesus was no longer a mere infant at the time of the flight, picturing Him as "two years old."

At this point in the Latin form (and one surviving Greek manuscript of the material) there is a passing allusion to something that happens before the arrival in Egypt (which is only specified as being reached after this occurrence). "And as He was walking through a field of corn, He stretched forth His hand, and took of the ears, and put them over the fire, and rubbed them, and began to eat" (c1). The allusion serves no narrative purpose, makes no doctrinal point, nor serves as a jumping off point for a youthful incident.

## Pseudo-Matthew

In Pseudo-Matthew, Jesus is two years old at the time of the coming of the Magi (c16). Being warned that they were in danger, they did not return to Herod but left the country by another route than that by which they had come (16).

Herod was so outraged that he ordered them seized and executed (c17). Unable to locate them, this turned out to be impossible. As a result, he immediately ordered the murder of all children in Bethlehem two years of age or under. Being warned of this in a dream, Joseph fled with his wife and child into the desert and toward Egypt.

## Arabic Gospel

These events are only vaguely touched on in the Arabic Gospel. It speaks of Herod having attempted to use the Magi to determine Jesus' location out of the desire to see Him dead (c9). Then the text leaps to an angel telling Joseph to get the family into Egypt. The connection of the two is an obvious case of cause and effect, but the text does not bother to make it explicit.

CHAPTER 6

# *Egyptian Exile*

What was the underlying rationale behind the tales about Jesus in exile as an infant? Since it was not uncommon to seek out prophetic "precedents" for events in Jesus' adult life in the writings of the Torah and prophets, it is not unlikely that such a source was mined here as well. On the other hand, in the New Testament even the miraculous have a "down to earth" tone in their description and verbal extravagance is avoided. Not so in the apocryphal gospel accounts of Jesus' time in Egypt, where even the most fanciful figurative language is used to construct an equally extravagant "literal" historic event.

B. Harris Cowper, in his nineteenth century work on the subject, suggests several texts in particular,[1]

> The Psalmist says 'Praise the Lord from the earth, ye dragons,' so dragons come out of a cave and worship Jesus. The prophet speaks of wolves feeding with lambs, and of lions eating chaff with oxen, so lions and leopards and all sorts of wild beasts, form a sort of bodyguard for the Holy Family in the desert.
> The bride in Solomon's Song says, "I will go up to the palm tree, I will take hold of its boughs," so the palm tree bows down to Mary for her to have its fruit. The Israelites sang, "Spring up, O well!" and the prophet said, "waters shall break out in the wilderness," so a fountain gushes forth in the desert. The prophet said, "The idols of Egypt shall be moved at his presence," so the idols of Egypt fall and are shattered when Jesus comes thither.

These sources were supplemented, of course, by a retrospective "reading back" into infancy of what seemed like parallel miraculous interventions to those that occurred during Jesus' adult life: the blind see, the leprous are healed, the dead are raised — all adapted (more or less) to the reality that as a baby and little beyond it the mode of healing had to be carried out differently. The changing of the methodology of curing also opened the door for the elevation of Mary's role as one of an essential participant in the miracles.

To the extent that readers actually believed that these incidents occurred — or, more probably (for those who recognized that these were but pious fictions), events like these — one felt emotionally reassured of an unbroken continuity between what was manifested in adulthood and in infancy. By making that assumption, Jesus' childhood supernaturalness was simultaneously affirmed as being life-long as well. (But for the Gnostic appeal of childhood miracles, see later in this chapter.)

Even Jesus' teaching was given a miraculous twist: if water baptism was to produce spiritual salvation (Mark 16:16), then the water of Jesus' bath could be used to cure physical salvation from disease. The opportunity is also utilized to expand ideas far beyond the descriptions found in the canonical adulthood narratives. The physical appearance of demons is described. Diseases or difficulties not even hinted at in the canonicals are stirred into the brew: impotency and what appears to be vampirism, for example. The creative imagination is given wide reign in the hope of encouraging the faithful to greater fervency and dedication.

## *Flight into Egypt and Life While There*

Jesus' triumph over the Egyptian gods (referred to in both Pseudo-Matthew and the Arabic Gospel below) is taken for granted by Cyril of Jerusalem in the fourth century in his Jerusalem preaching, "When Jesus was about to travel to Egypt to overthrow the gods of Egypt made by human hands, the angel appeared once more to Joseph in a dream."[2] Hence by this time, at least in Cyril's circles, the tales of Jesus' supernatural acts while an infant in Egypt were a well established part of the accepted popular religious thought of the believing community.

### Infancy Gospel of James

James' account omits this period entirely. Joseph describes it very briefly, quoting Jesus Himself on the matter. After learning of Herod's murderous plans in a dream, "he rose and took Mary my mother, and I lay in her bosom. Salome also was their fellow-traveler. Having therefore set out from home, he retired into Egypt, and remained there the space of one whole year, until the hatred of Herod passed away" (c8).

### Infancy Gospel of Thomas

The Latin form of the Infancy Gospel of Thomas (and one Greek manuscript of the work) devotes one and a half chapters to Jesus' actions while in Egypt. They speak of how His literally childish actions got the family rejected out of both the home where they lived and the city as well.

In the first instance, Jesus took a dead, dried fish and placed it in a basin. He ordered it to "move about" in the water and it did. Then He ordered it to reject the salt in its body and enter the water, a command which it also obeyed. The neighbors happened to see it and "told it to the widow woman in whose house Mary His mother lived [and where was Joseph? RW]. And as soon as she heard it, she thrust them out of her house with great haste" (c1). Why is not explained. Perhaps she considered it an irrational act. Certainly one exercising such clear power with no constructive motive — from a baby no less! — would have been seen as automatically alarming and easily taken as a portent of harm that might be inflicted upon her household.

In the second instance (c3), Jesus and His mother were walking through the marketplace. A teacher was lecturing his students and was annoyed at Jesus' plain amusement. Demanding an explanation, Jesus explained that He had thrown a handful of grain into the midst of a dozen birds to see them fight for it. (Nothing in this requires it to be considered a miracle, but the Infancy Thomas presents the event in such a way that we are presumably to understand that the grain had appeared in Jesus' hands out of nowhere.) The teacher was so outraged that he had both mother and child kicked out of the city — an irrational act unless the text wishes us to understand that this was but the latest of a series of annoying miracles that served no constructive purpose but alarmed the community.

From our standpoint the most fascinating thing about this is that a miracle — any miracle — would be attributed to the direct action of a child that, chronologically, is still little more than a mere baby. The mindset needed to consider such credible would seemingly be one in which the infant is virtually an empty shell within which a fully mature "second" and adult being dwells. The hospitality of such a concept with Gnosticism's distinction between "Jesus" (the physical being) and the "Christ" (the inner anointed and different personality) is obvious. Perhaps what made the implicit dualism of conscious babyhood miracles acceptable from an "orthodox" standpoint was the fact that Jesus is simultaneously both personalities at the same time — even as a child, while Gnosticism did not picture Jesus as receiving the Christ until a grown man. Also, of course, the explicit verbal terminology used to describe the distinction is not utilized.

## Pseudo-Matthew

Turning to Pseudo-Matthew, four and a half chapters describe the journey to Egypt. Accompanying Jesus' parents are three other boys and one girl (c18). Since the parents are not mentioned, these are presumably other children they are helping escape the tragedy back in Bethlehem.

Either that or the author wants us to assume that they are all part of a small caravan traveling together for mutual encouragement and protection. Yet if the latter were intended it is odd that the concept is not further developed or even explicitly mentioned. For that matter, it is odd that these other children mysteriously disappear from the narrative as quickly as they appear. Having served their storytelling purpose in providing an excuse for the intervention of Jesus, their presence is no longer required.

His involvement came about in this manner. While resting in a cave en route, "many dragons" appeared and frightened the children. Jesus saw them, climbed down from His mother, and the creatures promptly gave reverence to Him.

At this tender age (between two and three) they were naturally fearful for their son's safety. Jesus reassured them with all the confidence of an adult pretending he is a child, "Do not be afraid, and do not consider me to be a little child; for I am and always have been perfect; and all of the beasts of the forest must needs be tame before me." Note the theological underpinning that is explicitly stated, "I am and always have been perfect." What I have done and been in the past I must continue to do and be in the present. Hence, at least in this particular instance, the childhood miracle is justified not on the basis of what the adult Jesus will do but what the *pre-incarnate* Jesus had always been doing, intervening to aid human beings in need of Divine assistance.

Both lions and panthers traveled with them to show them the way through the desert (c19). "Now at first, when Mary saw the lions and the panthers, and various kinds of wild beasts, coming about them, she was much afraid. But the infant Jesus looked into her face with a joyful countenance, and said: Be not afraid, mother; for they come not to do thee harm, but they make haste to serve both thee and me." Even wolves intermingled with the beasts of burden and yet none of the travelers were attacked nor did the animals attack each other.

On the trip's third day, Mary sought time to rest under a palm tree from the great heat (c20). His mother wished out loud for some of its fruit; in a different vein, Joseph wished that there were water for themselves and the animals. Jesus then fulfilled both their wishes. First he ordered the palm trees to bend so His mother might select from its fruit. After removing all its fruit, Jesus commanded a spring of "exceedingly clear and cool and sparkling" water to rise from the roots of the tree.

On the fourth day of the journey (the family apparently having camped out at what is now an oasis since the previous day), Jesus gave a special reward to the palm tree, "that one of thy branches be carried away by my angels, and planted in the paradise of my Father" (c21). An angel promptly carried out this promise and His parents were terrified by what they had seen. Jesus argued that they should rejoice instead since the palm would now be in a place "prepared for all the saints" in "paradise."

In an admission of Jesus' superiority to them though He is but a few years old, Joseph requested permission of his son to "go by the sea-shore, that we may be able to rest in the cities on the coast" (c22). Jesus responded that He would miraculously shorten the journey from the usual thirty days into one; furthermore, it would be completed that very day. "And while they were thus speaking, behold, they looked forward, and began to see the mountains and cities of Egypt."

The actual stay in Egypt is narrated in chapters 22–24 of Pseudo-Matthew. Not knowing anyone, they (oddly enough) do not ask if there is a local synagogue nor in what area of town fellow Jews might live or work. Instead they entered a major temple where there were a multitude of idols, one for every day of the year (c22). A monotheistic Jew's aversion to idolatry is cast aside for the opportunity to perform wonders against the pagan images.

When Mary and Joseph entered, all the idols fell down and shattered before them (c23). The governor of the city rushed to the temple and the priests were sure that he would take revenge on those who had made it happen (c24). Seeing the destroyed idols, he commanded his forces to honor Jesus instead. "Unless this were the God of our gods, our gods would not have fallen on their faces before Him; nor would they be lying prostrate in His presence: wherefore they silently confess that He is their Lord."

Unless they wished to share in a similar destruction — and he reminded them of what happened to the ancient Pharaoh who had attempted to exterminate the Jews — they needed to learn the lesson their gods of stone had provided them. "Then all the people of the same city believed in the Lord God through Jesus Christ."

## Arabic Gospel

The Arabic Gospel does not give us the age of Jesus when he left Palestine. When He returns, he is just turning four (c26). The large segment of text devoted to the stay (c10–25) in Egypt describes a large number of miracles that take place during this period:

(1) An idol that periodically gave revelation to the people spoke of how "a God has come here in secret, who is God indeed; nor is any God besides Him worthy of divine worship, because He is truly the Son of God" (c10). This caused widespread alarm throughout the land.

(2) The son of an idolatrous priest was healed of demon possession

by the touch of the cloths worn by the child Jesus (c11). "Then the demons, fleeing in the shape of ravens and serpents, began to go forth out of his mouth." The father rejoiced at this and suspected that there was a correlation between the child's arrival in Egypt and the strange fact that at the same time, the various idols of Egypt had been broken. (For comparison's sake, it should be noted that though the canonical gospels often speak of demon exorcisms, none of them ever attribute a bodily shape to the dispossessed creatures.)

(3) The family was protected from danger from plunderers who heard them approaching. The thieves were miraculously made to think that they were hearing the "king going out of his city with his army and his chariots and his drums" (c13). In other words, they were up against a vast multitude rather than easy victims.

(4) A female adult demoniac was so powerful that she could break her chains and endangered others by throwing stones at them. When "Mary saw her, she pitied her; and upon this Satan immediately left her" out of fear of both Mary and her offspring (c14). Such intervention by Mary as a miracle-working intercessor would become vitally important to the evolution of later theology.

(5) In another city, a bride who could not speak sought out the family. She reached out her hands for the child Jesus and, while holding Him, her burden of being incapable of speaking was removed (c15).

(6) In another town a woman had been assaulted by the Devil while bathing. The demon did this "in the form of a serpent, [who] had leapt upon her and twisted himself round her belly; and as often as night came on, he tyrannically tormented her" (c16). (The idea of demoniac sexual assault may be discretely implied in this as well.) She happened to see the child Jesus, asked permission to hold him, and while doing so Satan "fled and left her."

(7) The cured woman washed Jesus the next day and poured some of the water on a girl who was leprous. The leprous girl was promptly cured and obtained permission to travel with the family of Jesus (c17).

(8) This girl happened to meet a princess who poured out her own secret (c18): When at last she produced a son for her husband, the infant was born leprous. The prince ordered her to adopt out the child or kill it. As her personal punishment, he would never look upon her again. Learning that the girl had been cured by the bathwater of Jesus, she arranged a banquet for Jesus' family. The next day she herself washed Jesus and poured the water on her son who was promptly healed.

## 6. Egyptian Exile

(9) In yet another town the family was the guest of a man who was under a witch's curse and was impotent. As the result of staying the night, his sexual inability was removed (c19).

(10) On another occasion Mary asked the girl who was traveling with them to seek out the reason that three women were so deep in mourning: a spell had turned their brother into a mule because of "jealousy" at the very time that his nuptials were being prepared (c20). They had tried everything they could to reverse the spell: "there is no wise man, or magician, or enchanter in the world that we have omitted to send for; but nothing has done us any good."

She had them repeat the story to Mary, confident (based on her own experience) that healing was quite possible (c21). Grieving at their fate, Mary placed Jesus on the mule's back and urged Him, "My son, heal this mule by Thy mighty power, and make him a man endowed with reason as he was before." This promptly occurred. The three sisters recognized that their brother still needed a wife and that the girl who had intervened on his behalf needed a husband (c22). So they requested permission for the two to be married and a joyous feast was held to celebrate the joining of them together.

(11) While crossing a robber-infested desert by night, two of the robbers happened to see the family (c23). For reasons unspecified, one intervened with the other and even offered him a large amount of money not to inform their colleagues. (Since we are in the midst of various miracles, at least a miracle of good will must be intended if not something more specific.) Mary is so happy at the help that she promised, "The Lord God will sustain thee by His right hand, and will grant thee remission of thy sins."

For the first time in this series of Egyptian stories, Jesus no longer acts like a child. He responds, "Thirty years hence, O my mother, the Jews will crucify me at Jerusalem, and these two robbers will be raised upon the cross along with me, Titus on my right and Dumachus on my left; and after that day Titus shall go before me into Paradise."

The text makes no effort to explain how two Egyptian thieves are going to end up dying in Jerusalem. Not to mention the fact that if they are at least twenty years old already, their deaths will not occur until they are in their fifties—a difficult though not impossible age to still be involved in such treacherous doings. Theologically speaking, Mary's assumed right to assure or promise one redemption is more important than the improbability that the paths of the thieves will cross that of Jesus decades into the future.

(12) In another place Jesus miraculously produced a fountain for Mary to wash His clothes (c24). "And from the sweat of the Lord Jesus which she sprinkled there, balsam was produced in that region."

In this most detailed of all the infancy gospels in regard to Jesus' Egyptian wonders, these were but a small sample. "Thence they came down to Memphis, and saw Pharaoh, and remained three years in Egypt; and the Lord Jesus did in Egypt very many miracles which are recorded neither in the Gospel of the Infancy nor in the Perfect Gospel" (c25).

What these miracles tend to have in common is that they were (usually) unsolicited, i.e., they do not grow out of specific requests for healing. Faith is certainly not explicit, and creative imagination must be used to put it even implicitly in any but one or two of the cases.

They also are narrated in such a manner that the infant Jesus usually only has to act like an infant rather than as an adult masquerading as an infant. Although the tales themselves are often fantastic, they at least permit a child to live and act in a manner appropriate to His chronological age and do not require him to act inappropriate to it. The one exception is the prediction about the robbers who would die on the crosses around Jesus.

## *Return to Palestine from Egypt*

### History of Joseph the Carpenter

Herod's death is unmentioned in James, but Joseph begins by referring to how "Herod died by the worst form of death," thereby

> atoning for the shedding of the blood of the children whom he wickedly cut off, though there was no sin in them. And that impious tyrant Herod being dead, they returned into the land of Israel, and lived in a city of Galilee which is called Nazareth. And Joseph going back to his trade of a carpenter, earned his living by the work of his hands; for, as the law of Moses had commanded, he never sought to live by another's labour (c9).

### Infancy Gospel of Thomas

In the Latin Infancy Thomas, the expulsion of Jesus and his mother due to his annoying childish miracles (c1–2) leads to an angel appearing to Mary and commanding that they return to their homeland (c3). She proceeded to do this. In a failure in narrative continuity, Joseph's departure is then described as if a separate action entirely. When he returned "out of Egypt after the death of Herod," he decided to keep Jesus "in the desert until there should be quietness in Jerusalem on the part of those who were seeking the boy's life."

## Pseudo-Matthew

The duration of the stay in Egypt is described as a short time by Pseudo-Matthew, whose only other reference to the subject is to quote the canonical scripture concerning an angel telling them that those who had sought to kill Jesus were now dead (c25). How they came to reside in Nazareth is not discussed at all. Chapters 26–31 record a series of miracles and then the next chapter begins, "After these things, Joseph and Mary departed thence with Jesus into the city of Nazareth; and He remained there with His parents" (c32). This could easily be read as indicating that the earlier actions had occurred in a different town of Galilee and that their son's actions had made it prudent to move on to another community, that of Nazareth. These earlier actions, however, are in the same broad geographic area; they are vaguely pictured as being "in Galilee as well" (c26).

## Arabic Infancy Gospel

The Arabic Gospel does not speak of why the family returned to their homeland (i.e., the death of Herod). Indeed, it seems to imply that they returned before knowing that their foe had died, "And when they had arrived at Judaea, Joseph was afraid to enter it; but hearing that Herod was dead [as if this were the first they had heard of it, RW] and that Archelaus his son had succeeded him, he was afraid indeed" (c26). The element of fear of Archelaus is, indeed, mentioned by the canonical account as the reason for what comes next here—the decision to go to Nazareth to abide—but the earlier decision to return is placed only after already knowing Herod was dead (Matthew 2:19–22).

# *Miracles of Healing and Protection While Still a Baby*

## Arabic Infancy Gospel

The Arabic Gospel narrates a series of miraculous healings that are described in such a manner that Jesus would seemingly not be able to move about on His own and act independently. Most of these miracles revolve around the wash-water of the baby. This and the fact that Jesus is not called upon to vocally or physically do anything argues for an age below that of normal physical mobility.

Where do these wonders occur? Although chapter 26 speaks of them taking up residence in "the city of Nazareth," the next chapter describes a miracle occurring in "the city of Bethlehem." The healing in chapter 28 occurs "in the same place" and that of chapter 29 "in the same city." Likewise chapter 30 speaks of "another woman there," i.e., in the same city of Bethlehem. The remainder of chapters 31–35 are more vague as to whether the locale remains the same, but the most natural reading would be that it does.

The references to entering Nazareth and being in Bethlehem are little more than two dozen words apart (c26, 27). Even a bungling writer would seem to have trouble making this blatant an error in location on his own initiative. The best alternative — though it still does not speak highly of the editor's capability — is that at this point he began copying from a new source and simply did not pay attention to the discrepancy in locales.

In support of this last hypothesis is the fact that in chapter 32 a cured leper says to another, "I also, whom you see come in my way, I went to Bethlehem. There going into a cave, I saw a woman named Mary, whose son was he who was named Jesus; and when she saw that I was a leper, she took pity on me, and handed me the water with which she had washed her son's body." Since the tradition was common of Jesus being born in a cave, this passing reference makes one suspect that these incidents have been lifted from a document purporting to describe Jesus' miracles while still in Bethlehem and before the flight into Egypt. In a similar vein is the instruction in chapter 33 for a woman to take another "to Bethlehem" to seek healing.

The Arabic composer is not the most clear-cut writer, having earlier omitted all mention of the warning to the Magi to not return to Herod nor explaining their failure to do so some other way. Nor does he mention at all their earlier meeting with Herod until after they have left on their homeward journey. Hence it is not inconceivable that a writer with this inexact a method of composition could even mean that the family dwelt for a while in Bethlehem before returning to Nazareth or, for that matter, returned to Bethlehem for a period in between stays in Nazareth. In other words, he intends for these wonders to be placed after the return as well. (But that would still leave the difficulty of residing in a cave near Bethlehem, a description that best fits the time of the birth itself.)

There are six wash-water miracles narrated after the return to Palestine and during this infancy period:

(1) The first two are tied in with the "many and grievous diseases infesting the eyes of the children, who were dying in consequence" (c27).

(Causing blindness one could understand, but causing death seems an odd association between this type of disease and the result.) A woman with a son "very near death" from this cause was given "a little" of Jesus' wash waters and, following Mary's instructions, "sprinkled it over her son. And when this was done his illness abated; and after sleeping a little, he rose up from sleep safe and sound."

(2) A neighbor of that woman had a son "now almost blinded" from the disease (c28). After telling her how her own son had been cured, "she too went and got some of the same water, and washed her son with it, and his body and his eyes were instantly made well."

(3) In another case there were two polygamous wives of the same husband living in the town (c29). (The author was clearly aware of Old Testament references to such practices. By the first century, however, there appears to have been few cases when such would actually have existed in Palestinian Jewish society. Theoretically still legal, its actual practice would have been very unusual.)

Both had sons suffering from serious "fever." One of them went to Mary and wished to trade a garment for a piece of clothing from Jesus. This cured his disease but the other mother's son died in the meantime. This produced intense hatred and the mother of the dead child repeatedly tried to kill the healed boy: she tried to cook him in a "very hot" oven with a good size fire "blazing under it." She then tried to drown the child in the water. Neither strategy worked. Finally she herself "got entangled in the rope" at the well, fell in, and broke her skull.

(4) So far these have all been children healed by bath water. Now comes "a leprous woman" who seeks Mary's help (c31). Mary gave her some of the dirty water as well and instructed her to pour "a little of this" over her body. She was immediately healed and gave thanks to God.

(5) The cured leper visited in another city (c32). There she met some women who were broken up in sorrow because of a girl whose marriage was cancelled at the last minute. The husband-to-be had discovered she had between her eyes "the mark of leprosy in the shape of a star." The visitor explained her own cure and they accompanied her back with "splendid gifts." These they gave to Mary and showed her the leprous girl who needed healing. Mary took one look and responded, "May the compassion of the Lord Jesus Christ descend upon you," handed them some of the bath water, and told them that the afflicted needed "to be bathed in it." This caused her to be healed and the suitor who had rejected her then decided to, indeed, marry her.

(6) A certain woman "repeatedly" saw Satan appear "in the form of a huge dragon, and prepared to swallow her. He also sucked out all her blood, so that she was left like a corpse" (c33) Since she is not dead the blood sucking references would suggest that he was "feeding" on her, so to speak, in the manner of legendary vampires. These attacks happened time and again.

A woman previously healed by Jesus' bath water contacted the afflicted woman's mother and convinced her to travel with the daughter to Bethlehem. The mother promptly acted on the suggestion and as soon as Mary heard the tale, she provided "a little of the water in which she had washed the body of her son Jesus." Mary "ordered her to pour it on the body of her daughter. She gave her also from the clothes of the Lord Jesus a swathing-cloth, saying: Take this cloth, and show it to thine enemy as often as thou shalt see him."

No explicit reference is being made of the afflicted's return to health, but that is surely taken for granted. The next time Satan appeared in the form of a dragon to assault her, she put the cloth she had received "on her head and covered her eyes with it." As soon as she did so "flames and live coals began to dart forth from it, and to be cast upon the dragon." The Satanic dragon immediately realized what was happening, "What have I to do with thee, O Jesus, son of Mary? Whither shall I fly from thee? And with great fear he turned his back and departed from the girl, and never afterwards appeared to her."

Only one miracle that clearly occurs during Jesus' "babyhood" results without the use of bath water as all or part of the healing technique. In this case a certain woman had seen one child die and the other at death's door (c30). She took the dying child to Mary and prayed to God that he might survive. Impressed by the intensity and sincerity of her words Mary instructed her, "Put thy son in my son's bed, and cover him with his clothes." Indeed by this time the child was dead, but she carried out the instruction anyway. "But as soon as the smell of the clothes of the Lord Jesus Christ reached the boy, he opened his eyes."

In these stories of the Arabic Gospel we do not have an explicit Mariology laid out in detail; rather her role in seeing that her son is put in a position to bring about the healing implies her role as the intermediary in obtaining miraculous help from Him. Even the healings via bath water were because it was Jesus' bath water rather than because of anything inherent in Mary herself. She had bathed him; she provided the water. Hence throughout she is the facilitator, the enabler, the one whose motherly concern causes it to occur.

## 6. Egyptian Exile

The indirect method still magnifies her profound importance. It is Mary who is spoken with (since Jesus is but a baby). It is Mary who offers up the solutions (is Divine revelation to her implied? or does it "merely" imply her profound understanding that anything connected with Jesus had healing potential if she but provided access to it?). And in each case Mary's solution works. Graft on to this the belief that the righteous dead can intercede for the living, and the rationale for "intercessional prayer to Mary" is clearly established.[3]

One of the rare lapses into explicitness occurs in connection with the last of the narrated miracles we examined. The woman reacted to it by applauding Mary's own spiritual status, "O Lady Mary, now I know that the power of God dwelleth *in thee,* so that thy son heals those that partake of the same nature with himself, as soon as they have touched his clothes."

CHAPTER 7

# *Youthful Years in Palestine*

At this point we pass from Jesus as a child to Jesus as a youth. Young, immature, and not always prudent, but blessed with supernatural capacities, He demonstrates Himself to be much like the gods of Greece and Rome—capable of great helpfulness yet also considerable vindictiveness as well. Indeed, the fact that a similar mixture of noble virtues and clear faults were found in the tales about gods and great heroes, has led to the speculation that some or all of these stories have been consciously adopted from contemporary pagan ones.[1]

For certain of the orthodox, Jesus' later supernatural manifestations would have required such phenomena to occur in childhood as well. The elements of growth and maturation would have been impossible for them to reconcile: the miraculous in His adulthood had to exist as a seamless whole with their presence in His childhood for His supernatural claims to have been genuine at all.[2]

For Gnostics the stories would have had an appeal as well in two very different ways. On the one hand, the interjection of blatant supernatural elements into even the youngest years permitted them to maintain the supernatural importance of Jesus in His youth in those years before He received the Christ into Himself,[3] an event they typically placed at His baptism.

If there were any cynically enough minded, they could even have utilized the miraculous excesses of His childhood as evidence of how vital it was to have that Christ element interjected into Him because only at that point did He receive the insight, wisdom, and capacity to rightly utilize those talents. If there were any who took that approach, they likely kept such controversial assertions for private discussions among themselves. The stories provided too useful a "bridge" to the orthodox to risk explaining them in a manner that would further undermine the tenuous relationship between "orthodoxy" and "dissent."

# Childhood Miracles of Self-Protection

## History of Joseph the Carpenter

The story of Joseph the Carpenter describes Joseph in his old age as tormented by doubts concerning his failures and mistakes, the kind of worries that so easily arise when one is near death. On his death bed, he confesses his lingering guilt about one childhood miracle of Jesus. Addressing his son, he says,

> Call to mind also, my Lord, that day when the boy died of the bite of the serpent. And his relations wished to deliver Thee to Herod, saying that Thou hadst killed him; but Thou didst raise him from the dead, and restore him to them. Then I went up to Thee, and took hold of Thy hand, saying: My son, take care of thyself. But Thou didst say to me in reply: Art thou not my father after the flesh? I shall teach thee who I am. Now therefore, O Lord and my God, do not be angry with me, or condemn me on account of that hour. I am Thy servant, and the son of Thine handmaiden; but Thou art my Lord, my God and Saviour, most surely the Son of God" (c17).

If this was Herod the Great, that Herod was long dead. If it was Herod, ruler of Galilee, why was there anything to fear from an unjust accusation being heard and rejected?

This is the only miracle narrated in Joseph. It can be read in one of two ways. It can be taken as indicating that it was the only childhood wonder of Jesus. Alternatively the fear of the case being heard by Herod could imply that Jesus had performed a number of punitive wonders such as those recorded in other apocryphal sources and that these would add "credibility" to the accusation of causing the other child's death. In that reading, the text bears possible witness to the existence of a significant body of childhood miracle legends that the author has not chosen to record.[4]

## Arabic Infancy Gospel

Chapters 27 through 34 of the Arabic Gospel describe incidents that occurred while Jesus was still an infant. Beginning in chapter 36 we have incidents that occur when Jesus has become a young boy. The incident recorded in chapter 35 is not clear-cut as into which of these segments of His life it should be placed. Probably the latter since Jesus is pictured as out playing with other children, indicating He had gained a degree of self-mobility and was trusted to be out on His own. (A not totally reliable criteria since, as we saw in the previous chapter, even as a baby and infant Jesus was sometimes pictured as possessing these abilities.) The incident is worth quoting in full because it involves a future apostle who was demon possessed,

> Another woman was living in the same place, whose son was tormented by Satan. He, Judas by name, as often as Satan seized him, used to bite all who came near him; and if he found no one near him, he used to bite his own hands and other limbs. The mother of this wretched creature, then, hearing the fame of the Lady Mary and her son Jesus, rose up and brought her son Judas with her to the Lady Mary.
> In the meantime, James and Joses had taken the child the Lord Jesus with them to play with the other children; and they had gone out of the house and sat down, and the Lord Jesus with them. And the demoniac Judas came up, and sat down at Jesus' right hand: then, being attacked by Satan in the same manner as usual, he wished to bite the Lord Jesus, but was not able; nevertheless he struck Jesus on the right side, whereupon He began to weep.
> And immediately Satan went forth out of that boy, fleeing like a mad dog. And this boy who struck Jesus, and out of whom Satan went forth in the shape of a dog, was Judas Iscariot, who betrayed Him to the Jews; and that same side on which Judas struck Him, the Jews transfixed with a lance.

The last few words either grow out of lack of attention to the scriptural text or medieval anti–Semitism: The execution squad was composed of Roman soldiers, not Jews. Any spear use was their doing and no one else's.

## *Playful Childhood Miracles*

### Infancy Gospel of Thomas

The Infancy Gospel of Thomas exists, in large part, to show the reader the childhood miracles performed by Jesus. Upon more than one occasion the adult Jesus collided with the religious authorities in the canonical gospels concerning the boundaries of behavior on the Sabbath. They insisted that such things as healing and plucking a few grains to eat while one passed through the fields constituted unlawful "work." On a comparatively far more trivial level, the Infancy Thomas has a similar incident during Jesus' childhood.

When He was just five years of age he was playing in a mountain brook and making pools of water from the stream (c2). These muddy pools He successfully ordered to become clear by His spoken command. Then he took clay and fashioned twelve sparrows. Jesus was engaged in this play along with other children. A certain fellow Jew saw it and protested that Joseph's "son is at the stream, and has taken clay, and made of it twelve birds, and has profaned the Sabbath."

Joseph rushed to the stream and demanded of his son why He was insisting on violating the Sabbath by doing "what it is not lawful to do?" Rather than answer him, Jesus "refutes" Him by performing a miracle. "And Jesus clapped His hands, and cried out to the sparrows, and said to them: Off you go!" Miracle trumps legal interpretation. In real life, it would probably have resulted in a nasty run-in with the religious authorities under the accusation that he had used demonic power to denigrate the holy day.

If this account were coming from an enemy of Christianity one would suspect that it was written to mock Jesus. Coming from a friendly source, however, it was likely written to mock Jesus' enemies who — if they were consistent — would have even attacked childhood game playing.

## Pseudo-Matthew

Pseudo-Matthew builds upon the same tale. Jesus makes twelve clay sparrows on the Sabbath day, is rebuked for violating the Sabbath, transforms them into living creatures and they fly away (c27). Public opinion was divided between those who condemned Jesus and those who "praised and admired Him." Certain of the critics reported "to the chief priests and the heads of the Pharisees" about the "great signs and miracles" being performed by Jesus "in the sight of all the people of Israel." Hence what had been a strictly local concern became one known to the national religious authorities.

## Arabic Infancy Gospel

The same incident is narrated in the Arabic Gospel, with the additional touch that the twelve sparrows had been arranged around "his fish-pond, three on each side" (c46). When an indignant youth destroyed the fish-ponds because it was the Sabbath, the clay objects were turned into actual birds at the clap of Jesus' hands.

A very similar incident (but conspicuously lacking any Sabbath or age reference) is found earlier in the book (c36). Here Jesus is seven and not five as in the other incident. The boys had made figures of "asses, oxen, birds, and other animals" (not previously mentioned) and each was bragging of his skill and ability. In this youthful game of one-upmanship Jesus boasted, "The images that I have made I will order to walk" and successfully made them do so.

The bird creation is developed in greater detail. "And He had made figures of birds and sparrows, which flew when He told them to fly, and stood still when He told them to stand, and ate and drank when He handed them food and drink." When the children reported this back to their parents they were warned never to play with him again for He had demonstrated that He was some kind of wizard — an expression, at the best, full of ambiguity about the ultimate source of such strange power and, at worst, implying that Jesus had the potential to use those skills for destructive behavior as well.

These stories build around the same core idea. In a different, irresponsible and essentially playful miracle recorded in the Arabic Gospel, Jesus dumped all the cloth that a certain dyer planned on using into "a tub full of indigo" (c37). The dyer reproached Jesus for ruining the material since each buyer would desire a different color.

Jesus offered to fix the situation by changing the colors to whatever was desired. "And immediately He began to take the pieces of cloth out of the tub, each of them that color which the dyer wished, until He had taken them all out. When the Jews saw this miracle and prodigy, they praised God." (Being impressed and startled would be quite understandable; it would be parallel to our reaction to a first class magician today. But that an idle wonder would cause people to "praise God" seems incomprehensible and presumably reflects the belief that any incredible wonder [of a non-harmful nature?] must have originated through the exercise of Divine power.)

In another tale not recorded in the prior accounts, we read of a day when the boys Jesus played with decided to hide themselves from Him (c40). Seeking them unsuccessfully, He asked at one home whether the boys were inside. The lady denied it. He insisted on knowing who was "in the furnace?" She replied that they were "kids" (note the play on words) and Jesus ordered them to come out and — in the form of animals — the boys did exactly that. Having receiving words of adoration from the woman, He granted her request to restore the animals into human form.

(Again, the difference in psychology in different ages is fascinating. We today would anticipate a reaction of shock, perhaps horror and indignation. We would anticipate a demand that the justice of the action be defended. The last thing we would expect would be praise in any shape or form! Yet we will run into this image of Jesus as childhood bully on various occasions in the incidents that follow. It is one that would not be unexpected in a polytheistic context and may add credence to the earlier suggestion that some or many of these stories were adopted from stories about the pagan gods.)

## Childhood Miracles to Benefit His Parents
### Infancy Gospel of Thomas

In Infancy Thomas we find "self-centered" miracles intended to benefit both of Jesus' parents. Two of these are narrated and in the interest of gender equality (so to speak) one is for each of them. At age six Jesus was sent by Mary to draw water (c11). He accidentally broke the pitcher and was miraculously enabled to carry the necessary water back in his unfolded cloak instead.

In Joseph's case we find that "His father was a carpenter and at that time made ploughs and yokes" (c13). A certain rich individual ordered a couch for his home. One of the cross pieces turned out to be too short and "they did not know what to do." (Replacing it with a different piece of wood would seemingly be the natural solution but that does not permit the interposition of a miracle.) Hence Jesus asked his father to put the two pieces of wood down together. Then "Jesus stood at the other end, and took hold of the shorter piece of wood, and stretched it, and made it equal to the other."

### Pseudo-Matthew

Pseudo-Matthew places the miracle of the broken pitcher in Jericho (the closing words of c32). Instead of Jesus accidentally causing the pitcher to drop, in this version another child hits the pitcher and causes it to smash (c33). Once again, He carries the water home in His cloak.

A miracle to help His father in his carpentry trade is also narrated (c37), but in much greater detail than Infancy Thomas. Joseph specialized in a number of forms of woodenware: he "used to make nothing else of wood but ox-yokes, and ploughs, and implements of husbandry, and wooden beds." After receiving an order for a couch, Joseph has the wood cut but one piece is shorter than the other. While holding the two pieces of lumber at one end, Jesus pulls the shorter one toward himself until they are both equally long.

### Arabic Infancy Gospel

Turning to the Arabic Gospel, we find that after going to a well, the pitcher somehow hit against something and broke (c45). Then Jesus "stretched out His handkerchief and collected the water, and carried it to His mother."

Could the underlying story have been borrowed from contemporary Jewish sources? The growing bridge between the church and synagogue at first makes this seem unlikely. Yet, oddly enough, Ezra, the ancient leader of the return from Babylon, is spoken of as having performed the same type of miracle in his own youth. The story is preserved exclusively in Coptic and Arabic and a Jewish origin is deemed likely.[5] The churchly writer may have borrowed from the Jewish author or vice versa or, for that matter, the two may have grown up spontaneously with no direct connection at all.

As to the Arabic Gospel we are analyzing, Joseph does not merely make an accidental mistake (as in the earlier narratives), he is pictured as a bungling incompetent who constantly requires Jesus' intervention,

> And Joseph used to go about through the whole city, and take the Lord Jesus with him, when people sent for him in the way of his trade to make for them doors, and milk-pails, and beds, and chests; and the Lord Jesus was with him wherever he went. As often, therefore, as Joseph had to make anything a cubit or a span longer or shorter, wider or narrower, the Lord Jesus stretched His hand towards it; and as soon as He did so, it became such as Joseph wished. Nor was it necessary for him to make anything with his own hand, for Joseph was not very skilful in carpentry (c38).

The detailed account concerns not a couch (as in the previous texts), but a throne. It had been commissioned by "the king of Jerusalem" (there was no such person in the first century, of course) and perhaps it fits the image of Joseph as an incompetent carpenter that it took him two years to finish the work on it — only to discover that it was not as big as he was instructed to build (c39). Jesus took one side and Joseph the other and they miraculously stretched it to the right dimension, thereby permitting Joseph to escape the wrath of the king.

## *Childhood Healings*

### Infancy Gospel of Thomas

Just as Jesus is recorded as performing varied acts of healing as an adult, Infancy Thomas speaks of how He had also done such earlier in life upon at least two occasions. In the first instance a young man cut off the bottom end of his foot with an axe (c10). The heavy bleeding endangered the man's life and Jesus pushed through the crowd, touched the foot, and it was immediately healed. "And the crowd seeing what had happened, adored the child, saying: Truly the Spirit of God dwells in this child."

In the second case, Jesus and another son of Joseph, James, were together as James collected wood (c16). While going about his task, a poisonous snake bit him and the pain was overwhelming. Death was clearly near at hand. Jesus recognized this "and blew upon the bite; and the pain ceased directly, and the beast burst, and instantly James remained safe and sound."

## Pseudo-Matthew

The same healing is also described in Pseudo-Matthew and takes place in Bethlehem while Joseph and Mary were living together in their own home. One day James was sent "into the vegetable garden to gather vegetables for the purpose of making broth" and Jesus happens to follow him.

A snake bit Jesus' brother and he cried out in intense pain. Jesus then "took hold of his hand; and all that He did was to blow on the hand of James, and cool it; and immediately James was healed, and the serpent died."

## Arabic Infancy Gospel

In the Arabic Gospel this healing occurs when James had gone out "to gather wood" (c43). Another serpent healing is narrated at greater length, however. This one begins with Jesus pretending to be king in front of his playmates and the children forcing passersby to join in their game of honoring Jesus as royalty (c41).

While this play acting was proceeding, certain men, accompanied by a boy, were in the countryside collecting wood (c42). Finding the nest of a partridge, the child attempted to take out the eggs when a poisonous serpent bit him. The adults found him near death and relatives came and took him back to the city. The route required them to pass by the place where Jesus was playing king, but the adults initially refused to proceed that way because of their sorrow and were brought into the game only by the kids pushing them toward Jesus.

Jesus saw them carrying the child and wanted to know what had happened. He then instructed them that they must go and kill the snake and they are forced by the children to accompany them. Finding the spot, Jesus called forth the serpent and commanded it, "Go away and suck out all the poison. Then the Lord Jesus cursed it, and immediately on this being done it burst asunder; and the Lord Jesus stroked the boy with his hand, and he was healed. And he began to weep; but Jesus said: Do not weep, for by and by thou shalt be my disciple. And this is Simon the Canaanite, of whom mention is made in the Gospel."

## *Childhood Resurrections*

### Infancy Gospel of Thomas

Although the pre-eminent resurrection in the New Testament is, of course, Jesus' own, the canonical gospels refer to occasional ones he performed on behalf of others. According to Infancy Thomas, the ability to raise the dead was one that He also possessed in His youth and exercised upon at least three occasions.

In the first instance, Jesus and a playmate were playing in an upper room and the child accidentally fell from there to the ground (c9). The parents saw it and threatened Jesus because they thought He was responsible. Jesus Himself jumped down to the ground and landed unhurt. He challenged the dead child to tell his parents what had really happened, that He had not been responsible. Zeno (the child's name) was immediately brought back to life, stood up, and assured his parents that Jesus had had no responsibility for the accident.

In the second instance, a neighbor's child "fell sick and died" (c17). Hearing the "great lamentation and commotion," Jesus quickly ran to the home and commanded the child to "live and be with thy mother." He was promptly restored to life and his first reaction was to laugh (presumably in joy). Jesus instructed her to "give it milk and remember me" and promptly returned to playing with the other children. The neighbors were torn between calling this strange child "God or an angel of God" since "every word" He spoke came true.

The third instance grew out of a building accident at a home under construction (c18). Jesus took the injured man by the hand and commanded, "Man, I say to thee, arise, and go on with thy work." The man immediately did. The crowd reacted by considering how "He has saved many souls from death [our emphasis, rw], and He continues to save during all His life." In other words such resurrections and miraculous interventions to prevent death had been a *pattern* throughout His years up to this point.

### Pseudo-Matthew

Pseudo-Matthew refers to the first example and tells us that it happened in Nazareth (c32). The details are more elaborate. While playing on the rooftop one of the several children pushed another off the roof and the fall killed the child. Jesus received the blame for it — not unexpected in light of Pseudo-Matthew's own record of Jesus' past behavior of inflicting corporeal pain on those who had "crossed" Him.

The parents protested to Jesus' own mother and father. Mary responded by demanding a straight answer from Jesus as to whether he had been responsible. Instead of answering her, He raised the boy from the dead and had him provide the answer.

In another incident, one that appears for the first time in Pseudo-Matthew, a miracle of resurrection is narrated that occurs at Capernaum (c40). In that city there was a very wealthy man by the name of Joseph who was approaching death. Widespread weeping over his calamity attracted the attention of Jesus. Because he bore the same name as His own father, Jesus instructed his parent to take the handkerchief he was wearing around his head and place it on the dead man's face.

When he did so he was to utter the words, "Christ heal thee." This Joseph did and the man promptly rose "and asked who Jesus was." (Dead but simultaneously conscious and able to hear the words? An improbability to most minds but a strange phenomena not unknown to near death experiences in the modern world.)

## Arabic Infancy Gospel

Childhood resurrections also have their place in the Arabic Gospel. Again we read of how a certain boy is pushed off the roof of a house while playing. Every one fled except for Jesus, who received the blame (c44). Since the people did not wish to believe His denial He insisted that, "if you do not believe me, come and let us ask the boy himself, that he may bring the truth to light." The child was then resurrected and affirmed Jesus' version. He even named the individual who had "cast me down from" the rooftop.

# *Childhood Duplication of Food*

## Infancy Gospel of Thomas

On two occasions the canonical gospels refer to Jesus miraculously feeding groups, one of five and one of four thousand. In Infancy Thomas, this capability also existed in Jesus' immature childhood years. Here, though, the miracle is not to benefit those waiting to hear Jesus' word but to assist the local poor (c12). At age eight he planted a few things by Himself yet, at the appropriate time, reaped and threshed a huge crop. Then he called "all the poor of the village to the threshing-floor" and gave to them what they needed while giving the remainder to His father.

## Pseudo-Matthew

The version of this in Pseudo-Matthew seems more selfish (c34). In this version He planted the grain, reaped it, and "gave it to His numerous acquaintances." No mention of the poor or His own parents.

# Childhood Protection of Others from Dangerous Animals

## Pseudo-Matthew

As part of his own contribution to the childhood mythology, Pseudo-Matthew speaks of an occasion when Jesus was eight years old and his family and others had traveled down a road from Jericho to the banks of the Jordan River (c35). There a lioness was discovered nursing her cubs, making it unsafe for anyone to use the road. Jesus (supernaturally) "knowing that in that [nearby] cave the lioness had brought forth her young, went into it in the sight of all." All the cubs began to play with Jesus and the grown lions bowed down to honor Him.

Those on the road at the time observed Him entering the cave and commented to each other that if "he or his parents had committed grievous sins, he would not of his own accord have offered himself up to the lion." (Would a person with "grievous sins" do so either? Since when did dangerous animals gain a perception of a human's moral character? To the medieval writers this is either a miracle of Divine protection and/or the assumption that only the morally evil would ever be harmed by a dangerous animal.)

After playing with the lions outside the cave as well as inside, Jesus rebuked the travelers for their dimness of insight, "How much better are the beasts than you, seeing that they recognize their Lord and glorify Him; while you men, who have been made after the image and likeness of God, do not know Him! Beasts know me, and are tame; men see me, and do not acknowledge me."

To add further drama to the occasion, Jesus crossed the Jordan with an escort of the lions "and the water of the Jordan was divided on the right hand and on the left" (c36). Then he sent the animals away, instructing them to avoid hurting any of these onlookers.

# Hurtful and Injurious Childhood Miracles

## Infancy Gospel of Thomas

Perhaps the most disconcerting elements in the childhood miracle accounts of Infancy Thomas concern the ones intentionally performed to inflict pain and suffering. Unlike the canonical wonders in which they are performed for the benefit of humans rather than to injure them, the Jesus of the childhood miracle stories transforms Him into some one like a polytheistic god: a being who feels free to inflict either good or bad as he solely determines according to the emotions and anger of the moment.

One incident narrated by Thomas follows up Jesus making ponds of water on the Sabbath day from the water of a stream, making clay sparrows, and causing them to come alive (c2). After seeing the birds fly off "the son of Annas the scribe" took a branch and burst the pools of water Jesus had made. Jesus responded with intense anger, "O wicked, impious, and foolish! what harm did the pools and the waters do to thee? Behold, even now thou shalt be dried up like a tree, and thou shalt not bring forth either leaves, or root, or fruit" and the boy's body immediately began to wither up (c3). The parents took their crippled (presumably dying) child to Joseph and rebuked him for having a son who would act in such a manner. So far as the incident goes, the boy is not restored to health. Indeed the restoration of this and Jesus' other victims only comes in chapter 8 — and that implicitly rather than explicitly.

Jesus at this point is supposed to be five years old (c2). Jesus the supernatural bully is about to become a murderer. Yet the ethical incongruity of this does not seem to have dawned upon either the writer or the users of the work since there is nowhere to be found a defense of the behavior. The action is simply presented as if a defense were totally unnecessary and the action totally appropriate.

In the canonical records we read of a withered *fig tree* (Matthew 21:18–19; Mark 11:12–14). Some believe that this incident may have been in the back of the author's mind.[6] This is quite possible though the callousness of equating human and ecological life seems more worthy of an extreme contemporary ecological crusader than a early medieval narrator.

## Arabic Infancy Gospel

The Arabic Gospel refers to this destruction of the water pools as being carried out by "the son of Hanan" (c46). Seeing the water disappear Jesus responds, "As that water has vanished away, so thy life shall likewise vanish away. And immediately that boy dried up." Death is not explicitly mentioned, leaving us uncertain whether the boy has actually passed away or is in such pitiful condition that he wished he were.

## *Supernatural Childhood Executions*
### Infancy Gospel of Thomas

If it was deemed credible in the theological and social world of Infancy Thomas to speak of Jesus' childhood ability to inflict bodily harm by supernatural power, it should, perhaps, not surprise us that it was also not considered contradictory to that supernaturalness to have Him produce actual deaths as well. If the incident in the preceding section could be interpreted as either extreme debilitating illness or death, there can be no element of doubt concerning what happens in the following cases.

When one boy ran into Jesus' shoulder from behind "Jesus was angry" and caused him to fall down dead (c4). We have the closest thing the book contains to a defense of such behavior in the people's response to the killing, "And some who saw what had taken place, said: Whence was this child begotten, that every word of his is certainly accomplished?" In other words, the destructive miracles demonstrate the power that lay behind every word of His. The reaction was an obvious one, but (working from Christian predispositions) one could equally well respond: The Devil might be even more likely to give to *his* child such destructive powers to do anything and everything that his juvenile temper might lead him. Would God?

The fact that the author and his audience did not react in this manner would seem to argue that they assumed that putting up with the sometimes uncontrolled use of those powers was the price society had to pay to have Him in their midst. These assumptions might be more plausible if they went hand-in-hand with an image of Jesus as a childhood teacher of right and wrong. This element is barely touched upon in the apocryphal gospels and leaves the impression that it rarely occurred (see the discussion of Jesus as childhood prodigy below). In that type of context, one could imagine the punitive actions as backing up the credibility of any teaching that departed from the expected norm. In these contexts, the miracles lack such a broader framework of reaction to rejection that would change them from wonders of naked power to actions that — at least theoretically — could be introduced as evidence that His teaching had to be heeded.

Infancy Thomas then tells us that Joseph rebuked Jesus in private for His behavior since it both caused suffering for others and led to hatred and persecution to His own family. Jesus (condescendingly?) responded that He would ignore the remarks because Joseph had been put up to them by the community, yet those behind them "shall bear their punishment." Immediately they were made blind, causing many to be "much afraid and in great perplexity." Again, we have the observation, "Every word which He spoke, whether good or bad, was an act, and became a wonder."

This latest indignity caused Joseph to grab Jesus by the ear and yank it hard. The child was perturbed and rebuked his father for not acting wisely. He demanded that he not trouble his son any more. Generously, one supposes, Joseph is struck neither blind, withered, nor miraculously put to death.

## Pseudo-Matthew

Infancy Thomas speaks of Jesus creating pools of water at age five and then making clay birds and then transforming them into real ones (c2). In Pseudo-Matthew a miracle of extermination occurs between the beginning of the narrative and the creation of model and then real sparrows.

As Pseudo-Matthew tells it Jesus was four years old on a certain Sabbath day and was playing in the Jordan River along with several other children (c26). He made seven pools of water with canals connecting them and caused the water to move in and out of them. One of the other children "a son of the devil, moved with envy" (because of hostility at Jesus' leadership of the group?) destroyed the canals and knocked down what Jesus had built. In retaliation Jesus struck him dead. "Then with great uproar the parents of the dead boy cried out against Mary and Joseph, saying to them: Your son has cursed our son, and he is dead."

Although endangered by an angry crowd of townspeople and convinced that Jesus was in the wrong, Joseph confessed his fear of rebuking His son to Mary and asked her to deliver the needed rebuke — though it is intriguing that it is not a rebuke for killing the lad but for causing "the hatred of the people" to be stirred up against them.

Even Mary approached the ticklish assignment with caution, asking, "My Lord what was it that he did to bring about his death?" The answer, "He deserved death, because he scattered the works that I had made." (Destroy the mere toys of a childhood God and you deserve death. Polytheists would seemingly have been more comfortable with such an assumption than monotheists.) Just as Joseph did not censure the behavior as wrong in itself but objects on utilitarian grounds, she takes the same approach, "Do not so, my Lord, because all men rise up against us."

Desiring to please her, Jesus "kicked" the dead body and ordered him to rise even though he is a "son of iniquity" and "not worthy to enter into the rest of my Father."

(Not worthy to enter heaven because he has destroyed a mere toy while Jesus has struck dead an immature child not much older than an infant? To the modern mind the "son of iniquity" is more properly Jesus Himself. What is the process of reasoning that made the medieval mind consider the childhood foe of Jesus worthy of such insult and punishment? Perhaps it grew out of the concept of inherited Adamic depravity: in other words the child had been born in the deepest sin and his behavior was merely the acting out of that pre-existing nature. He deserved death and this happened to be merely the excuse for delivering it. Probably cojoined to this is the idea that monarchs liked to encourage — at least implicitly — that anything a monarch did was beyond censure. As a man "born to be a king" Jesus had, even in childhood, such immunity to criticism.)

At this point the tale of the boy who is killed for running into Jesus is inserted from the Infancy Gospel of Thomas (c4). The boy's guilt is far heavier stressed, "Behold, suddenly from the opposite direction a boy, also a worker of iniquity, ran up and came against the shoulder of Jesus, wishing to make sport of Him, or to hurt Him, if He could" (Pseudo-Matthew c29). Jesus immediately struck him dead.

Joseph was terrified by the degree of public backlash due to Jesus' behavior and urged Him to reconsider acting in such a manner. In essence Jesus responds that they got what they deserved, "a father's curse can hurt none but evil-doers." However self-assured in the rightness of His behavior, Jesus recognized the prudence of backing off. "And the same hour Jesus seized the dead boy by the ear, and lifted him up from the earth in the sight of all: and they saw Jesus speaking to him like a father to his son." Even in resurrecting him, there is the element of contempt manifested in the original infliction of death.

## Arabic Infancy Gospel

The responsibility of the victim for his own death is also stressed in the Arabic Gospel version of the boy's demise. He "ran up against [Jesus] with so much force that He fell. And the Lord Jesus said to him: As thou hast thrown me down, so thou shall fall and not rise again. And the same hour the boy fell down and expired" (c47). (A fascinating example that shows that making moral equivalents things that are significantly different is not merely a modern phenomena: because Jesus has been knocked down "proves" it is okay for the person doing it to be permanently knocked down, i.e., be killed.)

# Jesus' Supernatural Brilliance as a Childhood Student

## Infancy Gospel of Thomas

The canonical gospels speak of Jesus' brilliance and perceptivity as an adult teacher (for example, Mark 1:21–22). In the world of Infancy Thomas, Jesus already possessed such capacities as a youth.

The first opportunity to demonstrate it appears in chapters 6–8. A local teacher by the name of Zacchaeus volunteered to become tutor. He explained to Joseph that Jesus was "a sensible child, and He has some mind. Give Him to me, then, that He may learn letters [the alphabet and to read]; and I shall teach him along with the letters all knowledge, both how to address all the elders, and to honour them as forefathers and fathers, and how to love those of his own age" (c6).

Zacchaeus had overheard (c6) Jesus' rebuke of Joseph's criticism of being a bully to the other children and striking their parents blind (c5). Hence implicit in this offer seems to be the idea that Zacchaeus thinks himself so talented that he will be able to set straight this unruly child, both in how He addresses His earthly father and in how He treats other children.

The first task is to learn the alphabet, from Alpha to Omega. (Since the manuscript is in Greek; those in other languages substitute the local equivalent.[7]) Jesus rebuked Zacchaeus for not even understanding the true meaning of Alpha, much less beta. Jesus noted that there are three points of the same length and each is interlocked with the others; implicitly the idea is that the letter carries with it the mystery of the Trinity.[8]

Jesus' insight thoroughly unsettled Zacchaeus' confidence as a teacher (c7). He begged Joseph to take him out of the class because he could not endure either Jesus' look of sternness nor could he fathom the depth of His thinking.

Jesus was amused by his discomfiture and laughed aloud at it (c8). "Now let thy learning bring forth fruit, and let the blind in thee see. I am here from above, that I may curse them, and call them to the things that are above" and immediately after these words all those "who had fallen under His curse" were healed. No apologies given, of course, and the implicit warning is there not to cross Him again. This they quickly deduced, "And no one after that dared to make Him angry, lest He should curse him, and he should be maimed."

The problem was that this supernatural creature who is capable of both healing and bullying is still assumed to be illiterate. After a period of time goes by, Joseph was convinced that another effort must be made to remove the difficulty (c14). The new teacher bogged down on the same subject as the predecessor: Jesus' insistence upon an explanation of the true, philosophical meaning of the letter Alpha. The teacher became so annoyed that he whacked Him on the head. Feeling the pain, Jesus cursed him and the man immediately passed out. This time Joseph gave an order to Mary, "Do not let [Jesus] go outside of the door, because those that make Him angry die." The connection of these two ideas makes one assume the teacher had died, but the following chapter shows that he was "merely" near death.

After the passage of more time, "a genuine friend of Joseph" decides that Jesus' need for an education was so great that he would volunteer to take the risk involved in becoming His tutor (c15). Jesus accompanied him happily enough, although the teacher was in considerable fear of what would happen next.

Jesus happened to see a book upon the desk, glanced at it and did not even attempt to read the letters on it (after all, He is illiterate). Even so, "opening His mouth, He spoke by the Holy Spirit, and taught the law to those that were standing round. And a great crowd having come together, stood by and heard Him, and wondered at the ripeness of His teaching, and the readiness of His words, and that He, child as He was, spoke in such a way."

The teacher recognized that, though technically illiterate, Jesus was full of such "grace and wisdom" that he did not need a formal education. Jesus laughed at this and assured him that he was quite right. Hence "for thy sake he also that was struck down [i.e., the previous teacher] shall be cured. And immediately the other master was cured." So far as the Infancy Thomas goes, Jesus grows up a functional illiterate. How its author fit this "truth" into the canonical claim that Jesus was quite capable of reading the scroll of Isaiah in the synagogue as an adult (Luke 4:16–20) would be intriguing to know.

## Pseudo-Matthew

At five years of age, Jesus encounters the teacher Zacchaeus in Pseudo-Matthew's account (c30). As in the earlier version, the teacher was convinced that he would be able to put Jesus on the straight and narrow road of proper childly respect and behavior. Jesus viewed the teacher's goal with disdain. After all, "I have no father after the flesh," "I was before the law" of Moses was ever written, and even know "how long your life on earth will be." Why, "I have seen Abraham, whom you call your father, and have spoken with him; and he has seen me."

(Good medieval theology but guaranteed to secure a first century child the label of demented. Hence medieval theological accuracy and perception is — surely knowingly — substituted for ancient societal reality by the author. Even in their own day the audience would have regarded as absurd any child speaking in such a manner — even assuming he or she was capable. Hence the author's conceptual guide for composition is what "should" have been able to be spoken — or what "could" have been said — and what, if it had been spoken, would have been "accurate and true." It becomes not merely a theological interpretation of history but theology in place of history.)

With the first effort to get Jesus under his teaching wing a failure, Zacchaeus made a second attempt (c30). Jesus' silence while teaching Him the alphabet so frustrated the teacher that Zacchaeus finally hit Him with a stick. Jesus protested, demanding why he had done it. Furthermore it was insulting: I know more than you, the teacher. Then Jesus challenged him to provide a proper philosophical explanation for each characteristic of the letters of the alphabet: their length, twists, and so forth. Jesus' ability to elaborate on such matters drove the teacher to despair.

Having come out on top and hearing public praise, Jesus was "smiling at him with a joyful countenance." Jesus provided a blessing to everyone afterward, "Let the unfruitful bring forth fruit, and the blind see, and the lame walk right, and the poor enjoy the good things of this life, and the dead live, that each may return to his original state, and abide in Him who is the root of life and of perpetual sweetness." Promptly "all who had fallen under malignant diseases were restored."

Unlike Thomas, where Jesus restored to life and well being those He had previously injured, Pseudo-Matthew makes no mention of such. Since he is utilizing the earlier work, he may well be working under the assumption that the breadth of the promise is such that their recuperation would be naturally incorporated within this much broader blessing of health and well being.

In Chapter 38 the parents are asked to send Jesus to school to learn His "letters" and become literate. The self-assured and arrogant teacher began to grill Jesus with the letters of the alphabet and Jesus refused to go any further than the first letter before demanding an esoteric explanation of its true meaning. "And upon this the master got angry and struck Jesus; and no sooner had he struck Him, than he fell down dead."

Joseph informed Mary that he was worried about all this. Oh, not that an innocent (howbeit foolish) man has been struck dead but that somehow some malicious individual would successfully strike Jesus dead through a body blow or other means. Mary rebuked her husband for daring to believe that such was in any way possible.

Again after being pressured by others, the parents sent Jesus to yet another tutor (c39). Inspired by the Holy Spirit, he removed the book from the teacher's hand. Rather than read from it, He spoke by Divine revelation a message not merely to those present but also "the people" who have (for reasons and by means unstated) appeared to hear Him speak. "And with such power He taught the people the great things of the living God, that the master himself fell to the ground and adored Him."

Hearing the report of something strange happening at the school, Joseph came running, fearful that yet another teacher had perished. He found the teacher still alive, praising Jesus' insight and wisdom.

An aside is appropriate here for it immediately follows the teacher's catastrophe just discussed. One of the few touches of credible realism in Pseudo-Matthew is Jesus' inability to live in one place only so long. After His record of baneful (the critic would say, malicious) miracles His welcome clearly wore itself out and His family had to move from place to place. In Chapter 26 the family is residing at an unidentified location in Galilee. In Chapter 32 "Joseph and Mary departed thence with Jesus into the city of Nazareth." In Chapter 40 "Joseph departed thence with Mary and Jesus to go into Capernaum by the sea-shore, on account of the malice of His adversaries." In Chapter 41 they move to Bethlehem. Only in the case of the move to Bethlehem is the change in home not preceded by one or more hurtful miracles.

## Arabic Infancy Gospel

Jesus' childhood brilliance is also stressed in the Arabic Gospel. In this case Zacchaeus is identified as being "at Jerusalem" (c48). (Are we to assume that the family is supposed to be living there at the time? Unlikely, for Chapter 50 references how they went to Jerusalem for a feast. Probably we are dealing with an authorial oversight or, less likely, are supposed to assume that the incident occurred during a visit to the city.)

Here, too, Zacchaeus believes it is high time for Jesus to begin his formal education. When Jesus refused to follow him through the repetition of the entire alphabet, the teacher threatened to beat Him for the refusal. Jesus responded with a learned philosophical discussion of the true meaning of the first two letters of the alphabet. Having done that, Jesus—without prompting—proceeded to recite all of its letters. Zacchaeus returned the child to His parents with the compliment that "this son of thine has no need of instruction."

A second teacher was then given the opportunity to further pursue the education (c49). When Jesus attempted to divert the conversation from a discussion of the letters of the alphabet to their true meaning, the teacher had no patience with the attempt to change the subject. He "raised his hand and flogged Him, [and] immediately his hand dried up, and he died. Then said Joseph to the Lady Mary: From this time, we shall not let him go out of the house, since everyone who opposes him is struck dead."

## *Jesus' Relationship to His Parents*

In the canonical gospels we read of Jesus staying behind at a feast in his twelfth year (Luke 2:41–50). While on the home bound trip with their large traveling company, they discovered Him missing and were compelled to make a hasty return to discover His whereabouts. This they resolved when they discovered Him listening to and discussing the Torah with the learned teachers in the temple. Jesus responded to their worries by asking where else would they expect Him to be than in the Temple. This is immediately followed by the assertion, "Then He went down with them and came to Nazareth, and was subject to them, but His mother kept all these things in her heart. And Jesus increased in wisdom and stature, and in favor with God and men" (2:51–52, New King James Version).

This is the only Biblical insight into the naturally intriguing relationship of Jesus with His parents. The Infancy Gospel of James cuts off his narrative before this point becomes relevant. In Joseph, however, we have Jesus waxing eloquent on the pattern of His childhood relationship with his mother and father,

> I passed all my life without fault. Mary I called my mother, and Joseph father, and I obeyed them in all that they said; nor did I ever contend against them, but complied with their commands, as other men whom earth produces are wont to do; nor did I at any time arouse their anger, or give any word or answer in opposition to them. On the contrary, I cherished them with great love, like the pupil of my eye (c11).

The canonical account stresses the obedience aspect but does not engage in this kind of verbal gilding of the lily. To the canonical writings it was quite adequate that Jesus was a fine, upstanding, obedient youngster. To the apocryphal Joseph, He must be a perfect youngster.

## Pseudo-Matthew

Another example of Jesus' relationship with His parents is found in Pseudo-Matthew and it is quite different in emphasis. There, in the closing chapter of the work (c42) we have parents and family so respectful that it borders upon fear — indeed, in light of the repeated malicious acts of this son of theirs (narrated in other parts of the work) paranoia would have been an entirely rational reaction.

The incident concerns a feast attended by His parents as well as two sisters and three brothers (James, Joseph, and Judah). Also attending was Mary's sister, Mary of Cleophas. (In terms of the narrative of Pseudo-Matthew this is quite credible: The two Mary' parents had been living as husband and wife for two decades after they had married when he was age twenty (c1). This would likely have placed the first Mary's birth in his mid- or late-thirties. In the earlier accounts, however, her parents are both depicted as very old, making it utterly improbable that any children were born afterwards to them. Hence this is one of those rare cases when Pseudo-Matthew has curbed earlier exuberance and turned his account in a more credible direction.)

At the feast Jesus—not the father, as was customary and proper in Jewish custom — was the one who "sanctified and blessed them" and was "the first to eat and drink." Why? Because

> none of them dared to eat or drink, or sit at table, or to break bread, until He had sanctified them, and first done so. And if He happened to be absent, they used to wait until He should do so. And when He did not wish to come for refreshment, neither Joseph nor Mary, nor the sons of Joseph, His brothers, came. And, indeed, these brothers, keeping His life as a lamp before their eyes, observed Him, and feared Him. And when Jesus slept, whether by day or by night, the brightness of God shone upon Him.

This holy terror of God, blessed by "the brightness of God" whenever He napped, and his family living in fear — would terror be too strong a word?— of His actions. This picture is considered as quite credible and honorable, presumably upon the grounds that Jesus must have possessed all the wisdom, intelligence, and prerogatives that He had as an adult though He was yet but a juvenile. Yet even as an adult the canonicals picture Him as dealing with friends and kin with a far gentler hand than this.

## Death of John the Baptist's Mother

So far as the canonical gospels go, John the Baptist disappears from attention from an unknown date in his youth until he begins his ministry. In the apocryphal tales, however, we read, in detail, of his father's death (as part of the effort of Herod to ferret out the new messiah). The death of his mother is regarded in Serapion's *Life of John*. The two Syriac manuscripts that survive are quite modern, one from the sixteenth and one from the eighteenth centuries.[9] If this is indeed the same work Serapion refers to, it was originally written in Greek, probably in the late fourth century.[10]

According to this version, John the Baptist was seven and a half at the time of the death, which would place Jesus at a little over seven Himself.[11] Although still so young, His omnipotent power to see everything permitted him to behold John in the wilderness crying his heart out over his dead mother. In sympathy Jesus Himself began to weep. He shared with His own mother the cause of His discomfort only when she inquired the reason for His distress. John, He explained, "is now weeping over her body which is lying in the mountain."

When Mary broke down into tears herself, Jesus assured her that she would be present with John and her dead relative within the hour. While speaking to her, a glowing cloud came down between them. Jesus instructed His mother to call Salome and when she arrived "they mounted the cloud which flew with them to the wilderness" where the body was lying. At that point Jesus ordered the cloud away. For unspecified reasons the cloud had made a "noise" in carrying them and John was fearful when he heard it.

Jesus' voice reached him to reassure him that there was nothing to be afraid of, that kinsmen had come to help. Turning, John saw them and they embraced. Then Mary turned to washing the body for burial. Afterwards she held John "and wept over him, and cursed Herod on account of the numerous crimes which he had committed."

The angels Michael and Gabriel appeared and Jesus ordered them to bring the souls of the deceased father of John and also Simeon, a priest, so that they could sing while the angels "bury the body." During the following week, they stayed with John and taught him how to survive in the wilderness. (So far as the apocryphal narratives go, Jesus was strictly a "city boy" yet He and his "urbanized" mother are able to instruct the child on the techniques of wilderness survival. Probably the author is assuming the presence of supernatural knowledge on the part of Jesus to be able to do so.)

When the time of teaching was over, Jesus then told Mary, "Let us now go to the place where I may proceed with my work." Being seven years of age the words hardly match a return to home; they more naturally fit a return to active ministry. It is quite possible that the author believed that Jesus was engaged in some type of systematic childhood teaching. Alternatively, he may have in mind the apocryphal accounts that speak of His miraculous childhood doings and have these in mind as His designated "work."

Mary immediately suggested that they return with John since he no longer had any one to care for him. Jesus insisted that this was not God's will. It was John's destiny that he remain in the wilderness until he began his own ministry. But for protection, "Instead of a desert full of wild beasts, he will walk in a desert full of angels and prophets, as if they were multitudes of people." In addition, Gabriel would be present to assure his safety.

Having provided for the young child, they mounted the waiting cloud. (Oddly, Salome, though supposed to have come with them, is never referred to after leaving their home.) Jesus assured Mary that "I shall not forget him" and "the clouds lifted them up and brought them to Nazareth."

## *Jesus' Jerusalem Pilgrimage at Age Twelve*
### Infancy Gospel of Thomas

The author of Infancy Thomas has the text of Luke 2:41–50 (referred to above) in front of him, for he freely utilized it even as he inserted his own interpretive glosses to magnify Jesus' intellect as He reached that turning point where he is going from childhood into the teenage years (and, in ancient Jewish thought, about to become a man).

Being part of a large traveling company of friends and fellow townspeople, a close eye was not kept on Him. Hence the parents had traveled a day's journey homeward before it struck them that their son was nowhere in the large group. They returned to Jerusalem, and on the third day found Jesus in the temple listening and asking questions of those giving instruction. So far Jesus was only demonstrating Himself to be a good Jew, interested in things of the scriptures and their proper interpretation.

Not content with this real life type situation, a major interpretive gloss is then added the canonical version, "And they were all attending to Him, and wondering that He, being a child, was shutting the mouths of the elders and teachers of the people, explaining the main points of the law and the parables of the prophets" (c19).

Infancy Thomas then echoes Mary's canonical query of why Jesus had inflicted such anguish upon His parents. The response is, similarly, that He had to be about His father's business. At that point comes another gloss, this one to magnify Mary's own importance, "And the scribes and the Pharisees said: Art thou the mother of this child? And she said: I am. And they said to her: Blessed art thou among women, for God hath blessed the fruit of thy womb; for such glory, and such virtue and wisdom, we have neither seen nor heard ever."

Then the text returns to the canonical version and speaks of Jesus returning to Nazareth with His parents and being subject to them.

## Arabic Infancy Gospel

The Arabic Gospel tells the story in even greater detail and with an exaggeration of Jesus' scriptural insight even more removed from the canonical account (chapters 50–53).

Once again it is at age twelve and Jesus is at the feast in Jerusalem, listening to and asking questions of the religious scholars in the temple. A question is put in Jesus' mouth that occurs in the canonicals only as part of an adult confrontation, "Whose son is the Messiah? They answered Him: The son of David. Wherefore then, said He, does he in the Spirit call him his lord, when he says, The Lord said to my lord, Sit at my right hand, that I may put thine enemies under thy footstool?" (c50).

Then Jesus is asked about the books He had read. In the accounts of the other apocryphal gospels—and implicitly in this one as well—Jesus is illiterate, refuses to learn how to read, and, presumably has no book learning at all. Yet He responds to the question about reading the books, "Both the books, said the Lord Jesus, and the things contained in the books. And He explained the books, and the law, and the precepts and the statutes and the mysteries, which are contained in the books of the prophets—things which the understanding of no creature attains to."

(There are three interpretive options: 1) Jesus' "reading" is metaphorical of supernaturally gained knowledge, just as in chapter 48 Jesus recites the letters of the alphabet without learning them; 2) Jesus had learned to read since His earlier rejection of doing so and had become an avid reader; 3) there is a major narrative incongruity that has passed unnoticed. Since the book refers to Jesus' knowledge of the alphabet the first is the most probable explanation, though that raises the question of whether, in that case, we can say that He was "reading" in any meaningful sense of the word.)

The questioner admitted he was in awe, "I hitherto have neither attained to nor heard of such knowledge: Who, pray, do you think that boy will be."

Not only was the twelve-year-old Jesus a master of scriptural lore, He was a master of secular knowledge as well. A "skilful astronomer" enquired of Jesus' knowledge of that subject (c51). Jesus responded in such detail that He made it obvious that His knowledge was exhaustive of that subject as well.

So Jesus has a comprehensive knowledge—though but twelve—of

both scripture and astronomy. What then of medicine (c52)? Jesus then poured out a detailed and thorough survey of all that was known on that subject. (Humility is not apparently His strong suit.)

At this point Mary and Joseph discovered Jesus' presence in the temple, having last seen Him three days before (c53). Jesus responded that He was where He was supposed to be, busy in His Father's house. The teachers present inquired whether she was Jesus' mother. When she responded that she was, they complimented her for being so fortunate as to have such a son.

## *Jesus Is Commissioned to Preach at Age Twelve*

The Gnostic Justin speaks of how an angel came to commission Jesus to preach while He was still young,[12]

> When he came to Nazareth, he found Jesus [there], the son of Joseph and Mary, as a twelve-year-old boy tending sheep, and told him from the beginning everything which had happened from the time of Edem and Elohim, and what was to happen in the future, and said: "All the prophets before you, allowed themselves to be seized. Take heed, Jesus, son of man, that you do not allow yourself to be seized, but proclaim this word to men, and tell them what concerns God and the good, and ascend to the good and seat yourself there by the side of Elohim, the father of us all." And Jesus obeyed the angel and said: "Lord, all this will I do," and he preached.

There are subtle word choices here that may well reflect the Gnostic agenda. Jesus is pictured as a "prophet," nothing more. He is to ascend to God "the Father of us all," in distinction with God as being uniquely and in a special sense Jesus' Father. If these differentiations be the intent of the author, then the use of "son of man" to describe Jesus could be intended to carry the connotation of "son of man only," i.e., nothing more. Nor is the reward promised for faithfully teaching God's will that of kingship or other special honor but simply a place by God's side. In the traditional Gnostic Jesus/Christ dualism only the Christ was entitled to the kingship; the most the Jesus element could hope for was heavenly reward.

There is a condition set for receiving the reward as well: not being "seized." If we take this literally, then Jesus would be denied a heavenly recompense if He permitted Himself to be arrested and executed. If so, since this had happened, He had forfeited the promised heavenly reward. (Which would permit further—and "justified"—Gnostic derogation of the importance of the earthly Jesus in contrast to the heavenly Christ.)

Since being "seized" is immediately followed with the admonition to faithfully preach God's "word to men," the idea could, alternatively, be that of not being captured by human traditions or thought that was contrary to what the true revelation demanded. In the canonical tradition, that would echo Jesus' rebukes of allowing such tradition to undermine or reverse obedience to the written scriptures (Matthew 15:1–9). In the Gnostic convention, since the full truth consisted of carefully guarded secret traditions, the admonition would seemingly carry the connotation of not permitting rival traditions or even scripture itself to undermine adherence to their distinctive doctrine.

In the canonical literature, Jesus does not begin to preach until about age thirty (Luke 3:23), after He is baptized by John. The idea of an early quasi-ministry, however, represents a mindset very congenial with those traditions that magnified the depth, breadth, and impact of His discussions in the temple at age twelve (see above). If such extravagant opinions of that event existed at the time of Justin, one can easily see this as a prophecy that was soon thereafter "fulfilled" by the pilgrimage.

## *Death of Joseph*

### History of Joseph the Carpenter

The death of Joseph is unmentioned in James, but in Joseph it is the core of the entire work, occupying the majority of the book (c10–29). Almost to the end of his life (c1), Joseph retained his intellect and physical strength,

> At length, by increasing years, the old man arrived at a very advanced age. He did not, however, labour under any bodily weakness, nor had his sight failed, nor had any tooth perished from his mouth. In mind also, for the whole time of his life, he never wandered; but like a boy he always in his business displayed youthful vigour, and his limbs remained unimpaired, and free from all pain. His life, then, in all, amounted to one hundred and eleven years, his old age being prolonged to the utmost limit (c10).

Since Mary is pictured as the embodiment of holiness in James, perhaps this is Joseph's attempt to picture the husband as the embodiment of the "secular" ideals of health and well being. The picture painted is reasonably imagined, more or less, of a man even into the sixties and seventies. At over a hundred, the idealization becomes a mere pleasant fantasy.

As the time of death neared, only the two daughters remained unmarried and in Joseph's household. Also present were the two brothers Judas and James the Less and, of course, Mary herself (c11). When the time of death approached an angel forewarned Joseph of it (c12). Nervous at facing the reality of what, until then, had been indefinite in the future, he pled for an angelic presence so that he could safely and securely face that hour (c13).

When he returned to Nazareth, disease struck and he quickly had to take to his bed (c14). His mental acuteness began to rapidly disappear. "He also loathed food and drink, and lost all his skill in his trade of carpentry, nor did he any more pay attention to it" (c15). (This contradicts chapter 29, which insists that "he worked at his trade of a carpenter to the very last day of his life.") Then came a lengthy prayer of self-denunciation that, if taken seriously, would have meant that Joseph had been a vile and despicable individual rather than the exemplar of uprightness that the book depicts him (c16).

On his death bed, Joseph shared his fears with Jesus (c17). In language even the apostles did not use until after the resurrection, he described Jesus as "my Saviour," "deliverer of my soul," "my protector," and the "sweetest name" he could ever utter. Jesus is "my God." He begged Jesus not to hold it against him that he had considered sending Mary away when he first learned of her pregnancy.

Mary poured out her own sorrow to Jesus about the approaching death. Jesus reassured her that for the two of them it would not be death but life that they would gain (c18). Sent by Him to keep an eye on His father (c18), Mary saw the signs of a rapidly approaching death (c19). In the last moments he could not speak but merely let out emphatic sighs (c19).

When the other children were summoned for the last moments, one daughter recognized the symptoms manifested by her father as those of "the same disease that my beloved mother died of" (c20). (Disease — not old age?) Both Jesus and Joseph beheld Death and Gehenna approaching and Jesus ordered them away (c21). Jesus prayed to God to send the angels Michael and Gabriel to escort the soul of Joseph to heaven (c22) and this came to pass in fulfillment of the prayer (c23). The hour of the physical death now being clearly obvious, Jesus reassured the other children of Joseph of their father's "life everlasting" and how "he has been freed from the troubles of this life, and has passed to perpetual and everlasting rest" (c24).

After their friends and acquaintances had come to pay their last respects, the body was prepared for burial. Jesus prayed for angelic intervention to come down and help with the body (c25). Jesus then promised the dead Joseph that his body would be perfectly preserved, "The smell or corruption of death shall not have dominion over thee, nor shall a worm ever come forth from thy body. Not a single limb of it shall be broken, nor shall any hair on thy head be changed. Nothing of thy body shall perish, O my father Joseph, but it will remain entire and uncorrupted until the banquet of the thousand years" (c26). Note here the concept (just short of explicit) of a millennial reign of Jesus.

Jesus then ordained that there would be a regular (presumably annual) day of remembrance of Joseph. Anyone who did good for "the wretched, the poor, the widows, and orphans" on that day would be rewarded during the thousand years (c26). Furthermore, whoever took the time to copy the account of Joseph's life would have all his sins forgiven.

When the crowd took the body to bury it, they discovered that it was hard as a rock and that the burial wrap could not be removed (c27). Jesus then poured out to God His sorrow over His earthly father's demise (c28). After embracing the body and crying over it, He permitted the friends of the family to place it in the tomb (c29).

Joseph had been a bachelor forty years and was married to his wife forty-nine years until her death (c14), making him near ninety at her death. One year later Mary came into his household and in the third year of her stay Jesus was born, making Joseph ninety-three. With Joseph dying in his 111th year, that made Jesus approximately eighteen.

## *Jesus Starts to Hide His Miraculous Abilities*

### Arabic Infancy Gospel

Of all the infancy gospels we have studied, only the Arabic refers to a cessation of the childhood miracles. This decision came after His visit to Jerusalem at age twelve, "And from this day He began to hide His miracles and mysteries and secrets, and to give attention to the law, until He completed His thirtieth year," when He was baptized in the Jordan (c54). Why He would undertake a policy of abstaining from miracles is unexplained.

One possibility is that the author believes such a scenario is necessary to explain why the canonicals present the people acting as if they were surprised at His adult wonders; there had to be a prolonged period of time for the stories of anything done in His early years to pass from general memory. (Actually in small and modest size towns it would have taken far longer than two decades for incidents as these to have vanished!)

Another possibility is that this is a discrete manner of saying that as Jesus grew, He learned maturity and self-control over His supernatural abilities. (In a society with widespread idolatry that would have left the embarrassing question of why Jesus should be considered superior to the ancient Greek and Roman gods since in His earlier years He had acted no better than they [with the notable exception of sexual promiscuity]. But by the time the book became popular, such paganism was on its way out or even safely a thing of the past. Hence if one begins with the assumption that Jesus started out with unlimited wonder-working powers, one merely needs to explain that He decided to repress the display of them as he matured since maturity is expected to be accompanied by greater self-control.)

## Jesus' Childhood Receipt of the Holy Spirit
### Pistis Sophia

Taking a short (and rare) break from its determined mystical interpretations of Jesus' post-resurrection discussions with His mother and certain other disciples, there is the record of a strange childhood event in the *Pistis Sophia*. As His mother recalls it (c61),[13]

> When thou wast small, before the Spirit came upon thee, while thou wast in a vineyard with Joseph, the Spirit came forth from the height, he came to me into my house, he resembled thee. And I did not recognize him and I thought that he was thou.
> And the Spirit said to me: "Where is Jesus, my brother, that I meet him?" And when he said these things to me, I was confused and I thought that he was a phantom to tempt me. But I took him, I bound him to the leg of the bed in my house, until I came out to you in the field, thou and Joseph, and I found you in the vineyard, as Joseph was hedging the vineyard with reeds.
> Now it happened, when thou didst hear me speaking the word to Joseph, thou didst understand the word and thou didst rejoice. And thou didst say: "Where is he that I may see him? Or else I await him in this place." But it happened when Joseph heard thee saying these words, he was agitated and we came up at the same time, we went into the house.
> We found the Spirit bound to the bed. And we looked at thee with him, we found thee like him. And he that was bound to the bed was released, he embraced thee, he kissed thee. And thou also, thou didst kiss him and you became one

The receipt of the Spirit at John's baptism was, in contrast, a receipt of "mercy" for the human race (c62).

This event from the *Pistis Sophia* is placed at a vague point in Jesus' youth, with no clear indication of when it occurred. The ambiguous reference to Jesus being "small" and the fact that He was helping His father in "a vineyard" rather than with the carpentry trade could easily point to a time when He was only five or six years ago. The successful wrestling and capturing of the Spirit (once one overcomes the inherent difficulty in imagining how one could accomplish this with a "spirit" being) would point to the human involved being larger and bigger than the creature, hence physically older than the spirit (although the identicalness of appearance could well argue that, in outward appearance, both were the same "age").

Why is such a receipt of the Spirit considered necessary by the author? Although the work does not describe Jesus' childhood wonders in Palestine, it would be easy to see in this youthful merger with the divine Spirit the conceptual explanation for why they were possible. Be that as it may, since we normally think of Jesus' first encounter with the Holy Spirit as being in connection with His baptism (which begins the next chapter) this incident—though vague as to its timing—serves as a useful "bridge" to what comes next since they are joined together by a special and important receipt of the Spirit.

## A Jewish Alternative Version of Jesus' Birth and Adolescence

The stories we examine in the current work are primarily those coming from sources claiming to be friendly to Christianity and revering Jesus. Most of the anti–Jesus material has long perished and little appears to have existed in lengthy narrative or apologetic form. Passing pagan and Jewish allusions have survived (the latter often obscured by the need to determine which Talmudic references are really to Jesus of Nazareth),[14] but successfully seeking for anything more is extremely difficult.

A bitterly controversial exception is the Testimonium Flavianum. In his *Jewish Antiquities* (13.3.3), the dominant text of Josephus' work describes Jesus as

(1) a miracle worker;

(2) a teacher of both Jews and Greeks—the latter is consistent with the gospel tradition only if Josephus had in mind the Samaritans or if one stresses the very modest teaching interaction with Gentiles mentioned in the canonicals;

(3) He was tried before Pilate;

(4) He died by crucifixion;

(5) those claiming to be His disciples still existed decades later.

The problem is how a Jew could refer to Him as "Messiah," question whether it was proper to refer to Him as a mere mortal, and mention Jesus appearing alive after three days in fulfillment of ancient prophecy. Scholars have run the gauntlet from acceptance of the genuineness of the entire passage, to the pro–Jesus references being interpolations, to total rejection of the entire text.[15]

Two scenarios might explain the genuineness of the questioned parts of the text. One is that Josephus had become so disillusioned with nationalism and the "disproving" on the battlefield of the feasibility of the military option against Rome, that he could now sympathize with a Man and a movement which had previously been rejected out of hand. A second possibility is that Josephus had become ultra-cynical and was rubbing salt into the wounds of his once comrades in the Great Revolt by praising a Man they despised. All the text absolutely requires is that he had become a friendly and awed outsider and that he recognized that in Jesus' fate and behavior were found events fully consistent with the Torah and prophetic literature he was versed in regardless of whether he "literally" believed that Jesus was "the" fulfillment of them.

Even the "explicit" reference to Jesus as "Messiah" would fit the cynicism scenario: The Romans had no problem with a dead Messiah such as Jesus. That was the way they wanted all Jewish "messiahs" to be—dead. In his disillusionment perhaps Josephus shared the sentiment and was discretely stressing what would happen to all future ones as well.

Jumping several centuries beyond Josephus—or further—one relatively lengthy Jewish narrative has survived, though it has been very neglected and ignored. This traditionalist Jewish version is called the *Toldoth Jeshu*. According to this account, Jesus' birth occurred in this manner: John was betrothed to Mary, the daughter of a neighbor whose wife had died. She was, indeed, a virgin and both families lived in Bethlehem. Joseph ben Pandera looked amazingly like him and, on one Friday evening, used the similarity to get her by herself and attempt a seduction. She resisted unsuccessfully.

Angered that her betrothed would act in such an improper manner, when John was back she rebuked him for his behavior. Knowing that the accusation was false and calculating that Pandera was the most likely individual to have successfully made such an impersonation, he repeated what had happened and his reasoning to Rabbi Simeon. When Mary's pregnancy became known, John was caught between the knowledge that the child was not his and the inability to prove the accusation against Joseph. Presumably in frustration at the situation, he ran away to Babylon.

When the child was born Mary named him Jesus because that had been the name of the brother of her mother. Although a student of the Law of Moses, he was stubborn and nonconforming. Appearing before his teachers with an uncovered head, this so upsets them that they call him a "bastard." (In other words, his behavior was proof of his illegitimacy.)

Doctrinal confrontations with Jesus later occur and the tensions escalated. His critics challenged Mary as to his legitimacy and she dodged a straight answer by insisting that he was the son of her runaway husband. Simeon recalls the accusations John had made before His flight and insisted that whatever sin was involved she was personally guiltless. As the story spread of His illegitimacy, Jesus fled to the city of Jerusalem.[16]

CHAPTER 8

# Jesus' Adult Life and Teaching Ministry

Heretics and theologians might be thoroughly enchanted (or repelled) by deep theological theorizing claiming to originate from Jesus. As preserved in works such as *Sophia Pistis* such speculation tended to be lengthy, obscure, and unrelated to the practicalities of living a moral and devout life in the current world; they, typically, were obsessed by cosmic "truths" and "insights" (elaborated at horrendous length) that, even if fully true, catered to one's theoretical knowledge rather than ability to live a better and more fulfilling life in the here and now. For most people, a simple, spiritually edifying account of "what happened" (or "could have happened") was of far greater interest. It had a larger inherent "market" and appeal to the masses.

Hence narrative not theory was the type of writing that was the most likely to gain favorable attention by a significant part of the believing community. But there were certain areas that were far more attractive to them than others. The "orthodox" accounts of Jesus' life that have survived center either on His birth or His death. In part this is to provide supplemental data (or, at least, speculation) which was not deemed necessary (perhaps not even appropriate) for the Biblical accounts to delve into, yet about which human curiosity cried out for more information.

Since the materials were written for the spiritual masses this was a natural area to emphasize. Furthermore, the body of His adult ministry represented far more dangerous territory. These were the segments of Jesus' life that were most likely to create the risk of intentionally or accidentally raising the specter of heresy or, through ignorance or inadvertence, misrepresenting the atmosphere, details, or even general background of the events of those years.

This avoidance tendency was reinforced by the twin ideas of a full canon (either in a literal sense or in regard to the life of Jesus) and the accompanying conviction of their authoritativeness in all matters they treated. Duplication of their subject matter put one in the uncomfortable position of probing matters on which there was already much data and opened one to the accusation of redundancy or pride in "challenging" the status, adequacy, or reliability of what was already available. It did not help that any work whose contemporary origin was admitted was directly in competition with narratives already accepted as far closer to the events and more authoritative than anything they could possibly compose.

Since the purpose of all but the consciously doctrinally self-serving versions was to "build up" the community's faith rather than to serve as lightning rods for dissent, confrontation, and controversy, there was a massive psychological disincentive to tackle the adult years of Jesus' life. Hence if one wished to have one's narrative gain a following in the church's "mainstream," this period had to be carefully avoided or treated with the greatest caution.[1]

Regardless of when one considers the full New Testament canon to have come into general acceptance, the canon of acceptable lives of Jesus was — so far as the evidence we have available — a religious "given" no later than the third decade of the second century. Indeed, the uniformity of a four-fold gospel standard is so clearcut that we must assume that it actually dates from significantly earlier.

Justin Martyr was using them as the authoritative collection about A.D. 150 in Rome. In Syria around 170, Tatian's *Diatessaron* combined them into a single document. The utilization of these exclusively and without resort to other sources also argues for a four-fold standard. Moving to Gaul a little later, we have Irenaeus not only embracing this standard but arguing that there needed to be only four on the grounds of the parallel with the number of directions, winds, etc. However weak the reasoning (which is more sermonic than anything else) it bears witness to the compulsion to recognize the complete adequacy of the life of Jesus as contained in the existing four authoritative gospels and four alone.[2]

From Rome in the center to Syria in the east and Gaul in the west, the uniformity is impressive long before Constantine or anyone else came on the scene who might have used secular or religious power politics to manipulate the choices.[3] True, other parts of the canon remained an issue in certain places, especially some of the shorter epistles. But the "life story" four gospel standard was essentially set in concrete as the universally recognized criterion. If one wished to reduce the number John would likely be targeted since Gnostic-type devotees considered it the only one of the four that they viewed with any favor.[4]

On the other hand, so long as there was no obvious heresy or contradition to this four gospel yardstick, there was the willingness to permit the continuing use of locally favored works in certain places as well. For example, Serapion had not previously encountered the "Gospel of Peter" and so permitted it to be used in one congregation in Syria because he considered the group fully orthodox — until he had occasion to examine the work and then prohibited it.[5] Even here one must tread with caution in assuming that because one tolerated the use of a narrative life-story "gospel" that it was regarded as on a level of authoritativeness or reliability with the Synoptics and John,[6] either by those in authority or by the users themselves.

Hence there was a distinction between works acceptable for use and those considered definitive in matters of faith and doctrine ("canonical," in the ultimate full development of the concept). As a the result there was a de facto standard by which to judge new and alleged old parallel works. Works might prove spiritually useful and beneficial yet not be viewed as on a level of authority and origin with the four gospels. Any perceived deviation from their teaching could easily be used by defenders of the four gospel consensus against even their utilization and when they merely duplicated what was already available there was little reason to encourage the use of the alternatives in the first place. As a result, the existence of a perceived adult life "standard" of what happened during Jesus' life discouraged the writing and reading of further such works even as efforts of pious fiction.

Yet a significant desire to avoid controversy enters the picture as well — as a secondary supporting motive to avoiding competition with the four fold gospel canon. Although the birth and childhood tales could be developed in a "heretical" direction (see our earlier discussion), this could be glossed over through ambiguity that could be interpreted in more than one direction.

It wasn't so easy in regard to the adult years of Jesus. In imagining doctrinal material one was easily opening the door to charges of quasi-orthodoxy or outward heresy even when it was not intended. Nor was this subject matter a route even those consciously attempting doctrinal innovation might wish to trod if they desired to propagandize among the non-"heretical" mainstream.

In detecting heresy, blatant "error" was the easiest to detect; a vivid imagination, however, permitted the skillful "hiding" of questionable materials by presenting the ideas in such a partially disguised form that only a careful "re-reading" of the words would actually uncover it. On the other hand, if buried in "non-controversial" areas such as the birth these would less likely be noticed, especially if one were careful to use rhetoric that could be taken in multiple senses or invent "life incidents" that could be superficially appealing to the mainstream while having a special "insider" meaning to those favoring dissidence.

The "orthodox" would tend to have a built-in bias in favor of the four gospels being adequate for the adult life in and of themselves. These were typically regarded as directly apostolic in the cases of Matthew and John. They were viewed as indirectly "apostolic" in nature in the case of Mark (as representing Peter's preaching) and Luke (as representing both his own research among disciples and apostolic eyewitnesses as well as Paul's own preaching). Hence there would be an automatic disincentive to create accounts of the adult ministry among the orthodox. Therefore it is not surprising that though various early church writers refer to specific incidents of the life, alternative "orthodox" narrative accounts of the life of Jesus have not survived. What little there is of the "Egerton Gospel" (Papyrus Egerton 2) appears to be perhaps the only example of this type of material and even there, there is much "quotation" rather than narration.[7]

Interestingly enough, the surviving major fragments of Jesus' teaching ministry and adult life that are derived from allegedly heretical sources put the stress on His purported teachings. On the other hand, summaries and short segments of individual events have been preserved by various ancient writers, sometimes because they wished to show the material to the public as heretical (or at least questionable) and in other cases probably because the extracted material had attracted their interest due to the subject matter. Because of the fragmentary nature of it, we will have to resort more to direct quotation of the text rather than summarizing it as we normally did in the previous chapters.

## Roman Allusions to Jesus' Life and Death

How the polytheists told the story is little known. We do know, for example, of the ancient tale of Jesus being fathered by a Roman soldier and the fact that accounts (perhaps faked) were available telling of the trial and execution of Jesus. Their actual texts have disappeared as well as that of any other events concerning Jesus' life that once may have existed. Scattered references to specific aspects of His life have survived and deserve at least passing mention so we can have a broader perspective of how non-Jewish non-Christians sometimes viewed Him.

Julius Africanus refers to how the first century historian Thallus wrote about the darkness at the time of Jesus' death, but Thallus' own writings have not survived and even Africanus' own summary concedes that the Romans had thought it to have been an eclipse. Nor does the church writer provide the context in which the remark was made. Was it a reference to an event at the approximate time of Jesus' death? Was it a reference to something that happened in geographic Palestine and it alone? Or was it a reference to an allusion to something that happened somewhere else and which Africanus assumed applied to Jerusalem as well? Was Jesus explicitly mentioned in connection with the alleged eclipse? Such are the unanswered questions. The allusion is admittedly tantalizing but because of its brevity, lack of context, and the loss of Thallus' own version leaves us with little tangible with which to work from.[8]

Writing apparently in the late first century, Mara bar Serapion speaks of how foolish it is to persecute the wise. He cites the example of the Greeks: they killed Socrates only to have his teaching live on in Plato. As to the Jews, they killed "their wise king" and were "ruined and driven from their own land [and] live in complete dispersion." Like Plato, he lived on in his teaching. That last assertion (seemingly implicitly rejecting the idea of a resurrection) argues he was not a Christian and, if his illustration derived from Christian teaching at all, he did not accept their assertions about that pivotal article of their faith. Indeed, the name of Jesus is not explicitly mentioned at all. The allusion being to anyone else, however, seems impossible.[9]

In the second century, Celsus effectively attacked the Christian faith. His works were sufficiently effective and popular that a century later Origen preserved a cross section of his remarks and assertions in his own *Contra Celsum*, written with the purpose of refuting them. According to Celsus, Jesus became a worker in Egypt and, while there, set out to master the magical arts. Utilizing these powers back in His homeland, he was able to work various wonders that impressed the masses as being the power of God in operation. This was to become a standard explanation in both Jewish and Gentile allusions to Jesus as to how he had been able to perform His miracles.[10]

Lucian of Samosata (died c. 200) wrote the *Passing of Pereginus*, a philosopher who spent some time as a Christian. Rapidly ascending to a place of leadership in Palestine, he became an expounder of their works and wrote a number of treatises on their behalf as well. Pereginus referred to how Jesus was crucified and how He had set Himself up as lawgiver for the movement.[11]

Tacitus (died c. 118) ruled as proconsul in Asia (112–113) and was the author of a series of histories of Rome and its possessions. He refers to how Jesus was sentenced to death by Pontius Pilate. Tacitus speaks, to his obvious horror, that the execution only temporarily squashed the movement of Jesus' followers and that he had seen it spread as far as Rome itself.[12]

# Jesus' Baptism by John

## Gospel of the Hebrews

According to the Gospel of the Hebrews, Jesus initially hesitated to go to John for baptism. A copy of the manuscript of the work was available at the library in Caesarea and Jerome quotes the exchange with Mary, "Behold, the mother of the Lord and His brethren said unto Him, 'John the Baptist baptizeth for the remission of sins; let us go and be baptized of him.' But He said: 'What have I committed, that I should be baptized of him, unless it be that in saying this I am in ignorance'" (*Against the Pelagians* III.2).[13] In other words, if I am to be baptized it has to be for a different reason than sin. The fact that He was baptized argues that there was such a reason though the text does not discuss what it was.[14] (Presumably the moral obligation of all to obey God and the practical problem in explaining why He was not baptized, if He declined.)

The same ancient author quotes the volume in describing the baptism itself (*Commentary on Isaiah* XI.2),[15]

> But in the gospel which is written in Hebrew and which the Nazarenes read, "the whole fountain of the Holy Spirit shall descend upon Him." And the Lord is spirit, and where the Spirit of the Lord is, there is liberty. And in the gospel referred to above I find this written: "And it came to pass as the Lord ascended from the water, the whole fountain of the Holy Spirit descended upon Him and rested upon Him, and said to Him, 'My son, in all the prophets I expected thee that Thou mightest come and that I might rest upon thee. Thou art my rest, thou art my firstborn Son, who reignest in eternity'"

The canonical accounts do not specify the "degree" to which Jesus received the Spirit at His baptism. The Hebrew Gospel, in contrast, placed a heavy emphasis on its totality. Similarly the canonical accounts only speak of a voice speaking from heaven — seemingly making it not the Spirit speaking, for the Spirit is spoken of as descending upon Jesus at the same time — and it is that voice (not the Spirit) who proclaims Jesus as the divine Son. Here it is the Spirit who makes the assertion and adds the remainder of the quotation attributed to it.

## Gospel of the Ebionites

The Gospel of the Ebionites provides an intriguing blend of canonical data and Ebionite doctrine and interpretation. As quoted by Epiphanius in his *Heresies* (30.13), the volume begins with the baptismal work of John,[16]

And after many other words it goes on: "The people having been baptized, Jesus came also, and was baptized by John. And as he came out of the water, the heavens opened, and He saw the Holy Spirit descending under the form of a dove, and entering into Him. And a voice was heard from heaven: 'Thou art my beloved Son, and in thee am I well pleased.' And again: 'This day have I begotten thee.' And suddenly shone a great light in that place.

"And John seeing him, said, 'Who art thou, Lord?' Then a voice was heard from heaven: 'This is my beloved Son, in whom I am well pleased.' Thereafter John fell at His feet and said: 'I pray thee, Lord, baptize me.' But He would not, saying, 'Suffer it, for so it behoveth that all should be accomplished.'"

Presumably the Spirit "entering into" Jesus is interjected to explain in what sense and in what manner God could say "this day have I begotten thee." This carries the apparent implication that prior to this entry of the Spirit, in some important and significant sense Jesus lacked the fullness of being the Divine Son. He is "adopted," so to speak, into that position at the time of His baptism.[17]

Since there is every reason to believe that John was performing the procedure in daylight, the claim that after Jesus was baptized there "suddenly shone a great light in that place" is unexpected and hard to visualize. Having put Jesus as the last to be baptized in the introductory words of the text, perhaps the Ebionites were implying that this was a night time baptism, done after the crowds had departed.

The imagery of a great light appearing at the baptism is, however, found in other sources as well. Tatian's *Diatessaron* appears to have referred to "a mighty light" that "flashed upon the Jordan" at the time of the baptism.[18] Using a different image that might be relevant here, Justin speaks of a "fire" in the Jordan at the point Jesus entered it.[19] The *Preaching of Paul* refers to how, during Jesus' baptism, "a fire was seen above the water."[20]

The concept even managed to infiltrate a very few Biblical manuscripts. In the Old Latin codexes Vercellensis and Sangermanensis an additional comment is added at Matthew 3:15, "And when Jesus was being baptized, a great light shone from the water, so that all who were assembled were afraid."[21]

Why is the image utilized in the Gospel of the Ebionites? A cultic practice of night baptism would be the most obvious, as we noted. Others have suggested that it was an application of the image of Jesus as "light of the world" into the baptismal account.[22] On a literalistic level this would be improbable: there is a vast difference between what Jesus "is" (in Christian belief) and what "happens" at some point in His life. On a symbolic level, however, one can imagine the concept being stretched in such a manner.

Another possibility is that it was an application of John the Baptist's description of the Messiah as one baptizing with both the Holy Spirit and fire (Matthew 3:11).[23] Against this is the fact that John describes the Messiah as giving rather than receiving the "fire." Furthermore the Ebonite gospel puts a positive "spin" on "fire" rather than accepting the more contextually appropriate interpretation in the canonicals of "fire" as Divine wrath (Matthew 3:10, 12), i.e., the Messiah would give both Divine blessings (the Spirit) as well as inflict Divine wrath ("fire"). (In spite of contextual scriptural indications, a positive construction of both expressions remains quite popular today so it would not be odd if many ancients similarly adopted on upbeat interpretation of the "fire.")

If the Baptist's allusion to the Messiah giving the Spirit and fire, is, indeed, the conceptual root of the Ebionite allusion then they probably reasoned something along this line: Just as Jesus received the Spirit at His baptism, in a similar vein He must have received the "fire" that He was to give as well. Hence the light/fire of our text.

## Jesus' Forty Days of Temptation

In the Gospel of the Hebrews, the description of this period of temptation is apparently first-hand. This would have the advantage of explaining how the disciples learned of its contents: Jesus described it to them.[24] According to Origen, Jesus is quoted in that Gospel as saying, "My mother, the Holy Spirit, took me just now by one of my hairs and carried me off to the great Mount Tabor" (*Commentary on John* II.2).[25] In his *Homily on Jeremiah* (15:4) the same text is again quoted, "My mother, the Holy Spirit, took me just now and carried me off to the great Mount Tabor."[26] In three other places the same text is also repeated but without reference to Mount Tabor in particular: *Commentary on Ezekiel* (XVI.13), *Commentary on Isaiah* (XI.9) and *Commentary on Micah* (VII.7).[27]

If the idea is of Jesus being taken to the general place of temptation, then this may represent commentary on the canonical idea of the Spirit leading or driving Him into the wilderness to endure the ordeal (Mark 1:12–13).[28] If it is referring to the specific temptation (less likely) of the Devil taking Jesus to an extremely high mountain and being offered the kingdoms of the world in exchange for worship this would represent a direct contradiction to the Biblical text (Matthew 4:8–10): there it is the Devil rather than the Spirit that does the conveyance.

Some have found Biblical precedent for the concept of being lifted by the hair and transported in Ezekiel 8:3 where Ezekiel is so carried to Jerusalem — unfortunately for the theory it is specifically called a "vision" and is not presented as if it "literally" happens as in the case of the temptations of Jesus. In the deuterocanonical literature one is more successful. In the story of Bel and the dragon (chapter 14 of the Greek form of Daniel) one reads of the prophet Habbakuk being transported by an angel in this manner in order to deliver food to Daniel (verses 33–39). Here the implication of "literalness" is certainly intended.[29]

In the Gospel of the Hebrews the key to the intent is probably found in the reference to Jesus being brought by "one" of his hairs: in other words, there was no opposition by Jesus, so effortlessly was He carried there.[30] The conception is clearly far from that of the Synoptics. Matthew (4:1) and Luke (4:1) refer to Jesus as being "led" to the place of temptation by the Spirit, rather than being miraculously transported. Mark (1:12) uses an even stronger word that properly means "driven."[31] The idea in the Synoptics is not so much that Jesus resisted the Spirit's going to the place of temptation but that the human element in His constitution recognized the danger and He went as a matter of duty rather than preference. In the Gospel of the Hebrews the reaction is dramatically different, either one of passivity or outright enthusiasm.

The physical location of the temptations at Mount Tabor, though ancient and common by at least the beginning of the fourth century,[32] is a most improbable one. The characterization of it in the Gospel of the Hebrews as "great," i.e., large, huge, is certainly hyperbole and it is hard not to dismiss it as blatant ignorance of the topography of Palestine.[33] A mount only 1,400 feet high is hard to dignify by such a label.[34] (Perhaps the description derives from a psychological deduction: do not "great" temptations require a physically "great" place for them to occur?) There was also a Roman encampment on the top during Jesus' lifetime, so the Mount was hardly likely to give the privacy and isolation assumed in the canonical versions.[35]

The concept of the Holy Spirit as mother deserves some attention as well. Initially it is an odd concept for we naturally think of Mary in that regard. On the other hand we have no problem with the dualism of Jesus having two fathers—"son of Joseph" as well as "Son of God." If we work from a "Trinitarian" approach, the spiritual "Father" role is already occupied and the only remaining term or analogy left to describe the Spirit's role would be as the "Mother" of Jesus. Alien to canonical terminology, it is an expression explicitly applied to Jesus in the *Secret Book of James* (5:6) and seems clearly implied in the Coptic (teaching/sayings) Gospel of Thomas (101) as well.[36]

## Jesus' Physical Appearance

The Acts of John depict Jesus as a person who would fit perfectly in a modern science-fiction novel: His physical appearance and nature varied from time to time and place to place and even in the visible perception of onlookers who saw him simultaneously. In chapter 90 (recounting a transfiguration, see below), He appears both as a normal sized man and as a giant.

The changes are, if anything, even more dramatic, when they are first called to be apostles. James saw Jesus as a child (c88). In contrast, John saw Him as "handsome, fair and cheerful-looking."[37] After this, Jesus helped them pull the boat up on the shore and was then perceived by them in yet more different forms (c. 89). To John He appeared "as rather bald-headed but with a thick flowing beard, but to James as a young man whose beard was just beginning." He never, during their years together, was seen to blink His eyes. (Pieter J. Lalleman takes this as a "traditional Greek way" of depicting Jesus' supernaturalness.[38]) Even the feel of His chest varied from "smooth and soft" to, at other times, "hard like a rock." This, understandably, perplexed John.

Looking back on those years, John tells his readers that "sometimes when I meant to touch him I encountered a material, solid body; but at other times again when I felt Him, His substance was immaterial and incorporeal, and as if it did not exist at all.... And I often wished, as I walked with Him, to see His footprint in the earth, whether it appeared—for I saw Him raising Himself from the earth—and I never saw it" (c93).

The fact that the two apostles beheld Jesus as of differing ages at the time of their call, has been interpreted by some to indicate the relative spirituality of the two men (or the spiritual communities owing allegiance to them). John beholds him as older because he "represents the mature believers."[39] Since John himself, as we have seen, beheld Jesus in various forms, this argues against the validity of this interpretation[40] unless we are to take the approach that the two different incidents are intended to make different points and this interpretation only explains one of them.

Paul G. Schneider is tempted by the theory that the manifestations are patterned after that of the Egyptian God Horus, who "manifested himself as an infant, a young man, a man and an old man to express his eternity and absolute permanence." This is the intent of the Acts as well, he argues, whether or not it is actually patterned after that source.[41] He finds appealing the theory that John, in contrast with James, symbolizes mature Christians as well but stresses that this is not intended in a derogatory manner. After all both are brothers. "Plus, with James and John [both] seeing progressively older manifestations of the Lord, the spirituality of both groups of Christians should be seen as maturing."[42]

The ever changing forms of Jesus tells us something of the theological core of the author's Christology. As Pieter J. Lalleman writes,[43]

> The fact that John never tells how the Lord normally looked, contributes to the impression that He should not be considered a real human being. He did not even have a semi-permanent mock body, but changed His appearance whenever He wished. This representation implies that His divine being can never adequately be expressed in a human form. In the eyes of our author, to believe that the Lord had a human body would amount to lessening His divinity. He rejects the immense paradox of the incarnation of the Logos (John 1).

In the canonical post-resurrection accounts we have cases where people did not recognize Jesus: the two men on the road to Emmaus (in Luke 24:13–35) is perhaps the best example. What we do not find is the element introduced here that Jesus could simultaneously appear different to different individuals. In the canonical account we can see the contextual usefulness of a disguised appearance: to have a candid discussion with the travelers under circumstances where the presence of the Jesus they remembered might well hinder their candor. In the Acts of John such factors appear missing and we seem to be faced with something more akin to a mere idle wonder.

As noted in our introduction to the historical background of these works, the Acts of John is a hodgepodge compiled from multiple sources. The incidents above — indeed, the entire section from chapters 87 through 105 — have been preserved only in a single manuscript, a Greek one.[44]

## *Jesus' Unique Physical Inability*

The accused heretic Valentinus claimed that Jesus' body had certain distinctive characteristics unlike the rest of the human race, "He was continent, enduring all things. Jesus digested divinity: He ate and drank in a special way, without excreting His solids. He had such a great capacity for continence that the nourishment within Him was not corrupted, for He did not experience corruption."[45]

Valentinus seems to be arguing that since Jesus' body did not suffer "corruption" (i.e., though dying His body did not decay because he was resurrected) in a similar manner the normal destructive "corruption" (decay) involved in digestion did not occur either. Others believe that an allusion is intended to the injunction in John 6:27. There Jesus told listeners not to "labor" for food that is consumed. The word "labor" translates a Greek word that covers both working and digestion.[46] A relevance here seems most unlikely since it is a command to others rather than a self-description of Himself. Furthermore it represented something they were capable of doing, while a human body can not survive without excretion of wastes.

The Greek word rendered "continent" and "continence" is broad in its description of moderation and restraint. It can be applied to any area of life from the amount one drinks to one's sex drive.[47] In regard to Jesus' bodily functions, Valentinus stretched the normal usage of the term from moderation into non-existence. From the canonical standpoint such speculation would seem fantasy. Jesus took for granted that whatever food any one took in (including Himself) enters the body, is digested, and then passes out of it (Matthew 15:17).

## Appointment of Apostles

Unlike the canonical gospels, in which the appointment of the twelve as apostles is spoken of as occurring after an unidentified period of membership as "disciples" in the broader Jesus movement, the Gospel of the Ebionites speaks as if the two happened simultaneously or, at least, the formal appointment was at a much earlier point. As Epiphanius quotes from the book in his *Heresies* (30.13),[48]

> And He came into Capernaum and entered into the house of Simon, surnamed Peter, and He opened His mouth and said, "As I walked by the sea of Tiberias, I chose John and James, the sons of Zebedee, and Simon and Andrew and Thaddaeus and Simon Zelotes, and Judas Iscariot; thee also, Matthew, when thou wast sitting at the receipt of custom, did I call and thou didst follow me. According to my intention ye shall be twelve apostles for a testimony unto Israel."

Oddly, though specifically mentioning "twelve apostles," the text only lists eight of them. This could be a transcription mistake by Epiphanius[49] or even of the manuscript utilized by that ancient writer.

## Healing of a Man with a Bad Hand

This healing is recorded in Matthew 12:9–13. Jerome quotes an addendum from the Gospel of the Hebrews in which "we read that the man with the withered hand, was a mason, who asked for help with these words: 'I was a mason, working for my bread with my hands. I pray Thee, Jesus, restore me to soundness, that I eat not my bread in disgrace'" (*Commentary on Matthew* XII.13),⁵⁰ i.e., because without the healing he would have to beg in order to survive.⁵¹ In the canonical account the request aspect is not mentioned and its inclusion, arguably, intensifies the implicit compassionate aspect of the healing.⁵²

## *Every Meal a Miracle*

In the canonical gospels we read of two large scale feedings by Jesus: one, a miracle that fed four thousand and another that fed 5,000. As the Acts of John tells it every meal (at least with His enemies so, presumably, with friends as well) involved a supernatural manifestation,⁵³

> And if ever He were invited by one of the Pharisees and went where He was invited, we went with Him; and one loaf was laid before each one of us by those who had invited us, and so He also would take one; but He would bless His and divide it among us; and every man was satisfied by that little piece, and our own loaves were kept intact, so that those who had invited Him were amazed (c.93).

## *Jesus' Miracles: A Hostile Interpretation*

There are three possible approaches to Jesus' alleged miracles by those who do not believe that they constitute vindication of His supernatural nature and/or His status as, at the minimum, a prophet of God. In the eighteenth to current centuries, the dominant explanation has been to claim that they never happened. This covers a gauntlet of explanations ranging from misunderstanding to conscious misrepresentation by the earliest believing community.

Although the ancient world was quite aware that "miracles" could be faked, neither pagan nor Jewish antagonists are known to have lodged such a charge. In the canonicals we read the accusation being made that Jesus' exorcisms were only possible due to the power of the Devil (Luke 11:15). This explanation had a ready come back even in that source. Since exorcisms were performed by those they agreed with, whose power made those possible?

For those favoring an explanation that could be applied with less danger of an embarrassing riposte such as this, the theory that "magical" powers were involved had a great deal of appeal. The explanation could work for those who believed that the powers being invoked were those of God

Himself, but they could also work for the more "secularly" inclined because these could be pre-existent powers independent of God and, perhaps, even utilized by God in His interaction with the human race. Being Jewish, that such powers would most effectively work when utilizing the name of Yahweh, their God, made great sense. (In light of their monotheism, one would hardly expect it to be that of Zeus or Jupiter!)

In the medieval *Toldoth Jeshu* this became the basis of Jesus' miracle-working powers. It was in the Jerusalem Temple itself that Jesus was able to learn "the Ineffable Name" whose invocation could make such wonders happen. The "brass dogs" at the place of sacrifice would transform themselves into animate objects and bark at any one who had learned this name, thereby "making them forget." To keep this from happening, Jesus had written it on leather and sewed the leather into the thigh to assure he would never lose it.

"He gathered around him in Bethlehem a group of young Jews and proclaimed himself the Messiah and Son of God."[54] To vindicate these claims, He invoked God's Name to heal both someone who was lame and a leper as well. The local Queen summoned Him because of this and convicted Him of "sorcery and beguilement" of the masses. (Perhaps this transfer of judgment from Pilate to a woman ruler is the author's method of avoiding the embarrassing admission that this was a time of Roman occupation and rule.)

Jesus overcame the conviction by resurrecting the dead and the Queen came to accept His credibility. Freed, "He went next to Galilee, where he continued to work miracles and to attract crowds."

The religious "sages" of the land were horrified at these successes. They appointed Yehuda Iskarioto (Judas) to discover the "Ineffable Name, as Jesus did" and thereby be able to equal him in miracle-working ability. Both then came before the Queen and "Yeshu [Jesus] flew in the air, but Yehuda [Judas] flew higher and caused him to fall to the earth."

Jesus was again convicted and this time was removed to imprisonment in Tiberias. By a bold military strike of their own, his supporters freed him from the "sages" and they fled northward to the city of Antioch.

## Jesus' Second Egyptian Stay

The canonicals refer to Jesus' family taking refuge in Egypt when He was an infant. The hostile *Toldoth Jeshu* makes no mention of this, but does refer to an Egyptian sojourn that occurred while He was an adult. Having been rescued from captivity and fleeing to Antioch, Yeshu than traveled to Egypt "where he learned spells."[55] This was as powerful a reinforcement of his magical powers as obtainable. An ancient Talmudic adage claimed that, "Ten measures of sorcery descended into the world: Egypt received nine; the rest of the world one."[56] Hence, to the extent that human sorcery could ever enhance and verify one's claims, Jesus now possessed the maximum humanly possible.

## The Second Transfiguration

In the Acts of John a transfiguration account speaks of how Peter, James, and John had gone with Jesus once again to the mountain where He liked to pray (c90). There they saw His flesh glowing with an indescribable light. John decided to approach Jesus since they were on especially close terms and as he did so he noticed that Jesus was stark naked. Not just naked but transformed into a giant, "And I saw that his feet were whiter than snow, so that the ground there was lit up by His feet; and that His head stretched up to heaven, so that I was afraid and cried out; and He, turning about, appeared as a small man and caught hold of my beard and pulled it and said to me, 'John, do not be faithless, but believing, and not inquisitive.'"[57]

The tug on the beard hurt for a month afterwards. So great was the immediate pain that John expressed concern that if "your playful tug" had inflicted such pain, how great would the anguish be if Jesus were truly cross? Jesus responded that He should no longer "tempt him that cannot be tempted." (But if He could not "really" be tempted how could anything said or done actually be a "temptation"?)

Seeing from a distance what was happening and upset because they could not hear what was being said, Peter and James motioned for John to rejoin them (c91). They wanted to know who Jesus had been talking with — the reference to "both" indicates that only two individuals had been observed, John and Jesus, though Jesus had been acting in such a manner as if speaking with someone else as well. Instead of answering them, John directed them to Jesus Himself for an answer.

J. K. Elliott calls this an alternative "account of the Transfiguration."[58] The fact that no mention is made of the appearance of Moses and Elijah (Matthew 17:3) argues against this, as does the fact that in the Acts of John only two individuals speak. The canonical account aims to enhance Jesus' exclusive role as authority figure as contrasted to such earlier ones as these. The absence of such material argues that this can, more properly, be considered a second transfiguration episode separate and distinct from the Biblical one. It is given not to enhance Jesus' superiority over previous authority figures but simply to enhance His own status in their eyes.

Although this reading seems the more probable, the Acts do indicate that Peter and James thought Jesus had been speaking to someone and — acting as if this had been the case — John dodged the question of what was happening entirely and referred them to Jesus if they wanted an answer. So the interpretation is certainly not an impossible one. However, even if we take this to be a three-figure joint appearance, we are left totally uninformed as to who the other two had been. There were several others whose joint appearance with Jesus would have enhanced the apostolic recognition of Jesus' great status: David and Ezra are two obvious ones. In any three-figure appearance, however, we would have expected the other individuals to be named for the "praise by association" that they would have given to Jesus and His ministry.

## A Rich Man Seeking Divine Acceptance Stumbles Over His Own Riches

The account of the rich young ruler in Matthew 19:16–24 speaks of how he is commanded to give his wealth to the needy poor. In the form of the story found in the Gospel of the Hebrews an addendum is added to the text to explain why it was so important for this man in particular to follow such a radical course. As Origen writes (*Commentary on Matthew* XV.14),[59]

> It is written in a certain gospel, which is styled "according to the Hebrews," if any one pleases to receive it not as an authority, but as an illustration of the subject before us: Another rich man said to Him: "Master, what good thing shall I do to live?" He said to him: "O man, fulfil the law and the prophets." He replied: "I have fulfilled." He said to him: "Go, sell all that thou possesseth, and distribute to the poor, and come, follow me."
>
> But the rich man began to scratch his head, and it did not please him. And the Lord said to him: "How sayest thou, I have fulfilled the law and the prophets, since it is written in the law: Thou shalt love thy neighbor as thyself; and lo! Many of thy brethren, sons of Abraham, are clothed in filth, dying of hunger, and thy house is full of many goods, and nothing at all goes out of it to them."
>
> And returning to Simon, His disciple, who was sitting by Him, he said: "Simon, son of Jonas, it is easier for a camel to enter the eye of a needle than for a rich man [to enter] into the kingdom of heaven."

This exchange has only survived in the Latin translation of Origen's commentary and is missing in the Greek.[60] Hence it is dismissed by J. K. Elliott as a pseudo–Origen statement rather than genuine.[61] Even so, it would indicate that the story was known to the later Latin writer who inserted it even if not to Origen himself.

## Healing of Contagious Leprosy

The canonical gospels make reference to the healing of individuals who had been burdened with "leprosy." In its Biblical usage, that term was broad enough to include a number of diseases, up to and including leprosy in the modern use of the term. None of the canonical accounts provide any indication of how many years a given individual had the disease nor the circumstances under which he came down with it. Turning to the Egerton Gospel (2), we find a case that actually ventures into this otherwise uncharted territory (conjectural reconstructions in brackets),[62]

> [They gave counsel to] the multitude to [? carry the] stones together and stone him. And the rulers sought to lay their hands on him that they might take him and [? hand him over] to the multitude; and they could not take him, because the hour of His betrayal was not yet come. But He Himself, even the Lord, going out through the midst of them, departed from them.
> And behold, there cometh unto him a leper and saith, Master Jesus, journeying with lepers and eating with them in the inn I myself also became a leper. If therefore thou wilt, I am made clean. The Lord then said unto him, I will; be thou made clean. And straightway the leprosy departed from him. [And the Lord said unto him], Go [and show thyself] unto the [priests].

Some regard this as a variant of the leper healing narrated in Mark 1:40–44.[63] If so, the emphasis on how the leprosy was contacted represents an unexpected addition.

## A Woman Accused of Sin

In John 7:53–8:11 there is the story of a woman taken in adultery who is brought to Jesus for judgment. Eusebius writes in his *Ecclesiastical History* that "He [Papias] gives a history of a woman who had been accused of many sins before the Lord, which is also contained in the gospel of the Hebrews."[64]

Although some like to think that this is a variant of John's canonical account there is a profound difference between one sin — even the serious one of adultery — and the series of sins referred to by Papias and the gospel of the Hebrews. One could hypothesize that what is in mind is a series of adulteries in particular (i.e., she was a known and habitual adulteress), but if that is the case in John's account it is odd that that is not specified as enhancing the credibility of the allegations against her.[65]

## A Challenge to Jesus' Ritual Purity in the Temple

Although the canonical accounts speak of various conflicts that Jesus had with religious authorities and experts in the Jerusalem temple, the Oxyrhynchus Papyrus 840 speaks of an otherwise undocumented one concerning ritual washings. The part that has survived reads (ellipses indicate missing text),[66]

> ...before he does wrong makes all manner of subtle excuse. But give heed lest ye also suffer the same things as they; for the evildoers among men receive their reward not among the living only, but also await punishment and much torment.
>
> And He took them and brought them into the very place of purification, and was walking in the temple.
>
> And a certain Pharisee, a chief priest, whose name was Levi, met them and said to the Saviour: "Who gave thee leave to walk in this place of purification and to see these holy vessels, when thou hast not washed nor yet have thy disciples bathed their feet? But defiled thou hast walked in this temple, which is a pure place, wherein no other man walks except he has washed himself and changed his garments, neither does he venture to see these holy vessels."
>
> And the Saviour straightway stood still with His disciples and answered him: "Art thou then, being here in the temple, clean?"
>
> He saith unto Him: "I am clean; for I washed in the pool of David, and having descended by one staircase I ascended by another, and I put on white and clean garments, and then I came and looked upon these holy vessels."
>
> The Saviour answered and said unto him: "Woe ye blind, who see not. Thou hast washed in these running waters wherein dogs and swine have been cast night and day, and hast cleansed and wiped the outside skin which also the harlots and flute-girls anoint and wash and wipe and beautify for the lust of men; but within they are full of scorpions and all wickedness. But I and my disciples, who thou sayest have not bathed, have been dipped in the waters of eternal life which come from ... But woe unto the...."

Since the canonical accounts speak of Jesus' willingness to forego ritual washings in a private setting (Mark 7:1–23), a similar policy of avoidance would be quite consistent when He and the disciples came to the temple. Yet there are at least two major differences: First of all, the practices Jesus and the disciples landed in conflict concerning involved the ritual washing of hands before eating and not the far more drastic act of the ritual immersion of the entire body before worshipping God.

Furthermore, there was a major conceptual difference inherent in the location: the everyday social, "secular" world versus the holy temple in

Jerusalem that was regarded as the epicenter of spirituality. Consistency would argue from the religious washing of part of the body to all of the body, using one as precedent for the other. On the other hand, even for one who abstained from pre-meal ritual ablutions, the unique "holiness" of the temple could argue that Jesus would not have necessarily followed the same policy in the two very different settings.

Furthermore, to what extent would some form of ritual washings have been required in the first century temple? (Note the important distinction between "required" versus "encouraged" or "desired" or even "existed.") Certainly facilities were potentially available, which could have promoted such a custom. The pool at Bethesda referred to in John 5 immediately comes to mind.[67]

John 13:10 refers to how, "He who is bathed needs only to wash his feet, but is completely clean..." (New King James Version). This has been cited as possible evidence of such a custom in the temple.[68] Contextually, however, the reference is to Jesus' desire to wash the disciples' feet rather than to any practice of the temple. The utilitarian context of the teaching would be that a person who has already bathed is going to get the feet dirty first because of the prevalence of bare feet or sandals in the society of that day. Hence to restore physical cleanliness it was merely a matter of washing the feet rather than the entire body.

Also in favor of a historical foundation for pre-worship immersion is the fact that priests who were actively engaged in temple duties were required to both bathe and change their garments before entering the temple. The problem is that this text's reference is the only direct ancient allusion to this being a general rule required of all temple users.[69]

Against the historicity of such a custom (and, therefore, the credibility of the narrative), at the various annual feasts such ceremonial activities would have been an impracticality for the majority of pilgrims. There were simply too many tens of thousands. Hence the custom of ritual washing for the masses is almost certainly unhistorical and the author of this fragment has either conjured it up out of whole cloth or has (due to a distance in time and, perhaps, geography) assumed that whatever was required of priests in such matters was also required of the masses.

To the extent that there was a theological purpose behind the story, the obvious one would be that Jesus applied his non-ritualism (as to non-Torah required activities) even to what happened in the Temple itself. In other words, He was consistent under any and all circumstances. It is less likely that the book of Hebrews' concept of Jesus as priest for all the people is intentioned. If that is the author's rationale, the point would be — and it would be one fully in keeping with the book of Hebrews' attitude

(7:11–18) — that even though a "true priest of God," His unique Melchizedek priesthood meant that He was in no way subject to the temporal requirements imposed upon the regular priests.

## Jesus' Final Passover with the Disciples

According to Epiphanius, the Gospel of the Ebionites interjected into the traditional canonical account a denial that Jesus wished to partake of the Passover with them. "'Where wilt Thou that we prepare for Thee to eat the Passover?' To which He replied: 'I have no desire to eat the flesh of this Paschal Lamb with you'" (*Heresies* 30.22).[70] This assertion would not go well with Epiphanius since it contradicts the canonicals (Luke 22:15). The remark is usually taken to reflect the Ebionite hostility to eating meat.[71]

CHAPTER 9

# Betrayal, Arrest, and Trial

Moving to the arrest and trial of Jesus, we again enter an area that could be creatively imagined with only modest danger of the author being accused of heretical content or intent. On the other hand, the actual arrest and death itself left little obvious maneuvering room to add material to the canonical versions. This difficulty was overcome by shifting the emphasis to what the affair seemed like from Pilate's perspective and those of his court and by recounting the reactions of the Sanhedrin.

In dealing with the crucifixion, the resurrection itself, and the period of post-resurrection appearances, there was much more room for the creative imagination to add to the canonical version. The orthodox were psychologically discouraged from taking full advantage of this period by the desire to keep their material fully compatible with the tradition they had received. Gnostic and other dissident movements did not suffer from that inhibition. Hence it is not surprising to discover that the expansion of the canonical version was also accompanied by efforts to make the traditional story more congenial to the doctrinal revisionists.

## A Jewish Account of the Events

The medieval Jewish *Toldoth Jeshu* places the death of Jesus under the reign of a Queen Helene, under whom (the story would have us believe) the religious authorities had the right to carry out executions not by the traditional one of stoning but by the Roman one of crucifixion.[1] This permits the death to be by a method embarrassing to Christians (since it was the method of executing common criminals) and yet dodging the embarrassing political reality that at the time the nation was an occupied Roman possession. Unlike the Christian tellings of the story, Jesus is not the innocent and guiltless party portrayed in the New Testament. Rather he is a troublesome rabble-rouser with violent followers who needed to be suppressed, not merely because of His doctrinal heresies but because He represented a threat to the political and social order.

In this version, prior to a Passover that fell on the Sabbath (4:1), Jesus arrived for the celebration from Antioch with His followers (4:10). He came riding into Jerusalem on a donkey and was praised by the crowds. He entered the temple along with 310 disciples (4:4). One, whose Aramaic name was Gaisa (thief/robber), offered to accept a bribe from the religious authorities for arranging His arrest.

Although Jesus was in the temple, Gaisa (some manuscripts read, "Judas") warned that all 310 were under a solemn oath not to reveal which of them was actually Jesus, so to disclose His identity he would make "obeisance" to Him when the arresting party arrived (4:8). When Judas had the opportunity to carry out this plan, the authorities successfully carried out their scheme for the arrest (4:10–11), and the band of 310 were unable to rescue their leader (4:17).

Jesus denounced the authorities as having bloodied hands and stressed that the ancient prophets had been killed too (4:18). The "insurgents" who followed Jesus sorrowed over the death they could not deliver Him from (4:18). It was the day before the Passover Sabbath and the crucifixion began at the sixth hour (4:19). The first tree broke into pieces and was unusable (4:20). The disciples thought it proof of Jesus' character (4:21); the authorities attributed it to Jesus' miracle-working power. (The earlier part of the book is quite candid that He worked a number of such wonders, explaining them, however, on the basis of what we today would call magical incantations.)

They resorted to the "stock of a carob tree" because it was technically a plant and, therefore, not protected by Jesus' invocation against the use of trees to kill Him (4:23). When the time for "afternoon prayer" arrived, the prohibition of being left out for the night was observed and His body buried by the governing officials (4:25).

## *Defenses of Jesus before Pilate by Friendly Witnesses*

In the Christian-originated apocryphal accounts, the picture is—not surprisingly—quite different from one favoring traditional Judaism. Yet they also differ from the New Testament version. The canonicals picture the hearings before Pilate as ones in which an angry group of opponents unjustly accuse Jesus before a hesitant governor, with nothing at all being said in His defense by friends or other witnesses.

There is much to be said for this depiction given the circumstances presented by the canonical text both explicitly and by implication. A faction of unknown size within the Sanhedrin was determined to railroad through Jesus' execution in the quickest amount of time possible lest there be a public backlash. In such circumstances, elemental prudence required that they take every step possible to assure the result by maximizing the number of their supporters present to support the action. These individuals were not of a disposition to tolerate any type of show of support for the accused and, even if the supporters had been daring enough to attempt it, it would have been extraordinarily difficult to safely get through the hostile crowd and gain attention from Pilate or his representatives in order to be heard.

The apocryphal Acts of Pilate overlooks these practical difficulties and assumes that a vigorous case was presented on behalf of the accused. The motive is surely to intensify the picture of the irresponsibility of the prosecutors by having individuals speak up in strong defense of some element of Jesus' life. (To the extent that one believed such actually happened, this intensified the guilt of Pilate as much as that of the religious authorities: not only was Jesus an innocent man, Pilate had heard the credible evidence to back it up. The Acts, however, clearly want us to put the moral guilt on only the accusers rather than the governor who permitted the defense case to be ignored.)

One element in their accusations was that Jesus was "born of fornication" (c2). This was rebutted by twelve "pious men of the Jews" who testified that they had been "present at the betrothal of Joseph and Mary." (In real life, of course, Pilate would have had not the slightest interest in such irrelevant issues as the alleged illegitimacy of Jesus' birth. Jesus' purported behavior, not His birth, was the concern of the governor.)

Although arguments from silence can be infamously treacherous, it remains extremely intriguing that only Jesus' legitimacy, not His virgin birth, is affirmed.[2] Did the author reject the concept? Or was he astute enough to recognize that, by its very nature, such could not be "proved" by eye-witnesses; that the most that could be hoped for from more or less "disinterested" testimony would be confirmation of a formal betrothal?

The dispute over whether to accept the testimony of these witnesses permits the interjection of yet another defense. Pilate orders the crowd out except for the twelve and inquires as to the reason for the insistent demand for the death of Jesus. They responded, " 'They are angry because He cures on the Sabbath.' Pilate says: 'For a good work do they wish to put Him to death?' They say to him: 'Yes.'" (c2).

As the result of this exchange, Pilate went out to the crowd "filled with rage" and attempted to dismiss the case (c3). Pilate pled with them, "Do not act thus, because no charge that you bring against Him is worthy of death; for your charge is about [miraculously] curing and Sabbath profanation" (c4). To prevent the case from being thrown out, they returned to the element of Jesus' claim to kingship and argued that this made Him a threat against Caesar as well as God.

Looking through the crowd Pilate observes "many of the Jews weeping, and says: 'All the multitude do not wish Him to die." The leaders insisted that the opposite was true.

Then Nicodemus stood before Pilate to defend Him (c5). Afterwards, another Jew spoke of how Jesus had seen him bedridden and had restored his health (c6). Another testified that he was born blind but had been given His sight by Jesus. A woman spoke of her unceasing menstrual flow that had been suddenly healed (c7). "A multitude both of men and women" cried that Jesus was a prophet and had conquered even demons—and raised the dead as well (c8). To hear the Acts tell it, it was an overwhelmingly pro–Jesus crowd that was present rather than the overwhelmingly anti–Jesus one found in the canonicals.

## *Roman Subordinates and Standards Give Honor to Jesus*

The Acts of Pilate speak of the governor ordering Jesus to be brought in. The military man carrying out the order recognized Jesus and used his very cloak for Him to walk into the room upon (c1). When Jesus entered Pilate's presence even the pagan military standards miraculously honored Him. "And Jesus going in, and the standard-bearers holding their standards, the tops of the standards were bent down, and adored Jesus." Those hostile to Him were indignant, claiming that the standard-bearers had wrongly and improperly bestowed honor upon the accused. The standard-bearers retorted that they were not Jews and were, in fact, slaves of the temple and they were hardly likely to have done any such thing. The standards had done it on their own.

Finding this a tad hard to believe, Pilate has the Jews pick out "twelve men powerful and strong." With six on each side, they were to hold the standards. (Orthodox Jews holding Roman pagan military standards? Hardly credible in a first century context except by brute coercion.) Once they took the standards into their hands, Jesus walked in between them. "And as He went in, the standards were again bent down and adored Jesus."

## Pilate's Challenge to the Jewish Leaders

The surviving section of the Gospel of Peter seems to begin just after Pilate has washed his hands as a sign of personal innocence and non-responsibility (1.1–2).[3] Apparently the preceding material had conveyed an implicit challenge to the Jewish tribunal and to Herod to do the same and to assume no liability for anything that happened next. Neither did so — if they had, they would, effectively, have concurred in carrying the proceedings no further since that was Pilate's preference. Failing to abort the proceedings by convincing everyone to disavow them, Pilate ordered them to do whatever he tells them, which (in light of what comes next) will be to crucify the accused.

This has been taken as an indication that the writer's agenda is one of putting exclusive blame on the Jews for the death of Jesus.[4] That element is certainly present in the work. In chapter 4.10–14 the thief's admission of Jesus' innocence of evil is addressed not at a fellow criminal being crucified but at the Jewish crowd. Similarly in 7.25–27 the apostles are pursued by the Jewish leadership even though the celestial phenomena at Jesus' death had convinced them that they had sinned.

Since Herod considered himself a Jew — however much he violated the precepts of the religion — he becomes a target as well. But the problem of Herod is more complex. Herod remained a Roman-approved ruler; hence any criticism of him inevitably involved an implicit criticism of Roman jurisprudence as well. Yet the reader could, psychologically at least, push this under a mental "rug" if he or she were determined to proceed on a "Jews alone" tangent rather than spread the blame around as the canonical accounts do. Indeed, the explicit demand by Pilate that they carry out his orders, and the accompanying acknowledgment in the following chapter that it will be crucifixion, puts the responsibility even more emphatically on Pilate's own shoulders than even the canonical's.

## Mary's Grief Over Jesus' Death

Although the canonical accounts refer to Mary as present at the crucifixion (explicitly only in John 19:25–27), they do not mention her grief — presumably because what other reaction would one anticipate? Greek Form B of the Acts of Pilate elaborates upon her grief in detail, however.

As it tells the story, the apostle John followed the crowd that was accompanying Jesus to the place of crucifixion (B/c10). When John informed Mary of what was happening, she cried out in frustration, "My son, My son, what evil then hast thou done, that they are taking thee away to crucify thee?" She was then escorted by John and several of the other women to where the procession was proceeding through the city.

Seeing the crown of thorns on His head and His bound hands, she fainted and passed out for "a considerable time." When she finally awakened, she lamented the abuse that had visibly been inflicted upon her Son. "She tore her face with her nails, and beat her breast. 'Where are they gone,' said she, 'the good deeds which Thou didst in Judea? What evil hast thou done to the Jews?'" Outraged, she cried out and challenged them to kill her before they killed her Son.

Reaching the place of crucifixion, her laments continued. Jesus consigned her into the care of John and she continued her bewailing of the bitter injustice being inflicted, the fickleness of His followers, and its personal impact upon her. "Without thee, my Son, what will become of me? How shall I live without thee? What sort of life shall I spend? Where are Thy disciples, who boasted that they would die with thee? Where are those healed by Thee? How has no one been found to help Thee?"

She cried out, unsuccessfully, for the cross to bend down so she could hold her Son for one last time. Hostile onlookers in the crowd had had enough by this point. They "came forward and drove to a distance both her and the women and John."

## *Crucifixion of the Wrong Man*

In the childhood miracles of Jesus there was the recurring image of power being utilized unrestrained by ethical theory or principle: someone annoys you; therefore they die. In at least one of the unorthodox views of Jesus' death this image arises again. To orthodox and unorthodox alike, the judicial execution on a cross was disconcerting and if it could be removed, what we today would call a "major public relations hurdle" would be removed in propagandizing among Gentiles.

One popular partial "solution" to this was to have the "Christ" merge with the physical Jesus at some point in life (usually the baptism) and then to leave to return to heaven before the death on the cross or even before the trial with Pilate began. Basilides took a quite different approach. He had Jesus (and not just the "Christ" element) escape death by trading identities with someone else. In death, He laughs at and mocks His enemies in a burst of childlike exuberance that ignores the fact that He has purchased His life at the price of another innocent man,[5]

And unto the nations belonging to them it [intellect] appeared on earth as a man, and He performed deeds of power. Hence He did not suffer. Rather, a certain Simon of Cyrene was forced to bear His cross for Him, and it was he who was ignorantly and erroneously crucified, being transformed by the other, so that he was taken for Jesus, while Jesus, for his part, assumed the form of Simon and stood by, laughing at them. For because He was an incorporeal power and was the intellect of the unengendered parent, He was transformed however He willed. And thus He ascended to the one who had sent Him, mocking them. For He could not be held back and was invisible to all (summary of Basilides' theory from Irenaeus, *Against Heresies* [1.24.4]).

## *Place of Crucifixion*

The Acts of Pilate provides a more exact description of the location of the execution than do the canonicals. Pilate delivers this death decree, "Thy nation has charged Thee with being a king. On this account I sentence thee, first to be scourged, according to the enactment of venerable kings, and then to be fastened on the cross in the garden where Thou wast seized. And let Dysmas and Gestas, the two malefactors, be crucified with Thee" (c9).

## *The "Departure" of Christ While Jesus Dies*

As the Gospel of Peter tells it, Jesus does not (as in the canonicals) bemoan His sense of abandonment by God but, rather, the loss of His own power (5.15–20). In the context of the darkness during the crucifixion we read that "many went about with lamps, supposing that it was night, and fell down. And the Lord cried out, saying: 'My power, my power, thou hast forsaken me,' and after these words he was taken up. And in that hour the veil of the temple of Jerusalem was rent in twain."

We seem to have here a version of the theory that the Christ entered the physical Jesus at His baptism and left it before the physical death on the cross.[6] The purpose of the theory was to show that the Christ escaped suffering.[7]

In the current context, the problem with applying this scenario to the text is that this withdrawal of Jesus' "power" (the inner Christ?) comes at the end of the suffering rather than before it begins. The fact that the departure of the "power" seems simultaneous with the death could also be evidence that the "taken up" referred to in the text is an unusual euphemism for death.[8]

The next words of Peter (6.21–24) certainly point to the loss of power and the death being simultaneous: it refers to the nails being removed. In other words, the death has occurred simultaneously/quickly after the departure of the "power" rather than as two separate events as in the classical form of the Christ/Jesus distinction theory. Furthermore, Jesus continues to be described as "the Lord" in the following section describing the removal of the body from the cross.[9] However much the author may believe in a Jesus/supernatural Lord distinction, the idea is conveyed in such a low-key manner that the account does not come into clear-cut contradiction to the theology that dominated the church. Hence this explains the popularity of this Gospel among some orthodox.[10]

In the canonical account, the parallel statement with Jesus' bemoaning the loss of His "power" is, "My God, my God, why have You forsaken Me?" (Mark 15:34, New King James Version). "Forsake" was interpreted by the Gnostics literally rather than in the sense of "abandoned": to them it was a plea by the fleshly Jesus as to why the "God" (Christ) part had "left me behind."[11] Admittedly, a good verbal dodge to reconcile scripture and Gnosticism, but if this were the intent, then the more natural way to express it would have been, "My Christ, my Christ, why have You forsaken Me?" Even less convincing of a Jesus/Christ distinction is the yet far more ambiguous, "my power, my power thou hast forsaken me" that is found in the Gospel of Peter.

Why then the substitution of this reading in Peter? Could something else be under discussion; could there be some other motive for the substitution? One might hypothesize embarrassment at Jesus' weakness: for Jesus to feel abandoned by God was simply too much for the author to accept. Hence the substitution of "power" as a euphemism for God. Alternatively, one could conjecture that Jesus is despondent at His fate and has found that His supernatural powers that could have been utilized to prevent it have deserted Him. He is unable to rescue Himself even if He wishes to.

John D. Crossan argues, in contrast, that "power" should be regarded as an intended synonym for God. He cites Mark 14:62 and Matthew 26:64 as parallel accounts from the trial of Jesus where "power" is used in place of the word God (though conceding that in Luke 22:70 we find the fuller, "right hand of the power of God," to show that it is explicitly the Divine power that is in mind).[12] It is often assumed that Jesus' words on the cross are a quotation from Psalms 22:1. Crossan notes that Aquila translated the initial words of that verse as, "My strong one, my strong one, why hast thou left me?"—the conceptual equivalent (or near so) of "power" used in the Gospel of Peter.[13]

## Earthquake at Jesus' Death

Whether as the result of the earthquake that occurred at the time or as a separate direct miracle, Matthew 27:50–51 speaks of the curtain in the temple being ripped apart when Jesus died. An earthquake of such ferocity could well produce other damage as well. Jerome, in an apparent reference to the Gospel of the Hebrews, observes that, "In the Gospel often mentioned we read 'that the very great lintel of the Temple broke and fell into pieces'" (*Commentary on Matthew* XXVII.51).[14]

This tradition was later embraced by other church writers.[15] Adam F. Findlay sees an allusion in this to Isaiah 6:4,[16] but in that scriptural text we are dealing with a vision rather than alleged reality and the posts of the door are shaken rather than broken. If there is a relationship at all, the Hebrews Gospel has built upon its idea, both literalizing it and altering it in the process.

## Jesus' Disciples Pursued After His Death

In 7.25–27 of the Gospel of Peter we have the paradoxical pursuit of the apostles by a religious leadership that feels guilty about what has happened to Jesus (due to the heavenly phenomena and earthquake that had occurred),

> Then the Jews and the elders and the priests, perceiving what evil they had done to themselves, began to beat themselves and to say: "Woe for our sins; the judgment has come nigh and the end of Jerusalem."
> And I with my companions was grieved, and being wounded in mind we hid ourselves. For we were being sought for by them as malefactors, and as wishing to set fire to the temple. And upon all these things we fasted and sat mourning and weeping night and day until the Sabbath.

The guilt element is uncanonical and, if it had existed, would surely have caused the religious authorities to call off the search for the apostles (another uncanonical element) and makes the posting of a guard at the tomb irrational (or seemingly so) since they "knew" Jesus was in the right (8.28–33). Of course the purpose of this claim is likely to paint their ethical improprieties in the blackest terms. On the other hand, even the worst reprobate normally retains sufficient common sense to recognize when it is time to "cut bait" and back off his or her indefensible actions. In other words the text pictures guilt of such an intensity that the account loses credibility when it insists upon further prosecutorial actions having been taken.

The connection of their alleged guilt feelings with fear for the future of the temple seems an odd interpretive jump with nothing in the context to justify it. Matthew 24's assertion of its ultimate destruction represented teaching given to the apostles and not to the public at large. So to a Christian-reading audience, acquainted with that prediction (not given in Peter), it would be a different story.

Even so, on a psychological level, if they felt guilty at all, such a leap might make sense. After all, they were custodians of the temple and what more appropriate way to punish its custodians than the destruction of the holy place entrusted to their care? There is nothing in Peter's context to suggest such was going through their minds and the text seems written with Christian assumptions in mind rather than those under which the Sanhedrin operated.

Oddly enough, the belief that they recognized their guilt was not unknown in wider circles—which makes one wonder whether that version of reality gave birth to what the Gospel of Peter narrates or vice versa. Ephrem's *Syriac Commentary on the Diatessaron* quotes the Jewish leaders, "Woe was it, Woe was it unto us: this was the Son of God: ...the judgments of the desolation of Jerusalem have come."[17] The Old Syriac Version even inserts it after Luke 23:48, "Woe to us: what hath befallen us? Woe to us for our sins."[18] One Latin manuscript of that scriptural text even includes the reference to Jerusalem, "Woe to us: what hath happened this day for our sins? for the desolation of Jerusalem hath drawn nigh."[19]

## *Pilate's Reaction to the Phenomena at Jesus' Death*

The Acts of Pilate follows the canonicals in speaking of the darkness during the crucifixion, the earthquake, and the splitting of the temple veil (c11). This was extremely disconcerting to Pilate and his spouse, but those who had pushed for the execution dismissed it as irrelevant: "And the centurion reported what had happened to the procurator. And when the procurator and his wife heard it, they were exceedingly grieved, and neither ate nor drank that day. And Pilate sent for the Jews, and said to them: 'Have you seen what has happened?' And they say: 'There has been an eclipse of the sun in the usual way.'"

This, of course, is totally inconsistent with their admission of guilt that we examined in the previous section. In all fairness, however, even if they had felt guilty they were hardly likely to admit it to the Roman ruler — or any grounds for guilt, such as these startling physical phenomena being supernatural in origin. To do so would be to permit Pilate to pass even greater blame onto them and thereby shed some of his own for his personal role in the proceedings.

## Joseph Asking for the Body of Jesus

### Gospel of Peter

Unlike the canonical account, the Gospel of Peter has Joseph asking for the body of Jesus before the crucifixion (2.3–5). The reason that Joseph made intercession was not a case of personal boldness overcoming fear but because he was "friend of Pilate and of the Lord" both.

Unlike the canonicals, Peter viewed Herod as retaining some kind of responsibility for the body since Pilate sent the burial request on to him. Herod responded that Jesus would have been buried anyway since it was not proper under the Jewish law to allow anyone to remain unburied before sunset of the same day. Roman ruler or not, Herod cites Mosaical statute for his decision. This would permit the reader to view him in an "evil Jew" stereotype rather than an equally plausible role of "evil Roman ruler." (The shift of the church's ethnicity from largely Jewish in the early decades to overwhelmingly Gentile in the following centuries would encourage the desire for such an interpretive shift.)

### Acts of Pilate

In the second Greek form of the Acts of Pilate the intervention to obtain the body is placed after the death and described in more detail. Joseph brings the idea to Nicodemus to "go to Pilate and beg the body of Jesus for burial, because it is a great sin for Him to lie unburied" (B/c11). Nicodemus confessed his own fear that Pilate would be angered by the request and would resort to some type of retaliation. He suggested a different procedure: If Joseph would make the request on his own, he would assist Joseph in the remainder of the burial.

After a prayer for his success, Joseph proceeded to an audience with Pilate. After greeting the governor, he urged him "not to be angry with me" at the request he wished to make. "And what is it that thou askest?" comes the natural reply. The body of Jesus, he responded.

Pilate was hostile to the request and acted as if the accusations against Jesus had been fully justified. "And what has happened, that we should deliver to be honored again the dead body of Him against whom evidence of sorcery was brought by His nation, and who was in suspicion of taking the kingdom of Caesar, and so was given up by us to death?"

Joseph fell to the ground and responded that hatred for a man should end at His demise. Furthermore, he reminded Pilate that he had been reluctant to grant the execution demand in the first place. Hence he should not "refuse my request." Backing down, Pilate gives the weeping and desperate Joseph permission to take the body he has requested.

He reported his success back to Nicodemus. "Then, having bought myrrh and aloes [weighing] a hundred pounds, and a new tomb, they, along with the mother of God and Mary Magdalene and Salome, along with John, and the rest of the women, did what was customary for the body with the white linen, and placed it in the tomb." The canonicals make no mention of John having any involvement with the preparation of the body for the burial. They also depict the women coming to do their part in preparing the body for permanent entombment as occurring on the first day of the week rather than Friday (Matthew 28:1, for example).

## *Punishment of Joseph for Burying Jesus*

As the only member of the Sanhedrin in the Acts of Pilate to break ranks and openly defend Jesus, it is not surprising that Nicodemus stirred up intense resentment. All the other defenders went into hiding (c12) but Nicodemus openly entered the synagogue on the Sabbath day. At the same time Joseph arrived, the one who had provided the tomb. Rather than attacking one of their own, they turned their attention to the outsider who would not be protected by any bonds of friendship, group loyalty, or obligation to them.

So far as Joseph was concerned, he was being criticized not for favoring Jesus but for his humanitarian act in arranging for the burial. On the other hand, if they wished to speak in terms of right and wrong, then they should have "repented of crucifying Him."

This affirmation of their guilt prompted his arrest. Though the trial had to be delayed until after the Sabbath was over, the critics anticipated it with fervor. "Thou shall not be deemed worthy of burial, but we shall give thy flesh to the birds of the air." He reminded them that they had wished God's wrath upon themselves and their descendants if their act against Jesus was unjustified and he feared that Divine wrath was, indeed, coming their way.

The reaction was quick and prompt,

> And the Jews, hearing these words, were embittered in their souls, and seized Joseph, and locked him into a room where there was no window; and guards were stationed at the door, and they sealed the door where Joseph was locked

in. And on the Sabbath, the rulers of the synagogue, and the priests and the Levites, made a decree that all should be found in the synagogue on the first day of the week. And rising up early, all the multitude in the synagogue consulted by what death they should slay him.

And when the Sanhedrin was sitting, they ordered him to be brought with much indignity. And having opened the door, they found him not. And all the people were surprised and struck with dismay, because they found the seals unbroken and because Caiaphas had the key. And they no longer dared to lay hands upon those who had spoken before Pilate in Jesus' behalf.

Later, in seeking further confirmation of Jesus' teaching and ascension in Galilee, the authorities discovered where Joseph had reappeared (c15). Through intermediaries they sent a letter confessing their sin in conspiring against him and expressed the hope of setting up a meeting. Joseph was agreeable and when it occurred they wished to know how he had managed to escape.

At midnight, he explained, he had seen a light as bright as lightning. In fear he fell to his knees. Jesus appeared before Him and instructed him to open his eyes. Still in fear, he recited "the [ten] commandments" and Jesus joined in the recitation with him. The reason for this was that everyone knew that if one encountered a spirit and it heard the commandments recited, it would flee.

Finding it difficult to believe it was really Jesus, Joseph requested that He show him the tomb He had been buried in. When Jesus did so, the doubts vanished and he knew for a certainty that it was truly Him. Jesus then transported him to his own home and commanded him to remain in hiding for forty days.

CHAPTER 10

# Triumph Over Death

## A Description of the Resurrection Event Itself

In spite of the New Testament's emphasis on the centrality of the death and resurrection as pivotal to Christian faith, nowhere is there an actual description of the resurrection itself. The Gospel of Peter attempts to fill this gap by devoting a significant amount of its short text to this missing information (9.34–11:43),

> And when the morning of the Sabbath came, a multitude came from Jerusalem and the region round about, to see the sealed sepulchre. And in the night in which the Lord's day was drawing on, as the soldiers kept guard two by two, there was a great voice in the heaven — and they saw the heavens opened, and two men descending from thence with great splendor and coming to the tomb. That stone which was put at the door, rolled away of itself and made way in part, and the tomb was opened and the two young men entered in.
>
> And when the soldiers saw this, they awakened the centurion and the elders, for they too had remained there to keep guard. And as they were telling what they had seen, they saw again three men come forth from the tomb, and two of them supporting one, and a cross following them, and of the two the head reached into the heaven, but the head of Him that was led by them overpassed the heavens, and they heard a voice from the heavens, saying: "Hast thou preached to them that sleep"— and a response was heard from the cross: "Yea."
>
> They therefore considered one another whether to go away and shew these things to Pilate. And while they yet thought thereon, the heavens again were seen to open, and a certain man to descend and enter into the sepulchre.

Peter suggests that only part of the detail was actually sleeping and that duty had been rotating among the soldiers as to who was awake at any given time. This makes inherent utilitarian sense since there was no need for all of them to be on duty at the same time in such a minimum risk assignment. On the other hand, for an inadequate number to be duty-ready against any emergency was potentially suicidal, for delegation of duty was a death penalty offense for Roman soldiers.

Who are the two helpers of Jesus at the tomb? Since the canonicals speak of the presence of angels (when the women come to the tomb on Sunday morning — Matthew 28:1–8, for example), it would be natural to make that correlation here as well. Yet they are pictured, simultaneously, as small enough to enter the tomb and yet massive enough that their heads hit the sky. This inconsistency is odd in language purporting to represent an objective historical event being narrated.

Equally strange is the question about preaching to the dead (those that "sleep") being answered "from the cross"— as if He were still on it or, equally odd, as if it is the cross itself that responds— the latter being the most common interpretation. However one may view the historical reliability of the canonicals in their depiction of angels and supernatural acts, having an inanimate object "talk" is unknown in their depictions of specific incidents.

Even if Peter intends to resort to symbolism within this "literal" context, such an admixture is also alien to canonical narrative. He is quite willing, of course, to utilize symbolism but conspicuously does not mix it in indiscriminately into purportedly literal events, making them both occur simultaneously and making the symbol itself an active participant.

It is quite possible that Arthur J. Dewey is correct in his suggestion that the gigantic size element is introduced to indicate the supernaturalness of the two beings.[1] Slightly different (but overlapping this approach) is the view that the size allusion is inserted to indicate their "importance,"[2] "exalted majesty,"[3] or "status."[4]

Certainly, the idea of supernatural beings being gigantic in stature was not unknown in other ancient religious literature. As Brook W. R. Pearson, and Felicity Harley observe,[5]

> *Ascension of Isaiah* 3:15–16 (end of the first century), describes how the angel Michael and "the Angel of the Holy Spirit" open the tomb and carry Christ forth. (The "Angel of the Holy Spirit" is also described as being involved in aiding the ascent of individuals through the heavens in 7:23.)
>
> In addition to this, Hermas, *Similitudes* 9.12.8 describes (perhaps significantly, not in a resurrection scene) the Son of God (who is the "Glorious Man" of the *Similitudes*) being supported by six angels on each side. Earlier, in *Similitudes* 9.6.1, the "Glorious Man" is described as "a man so tall that he rose above the tower," which is previously described as "higher than the mountains and the square, so as to contain the whole of the world" (*Similitudes* 9.2.1).

Another passage of apparent significance in connection to this is Hippolytus, *Ref.*, 9.13.2–3, which tells the story of how Elchasai received his revelation, describing the Son of God and the Holy Spirit as massive angelic figures.

Laying aside the matter of the angelic size, why are they present in the first place? In the canonicals they roll away the stone and inform the women disciples of the resurrection (Mark 16:1–8, for example). In Peter a new element is introduced. It refers to how the two were "supporting one," i.e., assisting Jesus out of the tomb. A revitalized body would not, illogically, be weak and temporarily need such support.

The Greek word rendered "supporting" is unique to this passage so far as ancient Christian writings are concerned. Its literal sense of physically supporting would be quite natural and expected in such a context. Jarl E. Fossum, however, argues for a symbolic usage of supporting in the sense of being there to assist rather than actually needing to assist. They are simply present as "his attendants" since the resurrected Jesus "is of course not so weak that he needs to be sustained...."[6] For parallel usage he appeals to the *Shepherd of Hermas* where two angels "took her [the church] by the elbows" into heaven. "Again, the Lady, who is the pre-existent Church, does not need to be carried to heaven by angels; the two 'men' are her courteous servants."[7]

Another aspect of the text deserving discussion is that concerning the teaching of the dead. A preaching of Jesus to the deceased is mentioned in 1 Peter 3:19 and 4:6. The following centuries began to see this as preliminary to the freeing of the "righteous dead" from Hades who had perished from Adam until Jesus' own death.[8] Certainly there is nothing in either Biblical passage that would convey the idea of the immediate release of anyone from the dead. This had to be deduced from other texts not mentioning preaching to the dead at all.

At a far later date the two Petrine texts began to be widely utilized to prove that the wicked dead were given a "second chance" through having the gospel preached to them, but that comes after the early and medieval centuries we are interested in. This approach came under automatic suspicion due to its earlier advocates. The guilty dead reading of the Biblical passages was associated, in particular, with the teaching of the heretic Marcion.[9]

As to the broader theory of the preaching of the Messiah to the dead, Justin Martyr went so far as to claim that Jewish copyists had removed an important prophecy from their manuscripts of the Septuagint. He quotes a prediction of Jeremiah that was no longer available in the circulated copies, "The Lord God, the Holy One of Israel, remembered His dead that had fallen asleep aforetime in the earth of burial, and descended to them to proclaim to them the good news of His salvation."[10] Irenaeus repeats the accusation of theological censorship on more than one occasion.[11] Even here it is "His dead" (i.e., God's dead) under discussion and not the dead who had rejected His will.

Likewise in the *Epistola Apostolorum*, Jesus declares, "I descended to the place of Lazarus and preached to the righteous and to the prophets, that they might come out of the resting-place which is below and ascend to that which is above."[12] The Christian *Odes of Solomon* (Ode 42) refers to this preaching as well, but it is unclear as to whether the preaching encompasses the "wicked dead" as well.[13]

"Christ's Descent into Hell"— the second broad section of the Gospel of Nicodemus— describes this preaching in great detail. Since this does not purport to picture anything happening on earth it is not directly relevant to the current work. It remains useful, however, to recognize that the Nicodemus account played a pivotal role in popularizing the concept among the broad spectrum of believers, and that even this was later developed in a way independent of this work's assumptions as to the nature of the after-life. As Friedrich Loofs notes,[14]

> In the gospel of Nicodemus the scene is the Hades, expressly distinguished from Tartarus, and the chief feature is the release of the Old Testament saints, the subjection of Satan being only an accompanying incident. To medieval theologians, and still more in the popular belief, it was hell to which Christ descended. It is true, the theologians declared that it was not the very *infernus damnatorum* to which Christ descended, but the forecourt, the limbo, where the Old Testament fathers dwelt. But many of the pictures have as their scene Satan's fortress, even the jaws of hell, and the victory over the devil comes already more into the foreground here than it did in the gospel of Nicodemus.

Oddly enough, as already noted, in the Gospel of Peter it is not Jesus Himself who responds to the question from heaven as to whether the dead had been preached to. Instead it is the cross that responds. Craig A. Evans suggests that by doing this, the text crosses a very important credibility line, "There is much in the Gospel of Peter that bears the stamp of enthusiastic Christian exaggeration unrestrained by realistic knowledge of Jewish piety and customs. And, of course, the description of the risen Christ, accompanied by a talking cross, is the stuff from which fables are made."[15] He notes the oddness of some scholars in claiming that this Gospel is pre-canonical when the canonical passion texts conspicuously lack such elements.[16]

On the other hand, the cross speaking reference could be a mildly sanitized version of the Jesus/Christ dualism doctrine. It could be the supernatural Christ *on* the cross that speaks while it is the human Jesus who is being assisted by the angels due to His physical weakness. The two beings have not yet been reunited as one as they had been before the death on the cross. To maximize acceptability among the mainstream orthodox, the fact that it is the Christ on the cross doing the speaking may have been left to be implied or may have been deleted for such a reason as the work was copied and circulated.

Whether this is the case or not, certainly the Gospel of Peter is open to the charge of reflecting a docetic theology, what with the lack of pain while on the cross (4:10) and the "power" going to heaven before the death occurs (5:19).[17] John D. Crossan argues that though this is one reasonable and credible reading of the Greek text concerning Jesus' lack of anguish (4:10), it is equally possible to read it in a figurative sense, "as if " Jesus felt no pain, i.e., He endured it in the silence one would expect of one enduring no suffering.[18]

If one is to take this approach, it would seem more advisable to use it as an indication that Jesus suffered stoically and unflinchingly, refusing to let the pain break Him. Even so, barring something in the text indicating that such symbolic stretching of "literal" language is intended, the connotation is far more likely to be that the writer believed that Jesus, literally, endured no suffering. Hence the significance of the "power" deserting Him could well be that that which protected Him from the pain was no longer present, the Christ had departed.

## *The Decision to Hush Up the Guards' Report*

### Gospel of Peter

In the Gospel of Peter 11.45–49, the centurion reports back to Pilate in words that the canonicals put in the mouth of the centurion at the actual crucifixion,

> When the centurion and they that were with him saw these things, they hastened in the night to Pilate, leaving the tomb which they were watching, and declared all things which they had seen, being greatly distressed and saying: "Truly He was the Son of God."
> Pilate answered and said: "I am pure from the blood of the Son of God; you [throwing the blame back to the religious authorities who had prosecuted Jesus, rw] have decided thus." Then they all drew near and besought him and entreated him to command the centurion and the soldiers to say

nothing of the things which they had seen. "For it is better," say they, "to commit the greatest sin before God, and not to fall into the hands of the people of the Jews and to be stoned." And Pilate commanded the centurion and the soldier to say nothing.

Oddly enough, Peter's account does not contain the canonical version that the soldiers (falsely) claimed they were all asleep.[19] Here they were simply ordered to keep their mouths shut and, in effect, to refuse to answer any question at all on the matter. From one perspective this is more credible than the canonical claim that they asserted they had been asleep. As already noted, every one knew that this was potentially suicidal for any Roman soldier if it actually were true.

On the other hand, the credibility of the narrative shifts back to the canonical because — again, in real life — there was simply no way that the ancient equivalent of "no comment" or "we are under orders not to say anything at all" was going to hold up. Some alleged "truth" had to be presented to satisfy public curiosity and to discourage the inevitable prying the soldiers would receive from other members of their detachment. The "sleeping" tale lacked credibility and the absurd claim that the disciples had stolen the body (in spite of the armed presence of trained Roman soldiers!) wasn't much of a cover story, but it was probably the best they could come up with under the circumstances. So long as Pilate was willing to co-operate and not take action against them for their "sleeping on duty," there remained a viable chance of minimizing the danger that a supernatural interpretation would be placed on the disappearance of the body.

Peter certainly makes a sound point in presenting a conversation occurring between Pilate and the Jewish religious officials as to how to explain the disappearance. There was no way that the officials' tale that the guards had been sleeping was going to escape Pilate's notice for long and they had to have Pilate's cooperation to make the scheme work. Some kind of meeting had to occur in the near term in order to co-ordinate the approach the two sides would take.

In light of the author's desire to maximize Jewish responsibility for Jesus' unjust death, Pilate's claim that "I am pure from the blood of the Son of God; you have decided thus" is clearly intended to shift the responsibility solely on to their shoulders. Observed from a more neutral standpoint — that neither side had much to be proud of — it was what we today call "buck passing." Crudely parallel to the "man at the desk where the buck stops" (i.e., the President of the United States), Pilate was blaming someone else for a decision he has accepted and ordered carried out.

## Acts of Pilate

The version in the Acts of Pilate strictly concerns the guards reporting to the Sanhedrin, and Pilate is only mentioned in connection with their pledge to protect them against possible retribution (c13). According to the soldiers in this version, there had been a "great earthquake and we saw an angel coming down from heaven and he rolled away the stone from the mouth of the tomb and sat upon it; and he shone like snow and like lightning." They heard the angel tell women that "the Lord" had "risen from the dead and is in Galilee." These events happened "at midnight" and they had been terrified into inaction and had made no attempt to seize anyone.

The response was a blunt, "As the Lord liveth, we do not believe you." The guards responded, "You have seen so great miracles in the case of this man and have not believed; and how can you believe us?" In other words, if what you've already seen was not enough it's not surprising you refuse to accept this embarrassing testimony as well. Even so what they spoke of they had really seen.

Summoning a council meeting, the religious leadership quickly reached a decision. They would pay "a considerable sum of money" to the soldiers. Furthermore, religious leaders pledged their intervention to protect the soldiers against possible retribution from the governor if he should take issue with them reporting that the body had been stolen by Jesus' disciples while they slept.

In a fascinating touch of modern world style political cynicism, they circulated a supplement to this story as well: that Jesus' "disciples have given a sum of gold to the guards of the tomb and have instructed them to say that an angel came down and rolled away the stone from the door of the tomb" (c14). Of course, only the Sanhedrin had the potential for protecting the soldiers from retribution and without that assurance any amount of bribe would have been too small for the risk of their own death. If a bribe was offered at all, it had to come from other than the disciples.

## *Appearance to Women at the Tomb*

As the Epistle of the Apostles tells the story, the women who first saw Jesus at His tomb were sent twice to the apostles to inform them of the resurrection. Furthermore, He instructed them to stop crying because He was alive and standing before them,[20]

> "But let one of you go to your brethren and say: Come ye, the Master is risen from the dead. Martha [Mary, Ethiopic] came and told us. We say to her: "What have we to do with thee, woman? He that is dead and buried, is

it possible that He should live?" And we believed her not that the Savior was risen from the dead. Then she returned unto the Lord and said unto him: "None of them hath believed me, that thou livest." He said: "Let another of you go unto them and tell them again." Mary [Sarrha, Ethiopic] came and told us again, and we believed her not; and she returned unto the Lord and she also told him. Then said the Lord unto Mary and her sisters: "Let us go unto them" (c10–11).

In the canonical accounts there is no mention of Jesus and the women arriving together when He finally appeared to the apostles. There is also the fact that, cynical though they were as to what had really happened, at least two of the apostles went to the tomb to investigate the women's report that it was empty (Luke 24:9–12; John 20:2–4). To integrate this version into the New Testament one would have required that at least two of the apostles had responded to the second female messenger.

## *Departure of the Apostles to Galilee*

The Gospel of Peter describes an angelic appearance to the women at the tomb. They are told of the resurrection and given the opportunity to inspect the empty tomb for themselves. To this is added the remark, " 'for He is risen and gone thither, where he was sent.' Then the women feared and fled" (13.57).

But where is this mysterious place to which Jesus has been "sent"? Apparently Galilee, for rather than placing any of the initial apostolic appearances in Jerusalem (as do the canonicals implicitly, since the initial appearances occur the same day [John 20:19]), Peter immediately shifts the scene to Galilee before anything more happens (14.58–60),

> Now it was the last day of the unleavened bread, and many were going forth, returning to their homes, as the feast was ended. But the twelve disciples of the Lord wept and were grieved; and each one being grieved for that which was come to pass, departed to his house. But I Simon Peter and Andrew my brother took our nets and went to the sea; and there was with us Levi the son of Alphaeus, whom the Lord....

Breaking off in mid-sentence, an unknown number of manifestations presumably occurred in the remainder of the narrative. In addition to the inconsistency with the canonical material there is also a psychological improbability as well. Since all the apostles were Galileans, one would assume that — whenever they returned to Galilee — they would do so as a group in the interest of traveling safety, companionship, and shared sorrow.

## Instruction to All the Apostles to Verify the Physical Reality of the Resurrection

### Letter to the Smyrnians

Although we normally think of only Thomas ("Doubting Thomas" as he has entered religious memory) as demanding to touch the physical wounds of Jesus, there was an ancient tradition that Jesus volunteered and instructed all the apostles to do so as well. Ignatius wrote in his *Letter to the Smyrnians* (III.1-2), "For I know and believe that after His resurrection He lived in the flesh. For when the Lord came to Peter and to the Apostles, He said to them: 'Lay hold, handle Me, and see that I am not an incorporeal spirit.' And immediately they touched Him, and believed, being both convinced by His flesh and spirit."[21] This incident may have been narrated in the Gospel of the Hebrews: Jerome mentions how that work refers to an initial apostolic belief that Jesus was now such an "incorporeal" being and that this misapprehension had to be removed.[22]

There is a certain inherent logic to such a command to the apostles in general. The other apostles had not anticipated a resurrection any more than Thomas in particular had. It was one of those occasions where it did not seem safe "to believe one's own eyes." If such did, indeed, happen, then Thomas' doubt (John 20:24-29) would not merely indicate a refusal to be credulous, but also carry the implication of stubborn obstinacy since the other apostles had already done what he now wished to do himself.

### Epistle of the Apostles

The Epistle of the Apostles speaks of how Jesus asked the women who came to anoint the body to send one of their number to the apostles and bring them to the tomb (c10). When the first effort failed, He had them send another one of their number. When that failed as well, He then led the women to the apostles (c11). Here, He singled out Peter and Thomas by name to touch the wounds in the hands and the side. Then He added a different instruction to Andrew, "Look on my feet and see whether they press the earth; for it is written in the prophet: A phantom of a devil maketh no footprint on the earth."[23] The source of this alleged prophetic utterance is unknown.[24] The apostles reacted to their verification of Jesus being real and alive by falling down, worshipping Him, and confessing their sin of unbelief (c12).

## Appearance to James to Convince Him to Break His Fast

1 Corinthians 15:7 mentions a separate appearance to James before Jesus appeared to all the apostles. Undiscussed in the canonical versions, Jerome tells us that the Gospel of the Hebrews provides a detailed account of this appearance,[25]

> The Gospel also entitled "according to the Hebrews," which I lately translated into Greek and Latin, and which Origen often quotes, contains the following narrative after the Resurrection:
> "Now the Lord when He had given the cloth to the servant of the priest, went to James and appeared to him." For James had taken an oath that he would not eat bread from that hour on which he had drunk the cup of the Lord, till he saw Him risen from the dead. Again a little afterward the Lord says: "Bring a table and bread," and forthwith it added: "He took bread and blessed and brake and gave to James the Just and said to him: 'My brother, eat thy bread, for the Son of Man is risen from them that sleep' " (*On Famous Men*, 2)

This story was quite popular among later medieval writers.[26]

The entire thrust — both of general theme and of details — that is found in the canonical gospels is that all the apostles and other disciples were in deep despair as the result of Jesus' death. Their dreams and hopes had been shattered. The last thing they expected was a resurrection. Hence there is a basic antithesis on this point between the canonical approach and the apocryphal: None would pledge to fast till the resurrection because none believed one was coming. For that matter, they had a fundamental difficulty in accepting even the idea of the death itself.

Some see this incident concerning James as patterned upon Jesus' own promise in Luke 22:16 not to eat again until the resurrection.[27] Actually the term resurrection or its equivalent is not utilized in the Lukian text though it is almost certainly what is in mind. Furthermore, the reference, contextually, is to eating the Passover again with the disciples rather than eating at all (verses 15–16).

Another seeming incompatibility of this account with the canonical ones is that Jesus gives the burial cloth to the servant of the priest, i.e., at the tomb itself. The Biblical text leaves the impression that only Roman soldiers were present, although the delegation of one or more individuals of their own would not have been an irrational or improbable act by the Sanhedrin clique behind the execution. In the context of telling the canonical story the presence of the Romans was the pivotal element, since by their soldierly trade they were the least likely to panic or otherwise be diverted from their duties.

More surprising is the omission of the appearance to the women and the fact that of the males it is James who is the first to be granted a sighting of the resurrected Jesus. This could be interpreted as the Hebrews' narrative method of asserting James as the leader of the apostles. Certainly in the sayings Gospel of Thomas (chapter 12) this supremacy of authority is explicitly claimed.[28] Perhaps we have here an attempt in semi- or unorthodox circles to creating a competing locus of authority to either the Pauline or Petrine ones.

## Post-Resurrection Period of Teaching

One characteristic of the Gnostic-type literature was to magnify the length of time Jesus remained on earth after the resurrection. (In the canonical record, Jesus has left earth permanently prior to Pentecost, fifty days after Passover [Acts 1, 2].) Presumably this approach functioned to explain how the unorthodox teaching could significantly differ either in content or emphasis from that which they had already received: it originated at a different point in time, when "fuller" knowledge was available.

Irenaeus (*Against Heresies*, 1.30.14; c. A.D. 180) sums up one form of Gnostic doctrine he was acquainted with in these words, "Now, after His resurrection He remained [on earth] for eighteen months. And because perception had descended into him [from above], He taught the plain truth. He taught these things to a small number of His disciples, who, He knew, were able to receive such great mysteries."[29]

The *Pistis Sophia* is even bolder. In the very introduction to the work (c1) it claims, "But it happened that after Jesus had risen from the dead He spent eleven years speaking with His disciples."[30] And then the text elaborates in detail that even this was only a small fraction of the total truth that was potentially available to mankind. Hence ample room for the "revealing" of yet additional sectarian truths, as the need might arise — a blank check for theological elaboration by recognized authority figures in whatever Gnostic movement one owed loyalty to.

## Ascension into Heaven

### Cyril of Jerusalem

The earthly period of Jesus' life ends at His final ascension into heaven, not to again reappear in fleshly form to the apostles (Acts 1:9–11).

Cyril of Jerusalem provides an interpretive gloss—rather than addition—upon the traditional account. He points to a specific geographic location and a description of the type of cloud into which Jesus disappeared: "The holy Mount of Olives from which He ascended to the Father bears witness. The rain-clouds which received the Master bear witness."[31]

## Epistle of the Apostles

The Epistle of the Apostles concludes with an account of Jesus' ascension and the physical splendor that accompanied it (c51). Oddly enough, Jesus tells them that in three days someone will be coming for Him and that He will depart with him, the implication seemingly being that it is the Heavenly Father Himself. Yet as soon as this prediction is uttered it comes to pass, "As He so spake, there was thunder and lightning and an earthquake, and the heavens parted asunder, and there appeared a light [bright] cloud which bore Him up. And there came voices of many angels, rejoicing and singing praises and saying: 'Gather us, O Priest, unto the light of the majesty.' And when they drew nigh unto the firmament, we heard His voice saying unto us: 'Depart hence in peace.'"[32]

The Biblical account is content to speak of the disappearance into a cloud and an angelic messenger reassuring them that He will ultimately be returning (Acts 1:9–11). The heavenly voice and command are absent.

## Acts of Pilate

In the Acts of Pilate three traditionalist rabbis—outsiders to the Jesus movement—happen to hear His final words and report them back to the Sanhedrin. These three individuals, though called rabbis in chapter 16 are identified as, respectively, "a priest," "a teacher," and "a Levite" in chapter 14. Unlike the canonicals, which place the ascension near Jerusalem (Acts 1:4), these Acts place it in Galilee. According to them,

> "We saw Jesus and His disciples sitting on the mountain called Mamilch; and He said to His disciples, 'Go into all the world, and preach to every creature: he that believeth and is baptized shall be saved, and he that believeth not shall be condemned. And these signs shall attend those who have believed: in my name they shall cast out demons, speak new tongues, take up serpents; and if they drink any deadly thing, it shall by no means hurt them; they shall lay hands on the sick, and they shall be well.' And while Jesus was speaking to His disciples, we saw Him taken up to heaven" (c14).

The Jerusalem religious authorities were not happy with this report and bound them with an oath not to repeat the story to anyone else.

They were called back to Jerusalem later and they reaffirmed their earlier account, "'How didst thou see Jesus taken up?' Adas says, 'While He was sitting on the mountain Mamilch, and teaching His disciples, we saw a cloud overshadowing both Him and His disciples. And the cloud took Him up into heaven, and His disciples lay upon their face upon the earth'" (c16). The other two rabbis, separately, repeated the same story.

## *The Imposture of Resurrection Exposed*

Since this work has been centered on the stories that evolved among those claiming to be Jesus' disciples, it is, perhaps, most appropriate to end on a tale that represents the very opposite. The others are designed to enhance the glory, honor, and prestige of Jesus' life, actions, and resurrection. This one is clearly intended to expose Him as a fraud and His disciples as either conscious or unconscious liars.

This version comes from the medieval Jewish tale *Toldoth Jeshu*,[33]

> The body was taken down while it was still the eve of the Sabbath — in order not to violate the prohibition, "His body shall not remain there for the night"— and immediately buried. A gardener, Yehuda, removed the body from the tomb and cast it into a ditch and let the water flow over it.
>
> The disciples, discovering that the body was not in the tomb, announced to the Queen that Yeshu had been restored to life. The Queen, believing the story, was tempted to put to death the Sages for having killed the Messiah. Indeed, all of the Jews mourned, wept and fasted, until Rabbi Tanchuma, with the help of God, found the body in a garden. The Sages of Israel removed it, tied it to the tail of a horse and paraded it in front of the Queen so that she could see the deception.
>
> The disciples of Yeshu fled [for fear] and mingled among all nations. Among these followers were twelve "apostles" who sorely distressed the Jews: one of these, Shimeon Kepha [Simon Peter] undertook to separate the disciples of Yeshu from the Jews and to give [the former] laws of their own.

If there is a historical kernel at all in this version, it might well be the reappearance of the disappeared body. After a few days in the ground without modern methods of preservation, one body of the right height and gender could easily look enough like all others after being dragged through the streets. If a body was needed to prove the mythology of the resurrection, doubtless one could be obtained.

Yet the canonicals, not known for holding back on narratives that would be embarrassing to the Sanhedrin, omits the accusation nor is there any indication in the limited pro-orthodoxy materials surviving from the early centuries that any one claimed to have viewed the body of Jesus after it disappeared from the tomb. So far as we can tell, the critics of the resurrection claim were content to rest on the accusation that the body was stolen.

# Notes

## Preface

1. For the view that the only real difference is that between "authorized" and "unauthorized" stories of Jesus' life, see R. Joseph Hoffmann, *The Secret Gospels: A Harmony of Apocryphal Jesus Traditions* (Amherst, New York: Prometheus Books, 1996), 13–14. On the other hand, his remarks about the Infancy Gospel of Thomas (29) imply that he recognizes some form of the qualitative distinction we have suggested.

## Introduction

1. Cf. Mary Clayton, *The Apocryphal Gospels of Mary in Anglo-Saxon England* (Cambridge: Cambridge University Press, 1998), 8.
2. Hoffmann, *Secret*, 23, 24.
3. William DiPuccio, "Annotated Index of Authors and Works of the Ante-Nicene, Nicene, and Post-Nicene Fathers," in the reprint edition of *Ante-Nicene Fathers: The Writings of the Fathers Down to A.D. 325*, volume 10 (Peabody, Massachusetts: Hendrickson Publishers, 1994), 270–271.
4. Hoffmann, *Secret*, 25.
5. *Ibid.*
6. *Ibid.*, 23.
7. Bernard Pick, *Paralipomena: Remains of Gospels and Sayings of Christ* (Chicago: Open Court Publishing Company, 1908).

## Chapter 1

1. For a detailed (and, in my judgment, inadequate) criticism of applying the term "infancy gospel" to this work, see John L. Allen, Jr., "The Protevangelium of James as an Historia: The Insufficiency of the Infancy Gospel Category," in *Society of Biblical Literature 1991 Seminar Papers*, edited by Eugene H. Lovering, Jr. (Atlanta, Georgia: Scholars Press, 1991), 508–518.
2. Gerd Ludemann, *Virgin Birth? The Real Story of Mary and Her Son Jesus* (Harrisburg, Pennsylvania: Trinity Press International, 1998), 136.
3. W. S. Vorster, "The Annunciation of the Birth of Jesus in the Protoevangelium of James," in *A South African Perspective on the New Testament*, edited by J. H. Petzer and P. J. Hartin (Leiden: E. J. Brill, 1986), 39. Cf. James H. Charlesworth, "Research on the New Testament Apocrypha and Pseudepigrapha," in *Aufstieg und Niedergang der Romischen Welt (Rise and Decline of the Roman World)*, 25.5.2, edited by Wolfang Haase and Hildegard Temporini (Berlin: Walter de Gruyter, 1988), 3920.
4. Ronald F. Hock, *The Life of Mary and the Birth of Jesus: The Ancient Infancy Gospel of James* (Berkeley, California: Ulysses Press, 1997), 21–22, effectively lays out the case for the work being apologetic in nature, but concludes (22–24) that it was actually written to praise Mary as an end in itself.

5. Vorster, "Annunication," 52. Cf. in a similar vein, Willem S. Vorster, *Speaking Of Jesus: Essays on Biblical Language, Gospel Narrative and the Historical Jesus*, edited by J. Eugene Botha (Leiden: Brill, 1999), 264.

6. Adam F. Findlay, *Byways in Early Christian Literature: Studies in the Uncanonical Gospels and Acts* (Edinburgh: T. & T. Clark, 1923), 159–160, 164–165.

7. B. Harris Cowper, *The Apocryphal Gospels and Other Documents Relating to the History of Christ*, Seventh Edition (London: David Nutt, 1910), liii–liv, also stresses that in honoring Mary the intent is also to give additional honor to Jesus.

8. Bart D. Ehrman, *The Orthodox Corruption of Scripture: The Effect of Early Christological Controversies on the Text of the New Testament* (New York: Oxford University Press, 1993), 24.

9. *Ibid*.

10. Vorster, *Speaking*, 249, bases his conclusions on the earlier work of Oscar Cullmann.

11. Vorster, *Speaking*, 249.

12. *Ibid*.

13. *Ibid*.

14. For the very different scenario that the apocryphal works depended upon a gullible reading audience for their success, see James Orr, *New Testament Apocryphal Writings* (London: Imdent & Company, 1902), viii–ix. To the extent that this enhanced their appeal, we must think in terms of centuries after the earliest works had already come into existence.

15. J. F. Elliott, *The Apocryphal New Testament: A Collection of Apocryphal Christian Literature in an English Translation* (Oxford: Clarendon Press, 1993), 49.

16. Stephen Gero, "Apocryphal Gospels: A Survey of Textual and Literary Problems," in *Aufstieg und Niedergang der Romischen Welt (Rise and Decline of the Roman World)*, 25.5.2, edited by Wolfang Haase and Hildegard Temporini (Berlin: Walter de Gruyter, 1988), 3978.

17. Oscar Cullmann, "Infancy Gospels," in *New Testament Apocrypha; volume 1: Gospels and Related Writings*, edited by E. Hennecke and W. Schneemelcher, English translation edited by R. McL. Wilson (London: Lutterworth Press, 1963), 370.

18. Elliott, *Literature*, 51, writing at a time when none earlier had been available.

19. Ludemann, 135. Vorster, "Annunciation," 39, speaks of a third or "early fourth century" origin. Cullmann (1:370) is receptive to a third century date.

20. Helmut Koester, *Ancient Christian Gospels: Their History and Development* (Philadelphia: Trinity Press International, 1990), 309–310.

21. Elliott, *Literature*, 48.

22. Koester, *Gospels*, 309.

23. Cullmann 1:370.

24. James H. Charlesworth, *Authentic Apocrypha: False and Genuine Christian Apocrypha* (North Richlands Hills, Texas: BIBAL Press, 1998), 70.

25. Cullmann 1:370.

26. Hock, *Mary*, 5, 38.

27. Elliott, *Literature*, 48.

28. *Ibid*.

29. *Ibid*.

30. *Ibid*.

31. Cf. Ronald F. Hock, *The Infancy Gospels of James and Thomas* (Santa Rosa, California: Polebridge Press, 1995), 77.

32. For example, Ehrman, *Orthodox*, 24; Vorster, *Speaking*, 250, 459; Stephen Benko, *The Virgin Goddess: Studies in the Pagan and Christian Roots of Mariology* (Leiden: E. J. Brill, 1993), 196; C. E. Stowe, *Origin and History of the Books of the Bible, both the Canonical and the Apocryphal* (Hartford, Connecticut: Hartford Publishing Company, 1867), 206.

33. Cf. Benko, 200, and Vorster, "Annunciation," 39.

34. Findlay, 157.

35. For a detailed argument that the work demonstrates acquaintance with the Old Testament, see Hock, *Gospels*, 21–22. For knowledge of the New Testament, see 22.

36. Hock, *Mary*, 15.

37. For other questions that the book answers that only make sense if Matthew and Luke were already in existence, see *Ibid.*, 32.

38. Clayton, 11–12.

39. Elliott, *Literature*, 49. P. A. van Stempvoort, "The Protoevangelium Jacobi: The Sources of Its Theme and Style and Their Bearing on Its Date," in *Studia Evangelica; volume 3: Papers Presented to the Second International Congress on New Testament Studies Held at Christ Church, Oxford, 1961; part 2: The New Testament Message*, edited by F. L. Cross (Berlin: Akademie-Verlag, 1964) pins down the date to the last quarter of the second century, between approximately A.D. 178 and 202–204 (425). Clayton (11) prefers to leave it somewhere between about 150 and 200.

40. For a detailed examination of these factors, see Hock, *Gospels*, 11–12 and Hock, *Mary*, 17–18. For a study of the possible use by Justin Martyr, see George T. Zervos, "Dating the *Protoevangelium of James*: The Justin Martyr Connection," in *Society of Biblical Literature 1994 Seminar Papers*, edited by Eugene H. Lovering, Jr. (Atlanta, Georgia: Scholars Press, 1994), 415–434. Oscar Cullmann (1:372) accepts an origin around A.D. 150, but with later additions. Bart D. Ehrman, *After the New Testament: A Reader in Early Christianity* (New York: Oxford University Press, 1999), 248, speaks of "soon after 150." Jacques Hervieux, *The New Testament Apocrypha*, translated from the French by Dom Wulstan Hibberd (New York: Hawthorn Books, 1960), 17, opts for A.D. 130–140.

41. Clare Drury, "Who's In, Who's Out," in *What about the New Testament? Essays in Honour of Christopher Evans*, edited by Morna Hooker and Colin Hickling (London: SCM Press, Ltd,

1975), 225; Vorster, "Annunciation," 33, 39.

42. For example, Benko, 196.

43. Elizabeth S. Fiorenza, *Jesus: Miriam's Child, Sophia's Prophet: Critical Issues in Feminist Christology* (New York: Continuum, 1994), 182.

44. Elliott, *Literature*, 64. For other internal and manuscript indications of expansion of the narrative (and its incorporation of once independent materials), see Cullmann (1:372–373).

45. Elliott, *Literature*, 49–50.

46. Vorster, "Annunciation," 39.

47. For a detailed analysis of such data, see Hock, *Gospels*, 12–13.

48. Ron Cameron, *The Other Gospels: Non-Canonical Gospel Texts* (Philadelphia: Westminster Press, 1982), 108–109.

49. Vorster, "Annunciation," 39.

50. Cf. Clayton, 12.

51. For a short analysis of the ancient translation history of the work, see Elliott, *Literature*, 111.

52. *Ibid.*

53. For a list, see *ibid.*, 111–112.

54. For a brief survey of the arguments, see Elliott, *Literature*, 111.

55. Hock, *Gospels*, 86, 101.

56. Maire Herbert and Martin McNamara, *Irish Biblical Apocrypha: Selected Texts in Translation* (Edinburgh: T & T Clark, 1989), 174.

57. Elliott, *Literature*, 68.

58. *Ibid.*, 69.

59. Harold Attridge, "The Infancy Gospel of Thomas" (introduction, notes, and draft translation), in *The Complete Gospels: Annotated Scholars Version* (Revised and Expanded Edition), edited by Robert J. Miller (Sonoma, California: Polebridge Press, 1992), 369.

60. Gero, 3982.

61. *Ibid.*

62. For a discussion, see Cullmann, 1:388–390.

63. See Cameron, 122; Elliott, *Literature*, 69. Herbert and McNamara, 175, opts for Greek, however.

64. Elliott, 69.

65. Attridge, 369, and Hock, *Gospels*, 90.
66. Koester, *Gospels*, 312.
67. A composition in the fifth century is considered by Stephen Gero (3982) as the earliest likely date.
68. Attridge, 370.
69. Findlay, 175–176, believes the surviving Infancy Thomas to be an abridgment of a gnostic original.
70. Cf. Bart D. Ehrman, *The New Testament and Other Early Christian Writings: A Reader* (New York: Oxford University Press, 1998), 127.
71. Attridge, 369, 370.
72. For the text of the two allusions see Hock, *Gospels*, n. 35 (91–92).
73. David R. Cartlidge and David L. Dungan, *Documents for the Study of the Gospels*. Revised and Enlarged Edition (Minneapolis: Fortress Press, 1994) date the original composition as A.D. 125 (86).
74. Hock, *Gospels*, n. 35, 91–92 evaluates and (in my opinion, rightly) rejects the claim that there is an inadequate amount of detail in the accounts to identify it clearly as the Thomas narrative. He argues, however, that this detail also proves the entire Infancy Thomas' existence as a distinct document at this early a date — a distinct possibility but still not certain beyond reasonable doubt.
75. Cf. Elliott, *Literature*, 68.
76. With this as an explanation of why the Second Greek form is shorter than the first, see *ibid.*, 69.
77. Hock, *Gospels*, 101.
78. Elliott, *Literature*, 85.
79. *Ibid.*
80. *Ibid.*, 84.
81. Hervieux, 18.
82. Elliott, *Literature*, 86.
83. Cartlidge and Dungan, 91; Cullmann, 1:406; Elliott, *Literature*, 86.
84. Clayton, 18.
85. *Ibid.*, 18–20.
86. Elliott, *Literature*, 86.
87. *Ibid.*
88. *Ibid.*, 100.
89. *Ibid.*
90. Cullmann, 1:404.
91. *Ibid.*, 1:369.
92. Elliott, *Literature*, 101.
93. Montague R. James, *The Apocryphal New Testament* (Oxford: At the Clarendon Press, 1924; 1955 printing), 79.
94. *Ibid.*
95. Orr, xvii.
96. Ehrman, *Writings*, 124.
97. Christian Maurer, "The Gospel of Peter," in *New Testament Apocrypha; Volume 1: Gospels and Related Writings*, edited by E. Hennecke and W. Schneemelcher, English translation edited by R. McL. Wilson (London: Lutterworth Press, 1963) 179; F. Neirynck, "The Apocryphal Gospels and the Gospel of Mark," in *The New Testament in Early Christianity*, edited by Jean-Marie Sevrin (Leuven: Leuven University Press, 1989), 140.
98. Cameron, 76, and Neirynck, 140. Elliott, *Literature*, 150, prefers the eighth century.
99. Jay C. Treat, "The Two Manuscript Witnesses to the Gospel of Peter." In *Society of Biblical Literature 1990 Seminar Papers*, edited by David J. Lull (Atlanta, Georgia: Scholars Press, 1990), 392.
100. *Ibid.*
101. *Ibid.*, 392. On both the date of the manuscript and the grave also see Cartlidge and Dungan, 76. On the date in particular, also see Gero, 3985.
102. Treat, 392, and n. 7, 392–393.
103. Cameron, 76, and Craig A. Evans, "Images of Christ in the Canonical and Apocryphal Gospels," in *Images of Christ: Ancient and Modern*, edited by Stanley E. Porter, Michael A. Hayes, and David Tombs (Sheffield, England: Sheffield Academic Press, 1997), 64. Elliott, *Literature*, 150, accepts early third century.
104. Koester, *Gospels*, 215–216.
105. Neirynck, 141–143. Cf. Cameron, 76–77. Brook W. R. Pearson, and Felicity Harley, "Resurrection in Jewish-Christian Apocryphal Gospels

and Early Christian Art." In *Christian-Jewish Relations through the Centuries*, edited by Stanley E. Porter and Brook W. R. Pearson, Journal for the Study of the New Testament Supplement Series 192 (Sheffield, England: Sheffield University Press, 2000), n. 5, 73, consider the identification "almost certain."

106. For example, Evans, "Images," 64. Pearson and Harley, n. 5, 73, note that the identification of this with the GP is "less sure" than in the case of P. Oxy. 2949. James H. Charlesworth and Craig A. Evans, "Jesus in the Agrapha and Apocryphal Gospels," in *Studying the Historical Jesus: Evaluations of the State of Current Research*, edited by Bruce Chilton and Craig A. Evans (Leiden: E. J. Brill, 1994), n. 60, 503, considers the possibility of its origin in the Gospel of Peter as "far from certain." Treat, 393–398, analyzes in detail P. Oxy. 2949, but apparently considers this other fragment to be so improbable as part of the same work that it is not discussed at all.

107. Jean Danielou, *The Theology of Jewish Christianity*, translated by John A. Baker; volume 1 of *The Development of Christian Doctrine before the Council of Nicaea* (London: Darton, Longman & Todd, 1964), 21.

108. Cartlidge and Dungan, 176. For a date about a decade later as well as the text of the Bishop's remarks, see Koester *Gospels*, 217.

109. Cameron, 76.

110. Maurer, 180.

111. Arthur J. Dewey, "Gospel of Peter" (introduction, notes, and draft translation), in *The Complete Gospels: Annotated Scholars Version* (Revised and Expanded Edition), edited by Robert J. Miller (Sonoma, California: Polebridge Press, 1992), 399.

112. For details, see Treat, 393–398.

113. For a discussion of the two possibilities, see *ibid.*, 398.

114. Cf. the discussion of the stability of the Peter text in Koester, *Gospels*, 219.

115. Cartlidge and Dungan, 176. For another defense of this approach, see Arthur J. Dewey, 399–401. For a critique of this claim, see James H. Charlesworth, "Research," 3935–3940, and Philip Jenkins, *Hidden Gospels: How the Search for Jesus Lost Its Way* (New York: Oxford University Press, 2001), 95–97.

116. Marion L. Soards, "Oral Tradition Before, In, and Outside the Canonical Passion Narratives" in *Jesus and the Oral Gospel Tradition*, edited by Henry Wansbrough, Journal for the Study of the New Testament Supplement Series 64 (Sheffield, England: Sheffield Academic Press, 1991), 340, argues that the work is a combination of new materials plus reworked canonical data.

117. Dewey, 400.

118. Jenkins' book effectively argues that the ultra-early dating of the various New Testament apocryphal books usually reflects the theological agenda of those making the claims (for example, 16–18). In regard to the effort to place the Gospel of Thomas at a very early date and the role of the Jesus Seminar in furthering the effort in their publication *The Five Gospels*, see N. Thomas Wright, "Five Gospels but No Gospel: Jesus and the Seminar," in *Authenticating the Activities of Jesus*, edited by Bruce Chilton and Craig A. Evans (Leiden: E. J. Brill, 1999), 83–120. Of their attempts to evaluate the historical genuineness of various alleged sayings of Jesus found in the canonicals and Thomas, Wright sums up the problems many non-members have: "It is a compromise of pseudo-democratic scholarship, based on principles we have seen good reason to question, employing methods that many reputable scholars would avoid, ignoring a great deal of very serious (and by no means necessarily conservative) contemporary scholarship, making erroneous and anachronistic assumptions about the early church and its cultural context, and apparently driven by a strong, and strongly distorting, contemporary agenda" (118).

119. Cameron, 78, and Dewey, 400.

120. Charlesworth and Evans, 506.

121. *Ibid.*, 507.

122. Claudia Setzer, *Jewish Responses to Early Christians: History and Polemics, 30–150 C.E.* (Minneapolis: Fortress Press, 1994), 116–117. For internal narrative inconsistencies, see pages 122–123.

123. Charlesworth and Evans, 507–508.

124. For specific examples, see Charlesworth and Evans, 507.

125. H. T. Andrews, *An Introduction to the Apocryphal Books of the Old and New Testament*, Revised and Edited by Charles F. Pfeiffer (Grand Rapids, Michigan: Baker Book House, 1964), 124.

126. For a concise summary of details, see H. C. Kim, *The Gospel of Nicodemus* (Toronto: Centre for Medieval Studies, Pontifical Institute of Mediaeval Studies, 1973), 6–7.

127. Chapters 35 and 48, as cited by Felix Scheidweiler, "The Gospel of Nicodemus: Acts of Pilate and Christ's Descent into Hell," in *New Testament Apocrypha*; Volume 1: *Gospels and Related Writings*, edited by E. Hennecke and W. Schneemelcher, English translation edited by R. McL. Wilson (London: Lutterworth Press, 1963), 444.

128. *Ibid.*

129. *Ibid.*, 445.

130. Tertullian, *Apology*, chapters 5 and 21, as cited *ibid.*, 444.

131. *Ibid.*

132. *Ibid.*, 447.

133. Elliott, *Literature*, 166.

134. *Ibid.*, 165–166.

135. Cameron, 164.

136. *Ibid.*, 164–165.

137. Scheidweiler, 447.

138. Kim, 1.

139. *Ibid.*, and Scheidweiler, 447–448.

140. Scheidweiler, 448–449.

141. For similarities and differences between the Greek and the Latin, see *ibid.*, 476–477.

# Chapter 2

1. Cameron, 83, and Phillipp Vielhauer, "Jewish-Christian Gospels," in *New Testament Apocrypha;* Volume 1: *Gospels and Related Writings*, edited by E. Hennecke and W. Schneemelcher, English translation edited by R. McL. Wilson (London: Lutterworth Press, 1963), 159.

2. Elliott, *Literature*, 4.

3. Vielhauer, 119, and John S. Kloppenborg, "Gospel of the Hebrews" (introduction, notes, and draft translation), in *The Complete Gospels: Annotated Scholars Version* (Revised and Expanded Edition), edited by Robert J. Miller (Sonoma, California: Polebridge Press, 1992), 427.

4. In this analysis, a distinction is made between the "Gospel of the Hebrews" mentioned by Epiphanius and that of a different work discussed under the same title by other ancient writers. See A. F. J. Klijn, *Jewish-Christian Gospel Tradition*, Volume 18 of the *Supplements to Vigiliae Christianae* (Leiden: E. J. Brill, 1992), 27–30. Kloppenborg ("Hebrews," 427) speaks of a scholarly consensus that three original sources are actually covered by the title "Gospel of the Hebrews," but only subdivides his translation and discussion into two divisions, the "Nazoreans" and the "Hebrews" (without citing which specific citation belongs to the two separate sources that go under this title).

5. Elliott, *Literature*, 5. For examples, see Kloppenborg, "Hebrews," 428.

6. Elliott, *Literature*, 5, and Kloppenborg, "Hebrews," 429.

7. Vielhauer, 163.

8. Klijn, 30.

9. Vielhauer, 163.

10. Elliott, *Literature*, 5; Klijn, 30; and Kloppenborg, "Hebrews," 429.

11. Vielhauer, 144.

12. *Ibid.*, 140–144.

13. John S. Kloppenborg, "Gospel of the Nazoreans" (introduction, notes, and draft translation), in *The Complete Gospels: Annotated Scholars Version* (Revised and Expanded Edition), edited by Robert J. Miller (Sonoma, California: Polebridge Press, 1992), 426, 427.

14. Elliott, *Literature*, 5; Klijn, 29–30; and Kloppenborg, "Nazoreans," 427.
15. Elliott, *Literature*, 5; Klijn, 29–30; and Kloppenborg, "Nazoreans," 427.
16. Kloppenborg, "Nazoreans," 442.
17. On the difficulty of fitting all of the preserved fragments into the theology of the movement at an early date, see John S. Kloppenborg, "Gospel of the Ebionites" (introduction, notes, and draft translation), in *The Complete Gospels: Annotated Scholars Version* (Revised and Expanded Edition), edited by Robert J. Miller (Sonoma, California: Polebridge Press, 1992), 435.
18. For example, Elliott, *Literature*, 5.
19. *Ibid.*, 6. George Howard, "The Gospel of the Ebionites," in *Aufstieg und Niedergang der Römischen Welt (Rise and Decline of the Roman World)*, edited by Wolfang Haase and Hildegard Temporini, 25.5.2 (Berlin: Walter de Gruyter, 1988), 4049, suggests that the Ebionites did not invent the account out of whole cloth but adopted already existing traditions into a cohesive account that would be amenable to their theories.
20. Elliott, *Literature*, 6; Kloppenborg, "Ebionites," 436, and Vielhauer, 156. Ehrman, *Writings*, 135, opts for the "early" part of the century.
21. Howard, 4035–4036.
22. Elliott, *Literature*, 6.
23. *Ibid.*
24. Kloppenborg, "Ebionites," 436.
25. Jon B. Daniels, "Egerton Gospel" (introduction, notes, and draft translation), in *The Complete Gospels: Annotated Scholars Version* (Revised and Expanded Edition), edited by Robert J. Miller (Sonoma, California: Polebridge Press, 1992), 416.
26. For what little can be reconstructed of the text of this section, see *ibid.*, 417
27. See the analysis of H. Idris Bell and T. C. Skeat, *Fragments of an Unknown Gospel and Other Early Christian Papyri* (London: Trustees of the British Museum, 1935), 31–32.
28. *Ibid.*, 30.
29. H. Idris Bell and T. C. Skeat, *The New Gospel Fragments* (London: Trustees of the British Museum, 1955), 19.
30. Andrews, 112.
31. Cameron, 74.
32. Cartlidge and Dungan, 49.
33. Elliott, *Literature*, 37–38.
34. Joachim Jeremias, "An Unknown Gospel with Johannine Elements," in *New Testament Apocrypha;* Volume 1: *Gospels and Related Writings*, edited by E. Hennecke and W. Schneemelcher, English translation edited by R. McL. Wilson (London: Lutterworth Press, 1963), 94.
35. Daniels, 413.
36. For example, Birger A. Pearson, "Earliest Christianity in Egypt: Some Observations," in *The Roots of Egyptian Christianity*, edited by Birger A. Pearson and James E. Goehring (Philadelphia: Fortress Press, 1986), 133.
37. Neirynck, 161.
38. Bell and Skeat, *New,* 16–17.
39. Daniels, 413.
40. For example, Cameron, 53; Joachim Jeremias, "An Unknown Gospel of Synoptic Type," in *New Testament Apocrypha;* Volume 1: *Gospels and Related Writings*, edited by E. Hennecke and W. Schneemelcher, English translation edited by R. McL. Wilson (London: Lutterworth Press, 1963), 92; and Phillip Sellew, "Oxyrhynchus Papyrus 840"(introduction and notes), in *The Complete Gospels: Annotated Scholars Version* (Revised and Expanded Edition), edited by Robert J. Miller (Sonoma, California: Polebridge Press, 1992), 419.
41. Sellew, "Papyrus," 419.
42. Cameron, 53, and Bernard P. Grenfell and Arthur S. Hunt, *Fragment of an Uncanonical Gospel from Oxyrhynchus, Edited with Text and Commentary* (London: Published for the Egypt Exploration Fund by Henry Frowde/Oxford University Press, 1908), 8. Jeremias, "Synoptic," 93, believes either century is viable.
43. Elliott, 31–32.
44. Sellew, "Papyrus," 418.

45. Cameron, 53.

46. For the firsthand account by the person who discovered it, see Morton Smith, *The Secret Gospel: The Discovery and Interpretation of the Secret Gospel According to Mark* (New York: Harper & Row, Publishers, 1973), 10–17.

47. Cameron, 67.

48. John D. Crossan, *Four Other Gospels: Shadows on the Contours of Canon* (Minneapolis: A Seabury Book/Winston Press, 1985), 100–101, discusses in detail the problem of access. Also on the question of the work's genuineness, see Charlesworth, *Authentic*, 29–30, and Jenkins, 101–102.

49. Crossan, *Four*, 99.

50. Cameron, 67.

51. F. F. Bruce, *The "Secret" Gospel of Mark: The Ethel M. Wood Lecture Delivered before the University of London (11 February 1974)* (London: University of London/Athlone Press, 1974), 13; cf. 20; and Charlesworth and Evans, 527–528.

52. Morton Smith, *Clement of Alexandria and a Secret Gospel of Mark* (Cambridge, Massachusetts: Harvard University Press, 1973), 89.

53. *Ibid.*, 92.

54. Smith, *Discovery*, 29.

55. Salvatore R. C. Lilla, *Clement of Alexandria: A Study in Christian Gnosticism* (Oxford: Oxford University Press, 1971), 154.

56. *Ibid.*, 155.

57. *Ibid.*

58. *Ibid.*, citing *Stromata* 1.13.2; 2.10.1–3. Since 1.13 is not germane to the subject, the author apparently had overlooked a typographical error and means 1.12, which *is* relevant to the matter.

59. Clement of Alexandria, *Stromata*, in *The Ante-Nicene Fathers: Translations of the Fathers Down to A.D.325*, edited by Alexander Roberts and James Donaldson. Book 1 at: http://www.ccel.org/fathers2/ANF-02/anf02-57.htm#P4831_1447881 (June 2002). Book 2 at: http://www.ccel.org/fathers2/ANF-02/anf02-59.htm#P5786_1757970 (June 2002).

60. The author has an apparent typographical error and identifies this as 1.13, which is not a relevant passage.

61. As quoted by Jean Danielou, *Gospel Message and Hellenistic Culture*, translated by John A. Baker; volume 2 of *A History of Early Christian Doctrine before the Council of Nicaea* (London: Darton, Longman & Todd, 1973), 454.

62. Cf. *ibid.*, 457. For quotations on this as the purpose of writing, from the *Stromata* itself (1.11) and also Eusebius (*Ecclesiastical History* (6.13) see 451.

63. Ehrman, *Writings*, 131, for example, refers to the possible "homoerotic overtones" of the text.

64. Crossan, *Four*, 116–117.

65. See the discussion of the evidence in *ibid.*, 116–117, though the evidence does not read as strongly to my ears as his. Also see John D. Turner, "Ritual in Gnosticism," in *Society of Biblical Literature 1994 Seminar Papers*, edited by Eugene H. Lovering, Jr. (Atlanta, Georgia: Scholars Press, 1994), 155–157.

66. Crossan, *Four*, 117.

67. Bruce, 16. He believes that the fragment that has been preserved is a blatant pastiche based upon the gospel of Mark, with material adapted from John and Matthew as well. For details as to specific texts believed utilized, see 11–13.

68. Cameron, 68, and Helmut Koester, "Secret Gospel of Mark" (introduction, notes, and draft translation), in *The Complete Gospels: Annotated Scholars Version* (Revised and Expanded Edition), edited by Robert J. Miller (Sonoma, California: Polebridge Press, 1992), 410. A different view: Philip Sellew, "*Secret Mark* and the History of Canonical Mark," in *The Future of Early Christianity: Essays in Honor of Helmut Koester*, edited by Birger A. Pearson et al. (Minneapolis: Fortress Press, 1991), 242–257 (especially 256) argues that Roman Mark was expanded into Secret Mark and that our canonical Mark represents an even later composition based upon elements from both works.

# Chapter 3

1. Elliott, *Literature*, 303.
2. E. Schaferdiek, "The Acts of John," in *New Testament Apocrypha; Volume 2: Writings Relating to the Apostles, Apocalypses, and Related Subjects*, edited by E. Hennecke and W. Schneemelcher, English translation edited by R. McL. Wilson (London: Lutterworth Press, 1965), 193.
3. *Ibid.*, 195, and Elliott, *Literature*, 304.
4. Cf. Elliott, *Literature*, 303. For a discussion of the various specific sources, see 304–305.
5. Preferring Syria or Asia Minor is Schaferdiek, 192. Cameron, 88, opts for Syria. Pieter J. Lalleman, *The Acts of John: A Two-Stage Initiation into Johannine Gnosticisim* (Leuven, Belgium: Peeters, 1998), 256–266, in a detailed study of the arguments pro and con for the three areas, ultimately opts for Asia Minor and Smyrna in particular.
6. Schaferdiek, 192.
7. Schaferdiek, 192–193.
8. Elliott, *Literature*, 306.
9. The sometimes incorporeal nature of Jesus' body, for instance: See the discussion in Schaferdiek, 189.
10. Cameron, 88, also refers to the possibility of a first century date.
11. Schaferdiek, 192.
12. Elliott, *Literature*, 306.
13. Violet Macdermot, *Pistis Sophia* (Leiden: E. J. Brill, 1978), xi.
14. Henri-Charles Puech, "Gnostic Gospels and Related Documents," in *New Testament Apocrypha; Volume 1: Gospels and Related Writings*, edited by E. Hennecke and W. Schneemelcher, English translation edited by R. McL. Wilson (London: Lutterworth Press, 1963), 250.
15. Macdermot, xiv.
16. Puech, 250–251.
17. *Ibid.*, 252.
18. Hugo Duensing, "Epistula Apostolorum," in *New Testament Apocrypha; Volume 1: Gospels and Related Writings*, edited by E. Hennecke and W. Schneemelcher, English translation edited by R. McL. Wilson (London: Lutterworth Press, 1963), 189.
19. *Ibid.*
20. Cameron, 131.
21. Duensing, 190.
22. Cameron, 132.
23. Duensing, 190.
24. Duensing, 190–191.
25. Cameron, 133.
26. For a discussion of the ancestry of the text, see R. Joseph Hoffmann, *Jesus Outside the Gospels* (New York: Prometheus Books, 1984), 50–51.
27. Gero, 3992.
28. Morris Goldstein, *Jesus in the Jewish Tradition* (New York: Macmillan Company, 1950), 161.
29. *Ibid.*, 162–163.
30. Craig A. Evans, "Jesus in Non-Christian Sources," in *Studying the Historical Jesus: Evaluations of the State of Current Research*, edited by Bruce Chilton and Craig A. Evans (Leiden: E. J. Brill, 1994), 449.
31. Hugh J. Schonfield, *According to the Hebrews* (London: Duckworth, 1937), 29–30.
32. For the evidence as he sees it, see *ibid.*, 215–227.
33. Goldstein, 166.
34. For examples, see *ibid.*, 147.
35. *Ibid.*

# Chapter 4

1. Clayton, 15.
2. For a discussion of parallels between these chapters and 1 Samuel 1–2, see Willem S. Vorster, "The Protevangelium of James and Intertextuality," in *Text and Testimony: Essays on New Testament and Apocryphal Literature in Honour of A. F. J. Klijn*, edited by T. Baarda, et al. (Kampen: Uitgeversmaatschappij J. H. Kok, 1988), 265, 268, 273.
3. Elliott, *Literature*, 49.
4. Benko, 200–201. We have added in parentheses scriptural references from

Benko's footnotes to make his argument more complete.

5. Hervieux, 39.
6. *Ibid.*
7. *Ibid.*
8. *Ibid.*, 41; Donald F. Hock, *Gospels*, 47; and Ronald F. Hock, "The Infancy Gospel of James" (introduction, notes, and draft translation), in *The Complete Gospels: Annotated Scholars Version* (Revised and Expanded Edition), edited by Robert J. Miller (Sonoma, California: Polebridge Press, 1992), 387.
9. Hock, *Gospels*, 49.
10. For an interesting effort to prove that the canonical accounts are derived from Buddhism (as well as presenting parallels with the apocryphal gospels), one will find useful, Zacharias P. Thundy, "Intertextuality, Buddhism, and the Infancy Gospels," in *Islam, Buddhism, Greco-Roman Religions, Ancient Israel, and Judaism*, edited by Jacob Neusner, Ernest S. Frerichs, and A. J. Levine; Volume 1 of *Religious Writings and Religious Systems: Systemic Analysis of Holy Books in Christianity, Islam, Buddhism, Greco-Roman Religions, Ancient Israel, and Judaism* (Atlanta, Georgia: Scholars Press, 1989), 17–73. He quotes at length the Buddhist, canonical, and apocryphal sources on a number of themes, a course that permits one to compare the treatment of the matters in very different sources.
11. Hock, *Gospels*, 51.
12. *Ibid.*
13. As quoted by James, 489.
14. Hock, *Gospels*, 55.
15. Elliott, *Literature*, 51.

# Chapter 5

1. Hock, *Gospels*, 65.
2. On the suspension of time in other ancient sources, see Francois Bovon, "The Suspension of Time in Chapter 18 of Protevangelium Jacobi," in *The Future of Early Christianity: Essays in Honor of Helmut Koester*, edited by Birger A. Pearson et al. (Minneapolis: Fortress Press, 1991), 397–399.

3. J. K. Elliott, *The Apocryphal Jesus: Legends of the Early Church* (Oxford: Oxford University Press, 1996), 10.
4. *Ibid.*, 11. The concept of "freezing time" for some people or every one has been creatively utilized in science fiction but the genre and intents are clearly different.
5. As quoted by Findlay, 324.
6. Cf. *ibid.*, 324–325.
7. As quoted *ibid.*, 325.
8. *Ibid.*
9. Hock, *Gospels*, 67.
10. Hock, *Mary*, 12–13.
11. For a fascinating circumstantial case that the figure of the skeptical Salome in this incident is a free borrowing from polytheistic mythology, see Benko, 201–202.
12. *Stromateis* vii.16, as quoted Findlay, 325.
13. Benko, 202.
14. Hervieux, 97.
15. *Ibid.*, 97–98.
16. For the quotation of various ancient writers embracing this belief, see Findlay, 327.
17. Jaroslav Pelikan, *Mary through the Centuries: Her Place in the History of Culture* (New Haven: Yale University Press, 1996), 47–48.
18. Elliott, *Literature*, 49.
19. Hock, *Gospels*, 71.
20. For other medieval versions of the visit of the Magi (including the claim that it was depicted in the Gospel of the Hebrews), see the documents and translations in Klijn, 125–128.
21. Hock, "James," 395.
22. *Ibid.*, 381.
23. *Ibid.*, 381, 382.
24. Hock, *Gospels*, 77.

# Chapter 6

1. Cowper, xxx.
2. *Catechesis* 10.10, as quoted by Edward Yarnold, *Cyril of Jerusalem* (London: Routledge, 2000), 123.
3. Elliott, *Legends*, 32–33 as to the intent of the Arabic Gospel but without

mention of the belief that the righteous dead can intercede.

# Chapter 7

1. Findlay, 177.
2. Cf. Drury, 227, and Findlay, 178.
3. Cf. Findlay, 177.
4. Elliott, *Literature*, 68–69, believes that Joseph is attempting to dilute the image of Jesus as an irresponsible youthful miracle-mongerer that is founded in such works as the Infancy Gospel of Thomas.
5. Gero, 3982–3983.
6. Attridge, 372.
7. *Ibid.*, 374.
8. *Ibid.* He also notes that the text is extremely corrupt and makes little sense.
9. Cullmann, 407.
10. *Ibid.*
11. The quotations that follow are *ibid.*, 414–417.
12. Justin as quoted by Hippolytus in *Philos.* v.26, as cited by Cullmann, 402.
13. As quoted by Macdermot, 243, 245 (Coptic text on 242 and 244).
14. For a concise discussion, see Evans, "Sources," 443–449, 462–464, and Hoffman, *Gospels*, 36–50.
15. For a discussion, see Evans, "Sources," 466–477.
16. Chapter 1. For full text of the entire work as found in the Hebrew language *Codex Strasburg*, see Schonfield, 35–61.

# Chapter 8

1. For the idea of an authoritative canon being determinative after c. A.D. 180, see Grenfell and Hunt, 13.
2. Jenkins, 85.
3. *Ibid.*
4. *Ibid.*
5. *Ibid.*
6. *Ibid.*, 86.
7. Elliott, *Literature*, 38, points to the fact that what has survived is a composite of canonical and noncanonical material but orthodox in intent and content.
8. For text and discussion, see Evans, "Sources," 454–455.
9. *Ibid.*, 455.
10. For text and discussion of both Celsus and others who echoed the magical interpretation, see *ibid.*, 459–461.
11. For a discussion of Lucian, see *ibid.*, 461–462.
12. For text and analysis, see *ibid.*, 464–466.
13. As quoted by Pick, 3.
14. Cf. Kloppenborg, "Nazoreans," 443, and Findlay, 68–69.
15. As quoted by Pick, 3–4.
16. As quoted *ibid.*, 16–17.
17. Cf. Kloppenborg, "Ebionites," 438.
18. As quoted by Howard, 4043.
19. *Dialogue* 88.3, as quoted *ibid.*, 4043.
20. As quoted by Findlay, 46.
21. As quoted *ibid.*
22. *Ibid.*
23. *Ibid.*
24. Cf. Klijn, 54.
25. As quoted by Pick, 4.
26. As quoted *ibid.*, 4.
27. For the quotations, see *ibid.*
28. Kloppenborg, "Hebrews," 431.
29. For the use of the two texts see Jack Finegan, *Hidden Records of the Life of Jesus* (Philadelphia: Pilgrim Press, 1969), 150.
30. Findlay, 58–59.
31. Cf. Findlay, 59.
32. *Ibid.*, 59.
33. As it is *ibid.*
34. *Ibid.*
35. *Ibid.*, 59.
36. See Kloppenborg, "Hebrews," 431.
37. All quotes are from Schaferdiek, 2:225–227.
38. Lalleman, 172.
39. *Ibid.*, 170, summarizing the views of another scholar.
40. *Ibid.*
41. Paul G. Schneider, "The Acts of John: The Gnostic Transformation of a

Christian Community," in *Hellenization Revisited: Shaping a Christian Response within the Greco-Roman World*, edited by Wendy E. Helleman (Lanham, Maryland: University Press of America, 1994), 246.

42. *Ibid.*, 246–247.
43. Lalleman, 172.
44. Elliott, *Literature*, 304.
45. As quoted by Clement of Alexandria, *Miscellanies (Stromateis)*, 3.59.3, and translated byBentley Layton, *The Gnostic Scriptures* (Garden City, New York: Doubleday & Company, Inc, 1987), 239.
46. *Ibid.*, 238.
47. *Ibid.*, 238–239.
48. As quoted by Pick, 17.
49. Kloppenborg, "Ebionites," 438.
50. As quoted by 6. On later acceptance of this tradition of the man being a mason, see the original language and English translations in Klijn, 89.
51. Findlay, 74.
52. Kloppenborg, "Nazoreans," 444.
53. As quoted by Schaferdiek, 2:227.
54. Quotations in this section come from Hoffmann, *Gospels*, 51–52.
55. As quoted *ibid.*, 52.
56. Talmud b. Qidd. 49b, as quoted *ibid.*, 45.
57. All quotes are from Schaferdiek, 2:226.
58. Elliott, *Legends*, 59.
59. As quoted by Bernard Pick, 6–7.
60. *Ibid.*, 7.
61. Elliott, *Literature*, 10.
62. As quoted by Bell and Skeat, *Unknown*, 28.
63. Koester, *Gospels*, 212–213.
64. As quoted by Pick, 13.
65. For, in my opinion, inadequate argumentation that John has in mind ongoing, repetitious sin, see in Klijn, 117–118.
66. As quoted by Pick, 32–33.
67. Sellew, "Papyrus," 421.
68. *Ibid.*, 420.
69. *Ibid.*, 420–421, and Grenfell and Hunt, 12, 20, 21.
70. As quoted by Pick, 18.
71. Howard, 4036–4037.

## Chapter 9

1. All quotations in this section come from Schonfield's translation in *Hebrews*.
2. Gero, 3986.
3. All quotations from the work will come from Pick, 43–50.
4. J. Armitage Robinson, "The Gospel According to Peter: A Lecture," in *The Gospel According to Peter and the Revelation of Peter: Two Lectures on the Newly Recovered Fragments together with the Greek Text*, edited by J. Armitage Robinson and Montague R. James, Second Edition (London: C. J. Clay and Sons, 1892), 16.
5. As quoted by Layton, 423.
6. Cf. Ehrman, *Orthodox*, 144, 145.
7. Quoting Irenaeus on this as the motive of the teaching, Robinson, 21.
8. Dewey, 403, suggests this and the possibility of some type of "ascension" as the possible interpretations of the words.
9. Findlay, 102.
10. *Ibid.*
11. Ehrman, *Orthodox*, 144.
12. John D. Crossan, *The Cross that Spoke: The Origins of the Passion Narrative* (San Francisco: Harper & Row, Publishers, 1988), 221–222.
13. *Ibid.*, 222.
14. As quoted by Pick, 11.
15. For original texts and English translations, see A. F. J. Klijn, 94–95.
16. Findlay, 75.
17. As quoted by Robinson, 23.
18. As quoted *ibid.*
19. As quoted *ibid.*

## Chapter 10

1. Dewey, 405.
2. Danielou, *Jewish*, 21.
3. Ehrman, *Orthodox*, n. 18, page 260.
4. Charles A. Gieschen, *Angelomor-*

*phic Christology: Antecedents and Early Evidence* (Leiden: Brill, 1998), 32, where the concept is advanced tentatively. The angelic nature of the beings is referred to on 240.

5. Pearson and Harley, 74–75.

6. Jarl E. Fossum, *The Image of the Invisible God: Essays on the Influence of Jewish Mysticism on Early Christianity* (Gottingen: Vandenhoeck und Ruprecht, 1995), 88.

7. *Ibid.*, 88–89.

8. For a study of other texts that may take for granted such a preaching, see Friedrich Loofs, "Christ's Descent into Hell," in *Transactions of the Third International Congress for the History of Religions* (volume 2) [no editor named] (Oxford: At the Clarendon Press, 1908), 299–301.

9. For a discussion of the apparently intentional role reversal from Old Testament "saints" to ancient rejectors of God in Marcion's doctrine, see *ibid.*, 295–296. For concise summaries of Marcion's theology, see Robert M. Grant, *The Earliest Lives of Jesus* (London: SPCK, 1961), 11–12, and Robert M. Grant, *Jesus after the Gospels: The Christ of the Second Century — The Hale Memorial Lectures of Seabury-Western Theological Seminary, 1989* (Louisville, Kentucky: Westminster/John Knox Press, 1990), 50–51.

10. As quoted by Robinson, 25.

11. *Ibid.*

12. As quoted by Findlay, 112.

13. See the quotation of the text *ibid.*, 113.

14. Loofs, 292.

15. Craig A. Evans, "Images," 65.

16. *Ibid.*

17. Charlesworth and Evans, 508, and Evans, "Images," 65.

18. Crossan, *Cross,* 180.

19. For a negative evaluation of the claim that the Gospel of Peter's account of the guard at Jesus' tomb (8:28–11:49) is older than the canonical version or may even be the source of it, see Susan E. Schaeffer, "The Guard at the Tomb (*Gospel of Peter* 8:28–11:49 and Matthew 26:62–66; 28:2–4, 11:16): A Case of Intertextuality?," in *Society of Biblical Literature 1991 Seminar Papers*, edited by Eugene H. Lovering, Jr. (Atlanta, Georgia: Scholars Press, 1991), 499–507, especially 505–506.

20. As quoted by James, 488.

21. As quoted by Pick, 12.

22. *Commentary on Isaiah* XVIII (preface), as quoted by Pick, 13. For other ancient comments on this theme, see the texts in Klijn, 122–123. Also see William D. Stroker, *Extracanonical Sayings of Jesus* (Atlanta, Georgia: Scholars Press, 1989), 151, and n. 2, page 151.

23. As quoted by James, 488.

24. *Ibid.*

25. As quoted by Klijn, 80.

26. For texts in both Latin and English, see *ibid.*, 80–83.

27. Kloppenborg, "Hebrews," 434.

28. Cf. *ibid.*

29. As quoted by Layton, 180.

30. As quoted by Macdermot, 3.

31. *Catechesis* 10.19, as quoted by Yarnold, 127.

32. As quoted by James, 503.

33. As quoted by Hoffmann, *Gospels*, 52–53. For a longer version of this text, see Schonfield, 51–53.

# Bibliography

## Primary Works

"Acts of Pilate" (Greek and Latin forms). In *The Ante-Nicene Fathers: Translations of the Fathers Down to A.D.325*, edited by Alexander Roberts and James Donaldson. At http://www.ccel.org/fathers2/ANF-08/anf08-77.htm. April 2002.

"Arabic Gospel of the Infancy of the Savior." In *The Ante-Nicene Fathers: Translations of the Fathers Down to A.D.325*, edited by Alexander Roberts and James Donaldson. At http://www.ccel.org/fathers2/ANF-08/anf08-75.htm. March 2002.

Attridge, Harold. "The Infancy Gospel of Thomas." (Introduction, notes, and draft translation.) In *The Complete Gospels: Annotated Scholars Version* (Revised and Expanded Edition), edited by Robert J. Miller, 369–379. Sonoma, California: Polebridge Press, 1992.

Bell, H. Idris, and T. C. Skeat. *Fragments of an Unknown Gospel and Other Early Christian Papyri*. London: Trustees of the British Museum, 1935.

_____, and _____. *The New Gospel Fragments*. London: Trustees of the British Museum, 1955.

Cameron, Ron. *The Other Gospels: Non-Canonical Gospel Texts*. Philadelphia: Westminster Press, 1982.

Cartlidge, David R., and David L. Dungan. *Documents for the Study of the Gospels*. Revised and Enlarged Edition. Minneapolis: Fortress Press, 1994.

Clayton, Mary. *The Apocryphal Gospels of Mary in Anglo-Saxon England*. Cambridge: Cambridge University Press, 1998.

Clement of Alexandria. *Stromata*. In *The Ante-Nicene Fathers: Translations of the Fathers Down to A.D.325*, edited by Alexander Roberts and James Donaldson. Book 1 at: http://www.ccel.org/fathers2/ANF-02/anf02-57.htm#P4831_1447881. June 2002. Book 2 at: http://www.ccel.org/fathers2/ANF-02/anf02-59.htm#P5786_1757970. June 2002.

Cowper, B. Harris. *The Apocryphal Gospels and Other Documents Relating to the History of Christ*. Seventh Edition. London: David Nutt, 1910.

Cullmann, Oscar. "Infancy Gospels." In *New Testament Apocrypha*. Volume 1: *Gospels and Related Writings*, edited by E. Hennecke and W. Schneemelcher, 363–417. English translation edited by R. McL. Wilson. London: Lutterworth Press, 1963.

Daniels, Jon B. "Egerton Gospel." (Introduction, notes, and draft translation.) In *The Complete Gospels: Annotated Scholars Version* (Revised and Expanded

Edition), edited by Robert J. Miller, 412–417. Sonoma, California: Polebridge Press, 1992.

Dewey, Arthur J. "Gospel of Peter." (Introduction, notes, and draft translation.) In *The Complete Gospels: Annotated Scholars Version* (Revised and Expanded Edition), edited by Robert J. Miller, 399–407. Sonoma, California: Polebridge Press, 1992.

Duensing, Hugo. "Epistula Apostolorum." In *New Testament Apocrypha*. Volume 1: *Gospels and Related Writings*, edited by E. Hennecke and W. Schneemelcher, 189–227. English translation edited by R. McL. Wilson. London: Lutterworth Press, 1963.

Ehrman, Bart D. *After the New Testament: A Reader in Early Christianity*. New York: Oxford University Press, 1999.

_____. *The New Testament and Other Early Christian Writings: A Reader*. New York: Oxford University Press, 1998.

Elliott, J. K. *The Apocryphal Jesus: Legends of the Early Church*. Oxford: Oxford University Press, 1996.

_____. *The Apocryphal New Testament: A Collection of Apocryphal Christian Literature in an English Translation*. Oxford: Clarendon Press, 1993.

"Gospel of Pseudo-Matthew." In *The Ante-Nicene Fathers: Translations of the Fathers Down to A.D.325*, edited by Alexander Roberts and James Donaldson. At http://www.ccel.org/fathers2/ANF-08/anf08-68.htm. March 2002.

"Gospel of the Nativity of Mary." In *The Ante-Nicene Fathers: Translations of the Fathers Down to A.D.325*, edited by Alexander Roberts and James Donaldson. At http://www.ccel.org/fathers2/ANF-08/anf08-69.htm. March 2002.

Herbert, Maire, and Martin McNamara. *Irish Biblical Apocrypha: Selected Texts in Translation*. Edinburgh: T & T Clark, 1989.

"History of Joseph the Carpenter." In *The Ante-Nicene Fathers: Translations of the Fathers Down to A.D.325*, edited by Alexander Roberts and James Donaldson. At http://www.ccel.org/fathers2/ANF-08/anf08-70.htm. March 2002.

Hock, Ronald F. "The Infancy Gospel of James." (Introduction, notes, and draft translation.) In *The Complete Gospels: Annotated Scholars Version* (Revised and Expanded Edition), edited by Robert J. Miller, 380–396. Sonoma, California: Polebridge Press, 1992.

_____. *The Infancy Gospels of James and Thomas*. Santa Rosa, California: Polebridge Press, 1995.

_____. *The Life of Mary and the Birth of Jesus: The Ancient Infancy Gospel of James*. Berkeley, California: Ulysses Press, 1997.

Hoffmann, R. Joseph. *The Secret Gospels: A Harmony of Apocryphal Jesus Traditions*. Amherst, New York: Prometheus Books, 1996.

"[Infancy] Gospel of Thomas" (First Greek form/Greek Version A). In *The Ante-Nicene Fathers: Translations of the Fathers Down to A.D.325*, edited by Alexander Roberts and James Donaldson. At http://www.ccel.org/fathers2/ANF-08/anf08-72.htm. March 2002.

"[Infancy] Gospel of Thomas" (Latin form). In *The Ante-Nicene Fathers: Translations of the Fathers Down to A.D.325*, edited by Alexander Roberts and James Donaldson. At http://www.ccel.org/fathers2/ANF-08/anf08-74.htm. March 2002.

James, Montague R. *The Apocryphal New Testament*. Oxford: At the Clarendon Press, 1924; 1955 printing.

Jeremias, Joachim. "An Unknown Gospel of Synoptic Type." In *New Testament Apocrypha*. Volume 1: *Gospels and Related Writings*, edited by E. Hennecke and W. Schneemelcher, 92–947. English translation edited by R. McL. Wilson. London: Lutterworth Press, 1963.

———. "An Unknown Gospel with Johannine Elements." In *New Testament Apocrypha*. Volume 1: *Gospels and Related Writings*, edited by E. Hennecke and W. Schneemelcher, 94–97. English translation edited by R. McL. Wilson. London: Lutterworth Press, 1963.

Kloppenborg, John S. "Gospel of the Ebionites." (Introduction, notes, and draft translation.) In *The Complete Gospels: Annotated Scholars Version* (Revised and Expanded Edition), edited by Robert J. Miller, 435–440. Sonoma, California: Polebridge Press, 1992.

———. "Gospel of the Hebrews." (Introduction, notes, and draft translation.) In *The Complete Gospels: Annotated Scholars Version* (Revised and Expanded Edition), edited by Robert J. Miller, 430–434. Sonoma, California: Polebridge Press, 1992.

———. "Gospel of the Nazoreans." (Introduction, notes, and draft translation.) In *The Complete Gospels: Annotated Scholars Version* (Revised and Expanded Edition), edited by Robert J. Miller, 441–446. Sonoma, California: Polebridge Press, 1992.

Koester, Helmut. "Secret Gospel of Mark." (Introduction, notes, and draft translation.) In *The Complete Gospels: Annotated Scholars Version* (Revised and Expanded Edition), edited by Robert J. Miller, 408–413. Sonoma, California: Polebridge Press, 1992.

Layton, Bentley. *The Gnostic Scriptures*. Garden City, New York: Doubleday & Company, Inc, 1987.

Macdermot, Violet. *Pistis Sophia*. Leiden: E. J. Brill, 1978.

Maurer, Christian. "The Gospel of Peter." In *New Testament Apocrypha*. Volume 1: *Gospels and Related Writings*, edited by E. Hennecke and W. Schneemelcher, 179–187. English translation edited by R. McL. Wilson. London: Lutterworth Press, 1963.

Orr, James. *New Testament Apocryphal Writings*. London: Imdent & Company, 1902.

Pick, Bernhard. *Paralipomena: Remains of Gospels and Sayings of Christ*. Chicago: Open Court Publishing Company, 1908.

"Protoevangelium of James". In *The Ante-Nicene Fathers: Translations of the Fathers Down to A.D.325*, edited by Alexander Roberts and James Donaldson. At http://www.ccel.org/fathers2/ANF-08/anf08-67.htm. March 2002.

Puech, Henri-Charles. "Gnostic Gospels and Related Documents." In *New Testament Apocrypha*. Volume 1: *Gospels and Related Writings*, edited by E. Hennecke and W. Schneemelcher, 231–362. English translation edited by R. McL. Wilson. London: Lutterworth Press, 1963.

Schaferdiek, E. "The Acts of John." In *New Testament Apocrypha*. Volume 2: *Writings Relating to the Apostles, Apocalypses, and Related Subjects*. Edited by E. Hennecke and W. Schneemelcher, 188–259. English translation edited by R. McL. Wilson. London: Lutterworth Press, 1965.

Scheidweiler, Felix. "The Gospel of Nicodemus: Acts of Pilate and Christ's Descent into Hell." In *New Testament Apocrypha*. Volume 1: *Gospels and Related Writings*, edited by E. Hennecke and W. Schneemelcher, 444–483. English translation edited by R. McL. Wilson. London: Lutterworth Press, 1963.

Schonfield, Hugh J. *According to the Hebrews.* London: Duckworth, 1937.
Sellew, Phillip. "Oxyrhynchus Papyrus 840." (Introduction and notes.) In *The Complete Gospels: Annotated Scholars Version* (Revised and Expanded Edition), edited by Robert J. Miller, 418–421. Sonoma, California: Polebridge Press, 1992.
Smith, Morton. *Clement of Alexandria and a Secret Gospel of Mark.* Cambridge, Massachusetts: Harvard University Press, 1973.
Stroker, William D. *Extracanonical Sayings of Jesus.* Atlanta, Georgia: Scholars Press, 1989.
Vielhauer, Philipp. "Jewish-Christian Gospels." In *New Testament Apocrypha.* Volume 1: *Gospels and Related Writings*, edited by E. Hennecke and W. Schneemelcher, 117–165. English translation edited by R. McL. Wilson. London: Lutterworth Press, 1963.
Yarnold, Edward. *Cyril of Jerusalem.* London: Routledge, 2000.

## Secondary Works

Andrews, H. T. *An Introduction to the Apocryphal Books of the Old and New Testament.* Revised and Edited by Charles F. Pfeiffer. Grand Rapids, Michigan: Baker Book House, 1964.
Allen, John L., Jr. "The Protevangelium of James as an Historia: The Insufficiency of the Infancy Gospel Category." In *Society of Biblical Literature 1991 Seminar Papers*, edited by Eugene H. Lovering, Jr., 499–507. Atlanta, Georgia: Scholars Press, 1991.
Benko, Stephen. *The Virgin Goddess: Studies in the Pagan and Christian Roots of Mariology.* Leiden: E. J. Brill, 1993.
Bovon, François. "The Suspension of Time in Chapter 18 of Protevangelium Jacobi." In *The Future of Early Christianity: Essays in Honor of Helmut Koester*, edited by Birger A. Pearson et al., 393–405. Minneapolis: Fortress Press, 1991.
Bruce, F. F. *The "Secret" Gospel of Mark: The Ethel M. Wood Lecture Delivered Before the University of London (11 February 1974).* London: University of London/Athlone Press, 1974.
Charlesworth, James H. *Authentic Apocrypha: False and Genuine Christian Apocrypha.* North Richlands Hills, Texas: BIBAL Press, 1998.
_____. "Research on the New Testament Apocrypha and Pseudepigrapha." In *Aufstieg und Niedergang der Romischen Welt (Rise and Decline of the Roman World)*, edited by Wolfang Haase and Hildegard Temporini, 25.5.2, 3919–3968. Berlin: Walter de Gruyter, 1988.
_____, and Craig A. Evans. "Jesus in the Agrapha and Apocryphal Gospels." In *Studying the Historical Jesus: Evaluations of the State of Current Research*, edited by Bruce Chilton and Craig A. Evans, 479–533. Leiden: E. J. Brill, 1994.
Crossan, John D. *The Cross that Spoke: The Origins of the Passion Narrative.* San Francisco: Harper & Row, Publishers, 1988.
_____. *Four Other Gospels: Shadows on the Contours of Canon.* Minneapolis: A Seabury Book/Winston Press, 1985.
Danielou, Jean. *Gospel Message and Hellenistic Culture*, translated by John A. Baker; volume 2 of *A History of Early Christian Doctrine before the Council of Nicaea.* London: Darton, Longman & Todd, 1973.
_____. *The Theology of Jewish Christianity*, translated by John A. Baker; volume 1

of *The Development of Christian Doctrine before the Council of Nicaea.* London: Darton, Longman & Todd, 1964.

DiPuccio, William. "Annotated Index of Authors and Works of the Ante-Nice, Nicene, and Post-Nicene Fathers." In the reprint edition of *Ante-Nicene Fathers: The Writings of the Fathers Down to A.D. 325*, volume 10, 269–399. Peabody, Massachusetts: Hendrickson Publishers, 1994.

Drury, Clare. "Who's In, Who's Out." In *What about the New Testament? Essays in Honour of Christopher Evans*, edited by Morna Hooker and Colin Hickling, 223–233. London: SCM Press, Ltd, 1975.

Ehrman, Bart D. *The Orthodox Corruption of Scripture: The Effect of Early Christological Controversies on the Text of the New Testament.* New York: Oxford University Press, 1993.

Evans, Craig A. "Images of Christ in the Canonical and Apocryphal Gospels." In *Images of Christ: Ancient and Modern*, edited by Stanley E. Porter, Michael A. Hayes, and David Tombs, 34–72. Sheffield, England: Sheffield Academic Press, 1997.

———. "Jesus in Non-Christian Sources." In *Studying the Historical Jesus: Evaluations of the State of Current Research*, edited by Bruce Chilton and Craig A. Evans, 443–478. Leiden: E. J. Brill, 1994.

Findlay, Adam F. *Byways in Early Christian Literature: Studies in the Uncanonical Gospels and Acts.* Edinburgh: T. & T. Clark, 1923.

Finegan, Jack. *Hidden Records of the Life of Jesus.* Philadelphia: Pilgrim Press, 1969.

Fiorenza, Elisabeth S. *Jesus: Miriam's Child, Sophia's Prophet: Critical Issues in Feminist Christology.* New York: Continuum, 1994.

Fossum, Jarl E. *The Image of the Invisible God: Essays on the Influence of Jewish Mysticism on Early Christianity.* Gottingen: Vandenhoeck und Ruprecht, 1995.

Gero, Stephen. "Apocryphal Gospels: A Survey of Textual and Literary Problems." In *Aufstieg und Niedergang der Romischen Welt (Rise and Decline of the Roman World)*, edited by Wolfang Haase and Hildegard Temporini, 25.5.2, 3969–3996. Berlin: Walter de Gruyter, 1988.

Gieschen, Charles A. *Angelomorphic Christology: Antecedents and Early Evidence.* Leiden: Brill, 1998.

Goldstein, Morris. *Jesus in the Jewish Tradition.* New York: Macmillan Company, 1950.

Grant, Robert M. *The Earliest Lives of Jesus.* London: SPCK, 1961.

———. *Jesus after the Gospels: The Christ of the Second Century — The Hale Memorial Lectures of Seabury-Western Theological Seminary, 1989.* Louisville, Kentucky: Westminster/John Knox Press, 1990.

Grenfell, Bernard P., and Arthur S. Hunt. *Fragment of an Uncanonical Gospel from Oxyrhynchus, Edited with Text and Commentary.* London: Published for the Egypt Exploration Fund by Henry Frowde/Oxford University Press, 1908.

Hervieux, Jacques. *The New Testament Apocrypha.* Translated from the French by Dom Wulstan Hibberd. New York: Hawthorn Books, 1960.

Hoffmann, R. Joseph. *Jesus Outside the Gospels.* New York: Prometheus Books, 1984.

Howard, George. "The Gospel of the Ebionites." In *Aufstieg und Niedergang der Romischen Welt (Rise and Decline of the Roman World)*, edited by Wolfang Haase and Hildegard Temporini, 25.5.2, 4034–4053. Berlin: Walter de Gruyter, 1988.

Jenkins, Philip. *Hidden Gospels: How the Search for Jesus Lost Its Way.* New York: Oxford University Press, 2001.

Kim, H. C. *The Gospel of Nicodemus.* Toronto: Centre for Medieval Studies, Pontifical Institute of Mediaeval Studies, 1973.

Klijn, A. F. J. *Jewish-Christian Gospel Tradition.* Volume 18 of the *Supplements to Vigiliae Christianae.* Leiden: E. J. Brill, 1992.

Koester, Helmut, *Ancient Christian Gospels: Their History and Development.* Philadelphia: Trinity Press International, 1990.

Lalleman, Pieter J. *The Acts of John: A Two-Stage Initiation into Johannine Gnosticism.* Leuven, Belgium: Peeters, 1998.

Lilla, Salvatore R. C. *Clement of Alexandria: A Study in Christian Gnosticism.* Oxford: Oxford University Press, 1971.

Loofs, Friederich. "Christ's Descent into Hell." In *Transactions of the Third International Congress for the History of Religions* (volume 2), [no editor named], 290–301. Oxford: At the Clarendon Press, 1908.

Ludemann, Gerd. *Virgin Birth? The Real Story of Mary and Her Son Jesus.* Harrisburg, Pennsylvania: Trinity Press International, 1998.

Neirynck, F. "The Apocryphal Gospels and the Gospel of Mark." In *The New Testament in Early Christianity*, edited by Jean-Marie Sevrin. 123–175. Leuven: Leuven University Press, 1989.

Pearson, Birger A. "Earliest Christianity in Egypt: Some Observations." In *The Roots of Egyptian Christianity*, edited by Birger A. Pearson and James E. Goehring, 132–159. Philadelphia: Fortress Press, 1986.

Pearson, W. R., and Felicity Harley. "Resurrection in Jewish-Christian Apocryphal Gospels and Early Christian Art." In *Christian-Jewish Relations through the Centuries*, edited by Stanley E. Porter and Brook W. R. Pearson, 69–92. Journal for the Study of the New Testament Supplement Series 192. Sheffield, England: Sheffield University Press, 2000.

Pelikan, Jaroslav. *Mary through the Centuries: Her Place in the History of Culture.* New Haven: Yale University Press, 1996.

Robinson, J. Armitage. "The Gospel according to Peter: A Lecture." In *The Gospel according to Peter and the Revelation of Peter: Two Lectures on the Newly Recovered Fragments together with the Greek Text*, edited by J. Armitage Robinson and Montague R. James, 11–36. Second Edition. London: C. J. Clay and Sons, 1892.

Schaeffer, Susan E. "The Guard at the Tomb (*Gospel of Peter* 8:28–11:49 and Matthew 26:62–66; 28:2–4, 11:16): A Case of Intertextuality?" In *Society of Biblical Literature 1991 Seminar Papers*, edited by Eugene H. Lovering, Jr., 499–507. Atlanta, Georgia: Scholars Press, 1991.

Schneider, Paul G. "The Acts of John: The Gnostic Transformation of a Christian Community." In *Hellenization Revisited: Shaping a Christian Response within the Greco-Roman World*, edited by Wendy E. Helleman, 241–269. Lanham, Maryland: University Press of America, 1994.

Sellew, Philip. " *Secret Mark* and the History of Canonical Mark." In *The Future of Early Christianity: Essays in Honor of Helmut Koester*, edited by Birger A. Pearson et al., 242–257. Minneapolis: Fortress Press, 1991.

Setzer, Claudia. *Jewish Responses to Early Christians: History and Polemics, 30–150 C.E.* Minneapolis: Fortress Press, 1994.

Smith, Morton. *The Secret Gospel: The Discovery and Interpretation of the Secret Gospel According to Mark.* New York: Harper & Row, Publishers, 1973.

Soards, Marion L. "Oral Tradition Before, In, and Outside the Canonical Passion Narratives." In *Jesus and the Oral Gospel Tradition*, edited by Henry Wansbrough, 334–350. Journal for the Study of the New Testament Supplement Series 64. Sheffield, England: Sheffield Academic Press, 1991.

Stowe, C. E. *Origin and History of the Books of the Bible, both the Canonical and the Apocryphal*. Hartford, Connecticut: Hartford Publishing Company, 1867.

Thundy, Zacharias P. "Intertextuality, Buddhism, and the Infancy Gospels." In *Islam, Buddhism, Greco-Roman Religions, Ancient Israel, and Judaism*, edited by Jacob Neusner, Ernest S. Frerichs, and A. J. Levine, 17–73; volume 1 of *Religious Writings and Religious Systems: Systemic Analysis of Holy Books in Christianity, Islam, Buddhism, Greco-Roman Religions, Ancient Israel, and Judaism*. Atlanta, Georgia: Scholars Press, 1989.

Treat, Jay C. "The Two Manuscript Witnesses to the Gospel of Peter." In *Society of Biblical Literature 1990 Seminar Papers*, edited by David J. Lull, 391–399. Atlanta, Georgia: Scholars Press, 1990.

Turner, John D. "Ritual in Gnosticism." In *Society of Biblical Literature 1994 Seminar Papers*, edited by Eugene H. Lovering, Jr., 136–181. Atlanta, Georgia: Scholars Press, 1994.

van Stempvoort, P. A. "The Protoevangelium Jacobi: The Sources of Its Theme and Style and Their Bearing on Its Date." In *Studia Evangelica;* volume 3: *Papers Presented to the Second International Congress on New Testament Studies Held at Christ Church, Oxford, 1961; part 2: The New Testament Message*, edited by F. L. Cross, 410–426. Berlin: Akademie-Verlag, 1964.

Vorster, W[illem] S. "The Annunciation of the Birth of Jesus in the Protoevangelium of James." In *A South African Perspective on the New Testament*, edited by J. H. Petzer and P. J. Hartin, 33–53. Leiden: E. J. Brill, 1986.

_____. "The Protevangelium of James and Intertextuality." In *Text and Testimony: Essays on New Testament and Apocryphal Literature in Honour of A. F. J. Klijn*, edited by T. Baarda, et al., 262–275. Kampen: Uitgeversmaatschappij J. H. Kok, 1988.

_____. *Speaking of Jesus: Essays on Biblical Language, Gospel Narrative and the Historical Jesus*, edited by J. Eugene Botha. Leiden: Brill, 1999.

Wright, N. Thomas. "Five Gospels but No Gospel: Jesus and the Seminar." In *Authenticating the Activities of Jesus*, edited by Bruce Chilton and Craig A. Evans, 83–120. Leiden: E. J. Brill, 1999.

Zervos, Geirge T, "Dating the *Protoevangelium of James:* The Justin Martyr Connection." In *Society of Biblical Literature 1994 Seminar Papers*, edited by Eugene H. Lovering, Jr., 415–434. Atlanta, Georgia: Scholars Press, 1994.

# Index

Abacuc (prophet) 72
Abiathar (high priest) 61
Abraham (father of Jewish nation) 108
Agobard (Bishop of Lyons) 49–50
Acts of John: authorship and date 47–48; Christology of 134; contents and manuscripts 47; on regular miracles to feed the disciples 136; second transfiguration of Jesus 138; on varying physical size of Jesus 133
Acts of Pilate *see* Gospel of Nicodemus
Acts of the Martyrdom of Julian 29
*Against the Pelagians* 7
Alexandria (Egypt) 39–40
Ambrose: and Gospel of the Ebionites 37
animal sacrifices 53
Anna (mother of Mary): death of 112–114; despair at not having borne a child 53; later children of 112; miracle made possible bearing Mary 54, 56; miraculous inspiration of by Holy Spirit 56
the Annunciation 61–62
*Ante-Nicene Fathers*: importance of 5
anti-Christ 20
Antioch 30; Jesus flees to 137; Jesus travels from to Jerusalem for Passover 145
Apocalypse of Peter 29
apocryphal gospels: attitude toward Mary 15; changing nature of miracles in 2; changing text of 6; connection with polytheistic mythology of gods 96; designed as pious fictions rather than history 15–16; difference in description of trial of Jesus 145; difference with canonical gospels in type of miracles described 21; existence of canonical standard as obstacle to popularity 125–127; Gentile audiences in mind as readers 15; and Gnostics 92; as interpreters of scriptual text 5–6; mind-frame of authors 6; motives in writing 1, 3, 4; necessity of miracles in 92; possible Jewish sources for some stories 98; "sayings" collections 7; as seed ed for doctrinal evolution 1; tenuous connection with genuine historical data 14–15; use of by church leaders 6–7; why childhood and death emphasized in 124
apostles: call to be 133; pursued by religious authorities immediately after Jesus' death 152
Aquila (ancient bible translator) 151
Arabic Infancy Gospel: authorship 28; date 28; as "fully" developing apocryphal tradition 4; manuscripts and translations 28; popularity 4; relationship to Pseudo-Matthew 24; summary of contents 27–28
Arabic language works: History of Joseph the Carpenter 19; Infancy Gospel of James 16; Infancy Gospel of Thomas 22; stories concerning Ezra 98
Archelaus (son of Herod) 87
Armenian language works: and Gospel of Nicodemus 35; Infancy Gospel of James 16
*Ascension of Isaiah* 30, 158
Asia (Roman province) 128
Askew Codex 48
Athene (goddess) 70
Augustus (Roman emperor) 68, 71, 73

Babylon 123
Basilides: argued Jesus escaped crucifixion by changing into bodily form of someone else 149
beards 138
*Ben-Hur* 14
Bethesda (pool at) 142
Bethlehem 11; and Judaea 75; miracles in as a baby 88; narrative of Jesus' birth there 68–74; as place of Jesus' birth 15, 71; as a place of Jesus' residence as a youth 99, 110; slaughter of children at 76–78; visit of Magi at 74–76
Buddha 69

Caiphas (high priest) 156
Capernaum: childhood miracles of Jesus in 101; Jesus' family moves there 110; Jesus staying there as an adult 135
Carpocratians 41, 45
Celsus 128
Celtic language works: Infancy Gospel of Thomas 22
Christology: as affected by Marian emphasis 15
Christ's Descent into Hell *see* Gospel of Nicodemus
Clement, epistles of *see* First Clement; Second Clement
Clement of Alexandria: and Apocalypse of Peter 41; and continued virginity of Mary through and after childbirth 70; and Gospel of the Hebrews 37; and Infancy Gospel of James 18; and preaching of Peter 41; purported letter concerning Secret Gospel of Mark 41–45
*Contra Celsum* 128
Coptic language works: Epistula Apostolorum 49; Gospel of Nicodemus 35; History of Joseph the Carpenter 19, 21; Gospel of Thomas 132; Infancy Gospel of James 16; Pistis Sophia 48; stories concerning Ezra 98
Cromatius: and Pseudo-Matthew 25
Cyril of Jerusalem (fourth century): accepted childhood miracle stories about Jesus 80; on Jesus' ascension into heaven 167–168

David (king) 139
demon possession: of adult female 84; assaulted while bathing 84; of boy 83–84
*Diatessaron* 125; commentary on 153
docetic theology 161
Dumachus (one of two thieves crucified with Jesus) 85
dyers 96
Dysmas (one of two thieves crucified with Jesus) 150

Ebionites: denial of miraculous birth of Jesus 14; Infancy Gospel of James and their doctrine 13–14; preference for night baptism 130; vegetarianism of 37, 38, 143
Egerton Gospel: contents and connection with other works 38–39; characteristics of 127; date of composition 39; description of attempted stoning of Jesus 140; Jesus heals a leper 140; place of composition 39–40;
Egypt: adult Jesus takes refuge there 137; idols of 83; Jesus learned magic there 128, 137; Jesus performed many miracles in 86; king of 84; pharaoh over 86; synagogues 83; thirty day flight into shortened to three days 83
Elijah 20
Elizabeth (mother of John the Baptist): miraculously protected by angel 76; visited by Mary 63
Emmaus (town) 134
Enoch 20
Ephrem: *Syriac Commentary on the Diatessaron* 153
Epiphanius: and Gospel of Nicodemus 33; and Gospel of the Ebionites 37, 38; *Heresies* 129–130, 135, 143
Epistle of the Apostles *see* Epistula Apostolorum
Epistula Apostolorum 49; appearance of resurrected Jesus to women at the tomb 163–164; description of Jesus' ascension to heaven 168; and Infancy Gospel of Thomas 22–23; on initial apostolic doubt that the resurrected Jesus had a physical body 165; on preaching to the dead 160

Ethiopian language works *see* Epistula Apostolorum
Eusebius 48; and Gospel of Nicodemus 33; and Gospel of the Hebrews 140
Exodus 83
exorcisms: as made possible by demonic powers 136; *see also* demon possession
Ezra (leader of Jewish return from exile) 139; childhood miracle of 97–98

First Clement 3
First Enoch 29

Gabriel (angel): attends death site of John the Baptist's mother 113; helps take Jesus' earthly father to heaven 118; Jesus as 62; protects John the Baptist while growing 114
Galilee 110; disciples in 156; Jesus' ascension to heaven from 168; Jesus in 163; working of miracles in 137
Gelasian Decree (sixth century): papal decree banning preservation of certain works 16
Georgian language works: Gospel of Nicodemus 35; Infancy Gospel of James 16; Infancy Gospel of Thomas 22
German language works: Infancy Gospel of Thomas 22
Gestas (one of two thieves crucified with Jesus) 150
Gnosticism: appeal of Jesus' childhood miracles 80, 81, 92; and Epistula Apostolorum 49; favoritism for gospel of John 125; and Infancy Gospel of Thomas 22–23; its interpretation of Jesus' words on the cross 151; and Jesus being commissioned to teach as youth 116–117; on length of Jesus' post-resurrection teaching ministry 167; and nude baptism 46; Valentinus 74
Gospel of Nicodemus: authorship 32–33; contents 32; date 33; description of Jesus' trial 146–147; description of Mary's grief at Jesus' death 148–149; difference in description of afterlife between the work and evolving medieval theology 160; guards report resurrection to Pilate 163; manuscript forms 34; on obtaining Jesus' body for burial 154; on place of Jesus' crucifixion 150; place of origin 34
Gospel of Peter: contents 29; date of origin 30–32; departure of apostles for Galilee after resurrection 164; departure of the Christ element from the physical Jesus while on the cross 150; description of resurrection event 157; description of trial of Jesus by Pilate 148; and Egerton Gospel (Papyrus Egerton 2) 39; manuscripts 29–30; on obtaining Jesus' body for burial 154; and Oxyrhynchus Papyrus 840 40; place of origin 30; pursuit of apostles 152; views of importance 11
Gospel of the Ebionites: date of origin 38; on apostles being appointed 135; place of origin 38; theology of movement and document 37–38
Gospel of the Hebrews: accepted as illustrative rather than authoritative 139; account of resurrection appearance to James 166; on baptism of Jesus by John 129; on healing of man with bad hand 135; on Holy Spirit as "mother" of Jesus 131; on initial apostolic doubt that the resurrected Jesus had a physical body 165; multi-documents carrying same title 36; origin 36–37; and Oxyrhynchus Papyrus 840 40; on sinful woman accused before Jesus 140; on temple destruction at Jesus' death 152;
Gospel of the Nativity of Mary 28–29
Gospel of the Nazoreans 37
Gospel of Thomas (Coptic sayings gospel) 7, 167

Harvey, Paul 4
Heliodorus: and Pseudo-Matthew 25
Hermas (ancient Christian writer) 158
Herod (family members of same name): death of 86; effort to kill Magi 78; as judge 93; kills father of John the Baptist 77; many evils of 113; partially responsible for disposition of Jesus' dead body 154; partially

responsible for Jesus' death 148; seeks Magi to come to Jerusalem 74; slaughter of Bethlehem children 76–78; two Herods confused 77
Hippolytus (ancient Christian writer) 159
History of Joseph the Carpenter: authorship of 19–20; and childhood miracles of Jesus 93; copying the story forgives all one's sins 119; date of 20–21; popularity 4; place of origin 19; summary of contents 19; translations of 19; *see also* Joseph (father of Jesus)
Holy Spirit: bodily incorporated into Jesus while a youth 120, 130; gave young Jesus such knowledge that literacy was not needed 108; gave youthful Jesus power to perform miracles 98; given to Jesus in "full" measure at baptism 129; "mother" of Jesus 131, 132
homosexuality 45–46
Horus (Egyptian god) 133

Ignatius: on apostles verifying Jesus having a physical body after the resurrection 165; and silence at Jesus' birth 69
Infancy Gospel of James: assumes existence of Matthew and Luke 17; claimed authorship of and difficulties connected with 12, 17; date of origin 17–18; and Ebionites 14; impact of pagan religious views on picture of youthful Mary 54; Jesus as secondary figure in 11, 13; manuscripts and translations of 16–17; Mary's role in 2–13; as meeting popular demand for more information about Jesus 14; original language of 16; place of origin 18; popularity of 4; as possible apologetic work 13, 14; reasons for opposition to 16–17
Infancy Gospel of Thomas: authorship 23; date written 23–24; manuscripts and translations 22–23; popularity 4; summary of contents 21–22; title of 22
Irenaeus 167; on Basilides' theory of how Jesus escaped death 150; charges that orthodox Jews had altered Old Testament texts on the Messiah preaching to the dead 160; and Gospel of the Ebionites 37; and Infancy Gospel of Thomas 22–23; on parallel of Eve and Mary 74; use of four gospels 125
Isaiah (prophet) 72

James the Less (brother of Jesus) 118
Jericho: Jesus' childhood residence in 97; in youthful years travels from to Jordan river 102;
Jerome 7; and Gospel of Nativity of Mary 29; and Gospel of the Ebionites 37; and Gospel of the Nazoreans 37; and Pseudo-Matthew 25–26
Jerome (works of): *Against the Pelagaians* 129; *Commentary on Isaiah* 129; *Commentary on Matthew* 135–136, 152; *On Famous Men* 166
Jerusalem 87, 164; baby Jesus predicts death at 85; Jesus flees to 123; king of 98; prophets in at time of Jesus' birth 72; queen of 137, 144; Zacchaeus a teacher in 110
Jesus— adult life and teaching ministry: appearance of great light at His baptism 130; appointment of apostles 135; attempt to stone 140; baptism by John 129–131; curing the sick on the Sabbath 146–147; discussion with a rich man seeking Divine acceptance 139–140; every meal a miracle 136; final Passover with the disciples 143; forty days of temptation in the wilderness 131–132; healing of contagious leprosy 140; healing of man with a bad hand 135–136; his ritual purity challenged in the temple 141–143; his second Egyptian stay 137–138; his second transfiguration 138–139; a hostile interpretation of His miracles 136–137; law-giver for believers 128; miracle work 163; performed miracles by magic 128; physical appearance 133–134; pulling beard of apostle John 138; receives "full" measure of Holy Spirit at baptism 129; Roman allusions to Jesus' life and death 127–128; sometimes had a beard 133; unique physical disability of 134–135;

varying physical size and appearance 133; a woman accused of sin 140
Jesus—arrest and death: burial 154–155; crucifixion of the wrong man 149–150; defenses of Jesus by friendly witnesses 145–147; "departure" of the Christ while physical Jesus dies 150–151; earthquake at Jesus' death 152; Jesus' disciples pursued after His death 152–153; Jewish account of the events 144–145; Joseph asking for the body of Jesus 154–155; Mary's grief over her Son's death 148–149; Pilate's challenge to Jewish leaders 148; Pilate's reaction to phenomena at Jesus' death 153–154; place of crucifixion 150; punishment of Joseph for burying Jesus 155–156; Roman references to darkness at death of 127–128; Roman subordinates and standards honor Jesus 147
Jesus—childhood and youth: ability to speak as a baby 62; ability to stand as a baby 71; annoying teachers 81; bath water cures leprosy 84; birth 68–74; brilliance as a student 107–111; commissioned to preach at age twelve 116–117; contempt showed toward those He resurrected 105, 106; dangerous animals escort 82; death of John the Baptist's mother 112–114; death of Joseph 117–119; demons cast out 83, 84; destroying idols in their temple 83, 84; executions of others 104–106; family members and visitors dared not eat until He had arrived 112; healings 98–99; helps teach John the Baptist how to survive in the wilderness 113; holding of miraculously cures others 70; hurtful and injurious childhood wonders 103–104; idol praises Jesus 83; illegitimacy of 146; inability to speak removed 84; Jewish alternative version of Jesus' birth and adolescence 121–123; making dead fish live 80–81, 86; making palm tree bend miraculously 82–83; making spring of water appear 82; making thirty day trip turn into three days 83; miracle stories accepted in Jerusalem in fourth century 80; miracles of self-protection 93–94; miracles to benefit His parents 97–98; miraculous sounds mislead would-be thieves 84; mule transformed back into its original human form 85; other children traveling with Jesus' family to Egypt 82; performed miracles by power of Holy Spirit 98; physical location of birth described 71; pilgrimage to Jerusalem at age twelve 114–116; plants crops to help others 101, 102; playful childhood miracles 94–96; plays in Jordan River 105; predicts future death in Jerusalem 85; preincarnation role as angel Gabriel 62; pretends to be king in a game 99; protection of others from dangerous animals 102; rationale for stories 79–80; receipt of the Holy Spirit 120–121; refused to learn how to read 108; rejects criticism of inflicting death upon others 104–105; relationship of childhood stories to pagan myths 92; relationship to His parents 111–112; removes impotency 85; return to Palestine from Egypt 86–87; resurrections 100–102; shepherds visit birthplace 72; slaughter of Bethlehem children in effort to kill Him 76–78; starts to hide His miraculous abilities 119–120; touching miraculously cures 73; visit of the Magi 74–76; walking 78

Jesus—resurrection: appearance to James to convince him to break his fast 166–167; appearance to women at the tomb 163–164; ascension into heaven 167–169; decision to hush up the Roman guards' report 161–162; departure of the apostles to Galilee 164; a description of the resurrection event itself 157–161; fakery of resurrection exposed 169–170; instruction to the apostles to verify physical reality of resurrection 165

Joachim (father of Mary): despair at not having fathered a child 53, 55; great charitableness of 55; later children of 112

John the Baptist: baptizes Jesus 129–130; effort to kill 11, 17, 76; mother of

# Index

63–64; murder of father 77; protected in wilderness 114; purpose of his baptism 129; sorrow of over death of his mother 112–114; taught by Jesus how to survive in the wilderness 113

Jordan River: Jesus plays in as child 105; waters divide so youthful Jesus can cross 102

Joseph (disciple of Jesus): arranges to obtain body of Jesus for burial 154–155; instructed to remain in hiding for forty days 156; retaliated against for obtaining the body 155–156

Joseph (father of Jesus): acknowledges Jesus as deity 93; age of at death 119; blamed for Mary's pregnancy 65–67; body immaculately preserved from decay after death 118–119; carpenter's trade 58; carpenter's trade causes lengthy absences 58; controversy over whether he was a widower 16, 23; death of 19, 93, 117–119; desires to have Mary marry one of his sons 61; fears Jesus' youthful tendency to strike dead those who cross Him 108, 109; feast day 21, 119; first wife died of disease 118; forced to move family from place to place due to malicious miracles of Jesus 110; incompetency of as carpenter 98; Jesus as his helper in carpentry trade 97; miraculously selected to be husband of Mary 58, 60; obeyed by Jesus 111; obscurity of in New Testament 4; rebukes Jesus for causing death of others 104–105, 106; rebukes Jesus for playing on the Sabbath 95; reluctance to marry Mary or any one else 58; seeks Jesus' permission to alter itinerary into Egypt 83; taken to heaven at death 118; told by angel he is to be Jesus' earthly father 63–65; unmarried daughters remained in his household 117–118; *see also* History of Joseph the Carpenter

Josephus (Jewish historian and war leader): summary of Jesus' life 121–122

Judas (brother of Jesus) 117

Judas Iscariot: appointed apostle 135; defeats Jesus in miracle working power 137; demon possessed as a child 94

Julius Africanus 127–128

Jupiter (the god) 137

Justin: and baptism of Jesus 130; and Gospel of Nicodemus 33; on birth of Jesus in a cave 72; on Jesus commissioned to teach by an angel 116

Justin Martyr: on preaching of Jesus to the dead 159–160; use of four gospels 125

Justinian (emperor) 50

Knox, John (bible translator) 5

Latin language works: Epistula Apostolorum 49; probable version of Infancy gospel of James, 16

Lazarus 160

*Legenda Aurea*: and Gospel of Nativity of Mary 29

leprosy: caught by eating with another person 140; causes decision not to marry 89; cured by Jesus' bath water 84, 89

Leucius (Charinus) 48

logos 134

Lucian of Samosata 128

Luther, Martin 50

Magi 11, 74–76; celebration of return home, 76; given gift by Mary 75; guided by miraculous star back to their homeland 75; ordered to be killed 78

Marcion 159

marriage 85

Mary (mother of Jesus): annunciation of Jesus' coming birth to 61–62; asks Jesus to heal others 85; baptized by John the Baptist (implied) 129; betrothal to Joseph 146; creates new greeting for temple residents, 56; feared by demons 84; fed by an angel 57, 65; gives birth to Jesus 68–74; gnostic theories of her role in birth of Jesus 74; grief at death of her Son 148–149; Jesus as her household helper 97; obeyed by Jesus as a youth 111; perpetual virginity 1, 12, 57, 59, 71; pregnancy 11; promises salvation to thieves 85; raped by Joseph ben Pandera 122; rebukes Jesus as a child 105; role as miracle facilitator 90–91; serves God in temple in Jerusalem during childhood 54, 56; theology of 15; to be excluded from temple due to age and menstruation 57–58, 59; to be excluded from temple for other reasons as well 59, 60; to be married to a widower 57; uniquely righteous of all women who ever would live 55, 91; vision of future near Bethlehem 71; visit of Magi 74–76; visits mother of John the Baptist 63; visits death site of mother of John the Baptist 112–114

Mary of Cleophas (sister of Jesus' mother) 112

masons 136

Michael (angel) 113, 118, 158

millennialism 119

miracles, possible non-miraculous explanations for 136–137

Moses (law of) 108

Mount Tabor 132

Nazareth: Jesus' parents move there 86, 87, 110; Mary's connection with 57; miracles in 88, 100; why Jesus' connection with 15

*Nicene and Post-Nicene Fathers* 5

Nicephorus (Patriarch of Constantinople) 36; on Acts of John 47

Nicodemus (disciple of Jesus): agrees to help bury body of Jesus 154; defends Jesus before Pilate 147

*Odes of Solomon* 160

Origen: *Contra Celsum* 128; and Gospel of the Ebionites 37; and Gospel of the Hebrews 37; and Infancy Gospel of James: 18; on orthodox Jewish versions of life of Jesus 50

Origen (works of): additions to in Latin form 139–140; *Commentary on Ezekiel* 131; *Commentary on Isaiah* 131; *Commentary on John* 131; *Commentary on Matthew* 139; *Commentary on Micah* 131; *Homily on Jeremiah* 131

Oxyrhynchus Papyrus 840 ("Unidentified Gospel"): contents 40; date 40; text 141; use of text 40

P. Oxy. 2949 30

P. Oxy. 4009 30

papacy 16

Papias: reference to woman accused of sin before Jesus 140

Papyrus Bodmer V: date of 16; differences with later manuscripts of Infancy Gospel of James 18; title given Infancy Gospel of James 12

Papyrus Egerton 2 *see* Egerton Gospel

*Passing of Pereginus* 128

Passover 143

Peter (apostle): appointed 135; as fisherman 164; at second transfiguration of Jesus 138

Pharisees: Jesus eating with 136; Jesus challenged by 141

Pilate (Roman governor) 137, 146; accounts and purported letters of 4–5; challenges Jesus' accusers to back down 148; commands soldiers to keep silence concerning Jesus' resurrection 161; defense witnesses in hearings before 145–147; his reaction to physical phenomena at Jesus' death 153–154; Joseph seeks Jesus' body to bury 154; reference to by Tacitus 128

Plato 128

polygamy 89

Pistis Sophia 124; background information 48; childhood receipt of Holy Spirit 120–121; on post-resurrection teaching ministry of Jesus 167

Pontius Pilate *see* Pilate

poverty 139

*Preaching of Paul*: and baptism of Jesus 130

Protevangelium of James *see* Infancy Gospel of James

Pseudo-Matthew: authorship 25–27; date 27; manuscripts 25; original language 16; popularity 4; relationship to Arabic Infancy Gospel 24; reliance on James and Infancy Thomas 26; significance 25; summary of contents 24

ritual purification and washings 40, 141

Rome: Spread of Christianity to 128

Sabbath 157, 169; desecration by playing on that day 94; trial of Jesus' friend delayed because of 155
Salome (friend or servant of adult Mary) 113, 114
Salome (midwife) 72
Samuel (prophet) 54
Sanhedrin 32, 144, 146, 166, 169; members fear retaliation from masses over Jesus' death 162; receives first-hand rabbinic accounts of Jesus' ascension to heaven 168–169; receives report from guards at Jesus' tomb 163; retaliates for arranging burial of Jesus 155–156
Second Clement 3
*Secret Book of James* 132
Secret Gospel of Mark: contents and discovery 40–41; credibility of Clement of Alexandria's purported letter concerning 41–45; credibility of the Secret Gospel itself 45–46; views of importance 11
Serapion of Antioch (Bishop): and Gospel of Peter 30, 126
Serapion's *Life of John*: date and manuscripts 112–113
Simeon (high priest) 77
Simeon (priest) 113
Simeon (Rabbi) 122, 123
Simon of Cyrene: unknowingly crucified in place of Jesus 150
Simon the Canaanite (disciple of Jesus): as a child healed by Jesus of death from a snakebite 99
Slavonic language works: Infancy Gospel of Thomas 22
snakes 98–99
Socrates 128
Syriac language works: Arabic Infancy Gospel 28; importance of language to Eastern church 16; Gospel of Nicodemus 35; Infancy gospel of James, 16; Infancy Gospel of Thomas 22

Tacitus (Roman historian and proconsul) 128

Talmud: on skill of Egyptians in sorcery 138
Tatian: and Jesus' baptism 130; use of four gospels 125
Temple in Jerusalem 54; destruction mentioned in some ancient manuscript versions of Luke 23:48 153; Herod's temple 57; Jesus interprets the Jewish Law there 115; Jesus refuses ritual washings before entering 141; Jesus visits at age twelve 111, 114; learn secret name of God there 137; miracle working powers 137; prediction of its destruction 153; question of whether ritual washings required for visitors 142; slaves of 147; Solomon's temple 60; veil of 61
Tertullian: and Gospel of Nicodemus 33; on orthodox Jewish versions of life of Jesus 50
Thallus (Roman historian) 127–128
Tiberias (city): Jesus imprisoned at 137
Titus (one of two thieves crucified with Jesus) 85
Toldoth Jeshu: alleged resurrection of Jesus exposed as falsehood 169–170; background to 49–50; summary of Jesus' childhood and youth 122–123; trial and execution 144–145;
trinitarianism 20

Valentinus 74; on Jesus' body not needing excretory ability 134–135

Wise Men see Magi

Zacchaeus (childhood teacher of Jesus) 107, 108; connection with Jerusalem 110
Zacharias (father of John the Baptist): high priest status 63, 77; killed by Herod: 77
Zelomi (midwife) 71
Zeno (childhood playmate of Jesus) 100
Zeus (the god) 137

www.ingramcontent.com/pod-product-compliance
Lightning Source LLC
Chambersburg PA
CBHW032059300426
44116CB00007B/814